AUTOMOTIVE
WIRING
AND ELECTRICAL SYSTEMS

Tony Candela

S-A DESIGN

CarTech®

CarTech®

CarTech®, Inc.
39966 Grand Avenue
North Branch, MN 55056
Phone: 651-277-1200 or 800-551-4754
Fax: 651-277-1203
www.cartechbooks.com

Edit by Paul Johnson
Layout by Monica Bahr

ISBN 978-1-932494-87-7

Item No. SA160

Library of Congress Cataloging-in-Publication Data
Candela, Tony.
  Automotive wiring and electrical systems / by Tony Candela.
    p. cm.
  ISBN 978-1-932494-87-7
  1. Automobiles—Electric wiring. 2. Automobiles—Electric equipment. I. Title.
  TL272.C36 2009
  629.25'4—dc22
                                        2008044172

Printed in China
10 9 8 7 6 5 4 3 2 1

Back Cover (top left)
Digital multi meters (DMMs) are essential for automotive electrical work and allow users to measure voltage, current, and resistance. This hand-held device allows you to identify problems for simple and the most complex procedures.

Back Cover (top right)
These quick disconnect electrical connectors allow you to easily remove this dash panel when performing necessary electrical work.

Back Cover (middle left)
Installing an aftermarket tachometer is one of the most common add-on accessories for a high-performance vehicle.

Back Cover (middle right)
This shows how to heat the connection in order to get the solder to flow and form a solid connection that will last indefinitely.

Back Cover (bottom left)
Look closely at terminal 87 (front and center). Careful investigation proved that this particular relay was poorly manufactured. When the female connector was pushed onto a terminal, it broke the relay and it needed to be replaced.

Back Cover (bottom right)
A wiring harness is assembled. There are four sub harnesses in addition to the power and ground—left actuator harness, right actuator harness, switch harness, and keyless entry harness (with the red push-on connectors).

OVERSEAS DISTRIBUTION BY:

Brooklands Books Ltd.
P.O. Box 146, Cobham, Surrey, KT11 1LG, England
Telephone 01932 865051 • Fax 01932 868803
www.brooklands-books.com

Brooklands Books Aus.
3/37-39 Green Street, Banksmeadow, NSW 2019, Australia
Telephone 2 9695 7055 • Fax 2 9695 7355

CONTENTS

ABOUT THE AUTHOR

Tony Candela has been in the automotive aftermarket electronics industry for 20 years and has held positions in installation, sales, management, manufacturer's sales representation, and regional sales management. In his tenure, he has worked for two different aftermarket electronics manufacturers—Clifford Electronics and Rockford Fosgate.

Tony has written and given hundreds of seminars on the topics of installation, application, wiring, and basic automotive electronics. Tony uses the skills outlined in *Automotive Wiring and Electrical Systems* daily.

ACKNOWLEDGMENTS

Before starting, I'd like to thank a few folks. First and foremost, I'd thank my parents for teaching me that nothing worth doing is ever easy. Second, I'd thank my wife for allowing me to do pretty much everything a car guy would dream to do. From encouraging me to buy and work on the cars to attending yet another parking-lot car show with me, she's been there every step of the way. In addition, she's been instrumental to me in completing this book—I couldn't have done it without her! Finally, I'd thank my high school electronics teacher, Mr. Don Waters, for helping me pursue electronics as a career—it's been a fun ride!

Over the years, I've been fortunate to work with some of the best minds in this field and I'd thank the numerous people that have influenced me. Those would include Leon Permenter, B.J. Latting, Richie Steinbeck, Ragan Young, Jason Digos, Gary Biggs, Magnus Friedholm, Mark Fukuda, Greg Cobbs, Bryan Schmitt, Garry Springgay, Anthony D'Amore, and Steve Meade. I'd also like to thank Mike Morgan for his help and guidance on photography.

Finally, special thanks to a few that have pushed me to think outside the box—my friends Kip Lawson, Mark Lieber, Bill Basore, Ron Trout, and Todd Ramsey. This book is dedicated to the memory of my great friend Jackie Burwick.

INTRODUCTION

Thanks for picking up this book! The whole intent of my writing it is to demystify the practice of automotive wiring in general. I can't tell you how many times I've overheard people say that they hate wiring or that wiring is their least favorite part of a project. Since you've got this book in your hand, I'm sure you know exactly what I mean. I've never really understood why wiring has gotten such a bad rap—after all, it's really quite simple.

Over the years, I've learned the hard way how to do a job right the first time. Automotive wiring is not a topic to be taken lightly. In fact, a simple mistake can cause a fire in your prized vehicle. You'd be surprised if you knew what I've seen under the dashes of the nicest of cars over the years. You'd be even more surprised at how simple it is to avoid these pitfalls altogether and do it right the first time.

So, why did you pick up this book to begin with? I mean, after all, automotive wiring is like calculus to most

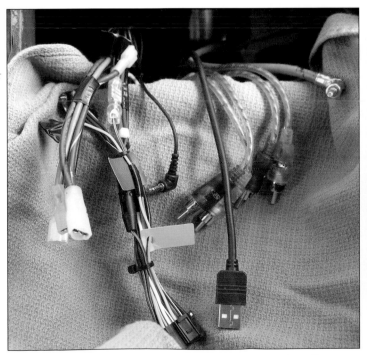

This book will show you how to professionally install a wide range of accessories, including stereo equipment.

Installing an aftermarket tachometer is a common upgrade for many vehicles. You will be shown how to wire it into the ignition system, install the ground wire, and make professional connections.

people! The answer is simple—you picked up this book because:

- You need help troubleshooting an electrical problem.
- You need help installing after-market electronics.
- You wanted to become the expert in this topic.
- Most importantly, you want to be able to do all of the above safely.

Again, this book is intended to demystify the practice so it won't read like a college-level physics book. After you've read it, you'll be able to do all of the above and so much more! To make the material easy to follow and learn, I've written the book so that each chapter provides you the knowledge needed to comprehend the following chapter. In addition, I've provided as many pictures and diagrams as I could, so that you can visualize my explanations. Finally, I've provided several step-by-step examples that you can do in your garage so that you can practice what you see in these pages.

Here's a quick run down of my qualifications for writing a book of this nature. As of this writing, I'm 38 years old and have been a car guy since as long as I can remember. Early on, my talents leaned toward auto-motive electronics—stereo systems, auto security, etc. I began installing car stereo systems in my parent's driveway at the age of 14, and by the time I graduated high school I was known as the "car stereo guy." Early on in my career, I spent seven years installing automotive electronics of all kinds to earn a living. Many years later, I'm still involved with the car stereo industry. During my 20 years in the profession, I've been fortunate enough to work for two different manufacturers—Clifford Electronics and Rockford Fosgate. And lastly, I'm a hot rodder!

Throughout this book I use my three personal vehicles as references so I thought I'd acquaint you with them now:

- 2004 Nissan Frontier Crew Cab Truck: Nothing special here, it's just a daily driver with aftermarket audio and security systems.
- 2003 Ford Mustang GT: It's loaded with go-fast goodies. It's got a centrifugal supercharger with water/methanol injection, full exhaust, an opened-up intake tract, hot ignition, upgraded clutch, and a built 8.8 rear differential with 4.10 gears. A fully tweaked suspension allows it to handle great in the corners. Finally, it's full of electronics of all sorts—3,000 watts of audio, a pair of 18-inch woofers, stealth radar detector, security, and a host of black boxes.
- 1972 Oldsmobile Cutlass S: This one started life as a 1/8-mile race car. It was first purchased as a rolling chassis. It was already back halved, tubbed, had a roll cage, full fiberglass front clip, and excellent paint and bodywork. I'm in the process of converting it to a street/strip car in full Pro Street theme. It now has a Roots supercharged 454-ci rat, TH400 with brake, and a narrowed 9-inch with a spool and 4.30s. Practical it ain't, but there are few things cooler than the looks you get when driving this thing on the street! The myriad of wiring problems on this car inspired me to write this book. I work on it every chance I get.

Somewhere in those three vehicles, and the thousands I've worked on in my past, I'm sure to find common ground with you. From vintage to current in-car electronics, this book covers a lot of ground.

UNDERSTANDING ELECTRICAL PRINCIPLES AND SIMPLE CIRCUITS

Before beginning, I should note that this book makes the assumption that the vehicle you own has a 12-volt negative ground charging system. That is, the vehicle is equipped with a 12-volt battery and its negative terminal is connected to the vehicle chassis. If you own a vehicle with a 6-volt or even a positive-ground charging system, the theory still applies but the specifics do not.

The objective of this chapter is to provide a foundation for the rest of the book. Everything you need to know is explained so that you have a firm understanding of basic automotive electronics. Every other chapter in this book is written on the assumption that you've read and understand this one.

High Current/Low Voltage

The single most important thing to keep in mind when working on a vehicle's electrical system is safety. Unlike the electrical system of your

A standard 12-volt negative ground application always has the battery negative connected to the vehicle chassis and engine block. Note that in this 2004 Nissan Frontier, a single cable does double duty.

home, automotive electrical systems are low voltage, so there is little if any danger from shock. In addition, an automotive electrical system can deliver incredibly high currents—far in excess of the 15 amps available at a typical outlet in your living room. Finally, this current is direct current or DC versus the alternating current or AC found in your home.

- Automotive Electrical—Low Voltage/High Current (DC)
- Residential Electrical—High Voltage/Low Current (AC)

I assume that if you're reading this book, then you've experienced first hand the results of a short circuit in an automobile. They can cause extreme damage quite quickly!

Now I know I promised this book won't read like college-level physics, but I need to address two laws right away. A good friend once told me, "They're laws, not just really good ideas." Well put. The two laws that are paramount to understand for automotive wiring projects and nearly all electrical projects are Ohm's Law and Kirchhoff's Law.

Ohm's Law

Ohm's Law is generally considered the foundation of electronics. Named after the person that first defined it, Georg Ohm, Ohm's Law simply states the relationship between voltage (E), current (I), and resistance (R).

Voltage
- Difference in potential
- Measured in volts
- Typically expressed as E in mathematical formula

Current
- Flow of electrons
- Measured in amperes (can be abbreviated as amps)
- Typically expressed as I in mathematical formula

Resistance
- Opposition to the flow of electrons
- Measured in ohms (interchangeable with the Ω symbol)
- Typically expressed as R in mathematical formula

Voltage is that which causes current to flow. Resistance is anything that impedes the flow of current. The higher the resistance, the higher the voltage required to allow a given amount of current to flow. This relationship between voltage, current, and resistance is expressed as:

$$I = E / R$$

If you know any two of the above, you can solve for the third. Using a little algebra, you can re-arrange this formula to get the following formulas to aid in solving for the unknown:

$$E = I \times R$$
$$R = E / I$$

Fortunately, the voltage available in a vehicle is somewhat fixed and typically is 12—12.6 VDC with the vehicle off and 13.0—14.4 VDC with the vehicle running.

Figure 1-1: This is Ohm's Law pie chart. Simply cover the variable you wish to solve and it shows you the correct formula to do so. For example, to solve for I, cover the I, and the resulting formula is E/R.

Now that you know Ohm's Law, let's put it to work to determine how much resistance an electronic fuel pump has if it requires 10 amps of current at 12 Volts.

$$R = E / I$$
$$R = 12 \text{ volts} / 10 \text{ amps}$$
$$R = 1.2 \ \Omega$$

The Power Formula

The Power Formula simply states the relationship between power, current and voltage. Power is an expression of work and is expressed in watts. Power is the product of current and voltage and the relationship is expressed as:

$$P = I \times E$$

Again, if you know any two, you can solve for the third. Once again, let's use a little algebra to re-arrange this formula to aid in solving for the unknown:

$$I = P / E$$
$$E = P / I$$

Figure 1-2: This is the Power Formula pie chart. As with the Ohm's Law pie chart, simply covering the variable you wish to solve for shows you the correct formula to do so.

Now that you know the Power Formula, let's use it to determine how much power the electronic fuel pump I spoke of above consumes:

$$P = I \times E$$
$$P = 10 \text{ amps} \times 12 \text{ volts}$$
$$P = 120 \text{ watts}$$

An easy way to put the idea of power into perspective is to understand the simple incandescent light bulb. For example, a bulb rated 60 watts consumes 60 watts of power to light the filament within the bulb. Not all of the power across the filament can be converted to light—some of the 60 watts the bulb consumes is converted to heat. This is why the bulb gets hot in use. The same applies to electronic circuits in all automobiles.

In a simple circuit, a certain amount of power is dissipated across the load. The remaining power is dissipated into heat in the wiring, switch(es), and connections. By minimizing the amount of power burned up into heat, we can get more power to the load.

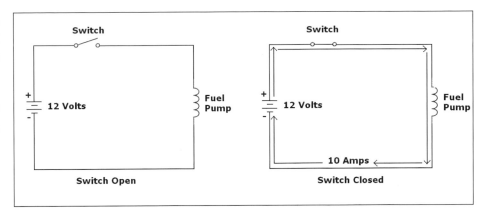

Figure 1-3: This is a simple electronic fuel pump circuit. Note that the circuits are the same, but the one on the left has the switch in the open position. No current can flow through the fuel pump until the switch is closed, as shown on the right.

Schematics

Electronic circuits are typically represented in wiring diagrams called schematics. A schematic is a simplified drawing of a circuit that uses symbols to represent the individual components of the circuit.

Reading a schematic is simple, but most do not have a key, as the symbols have been standardized.

Figure 1-4: Here is a key of the most commonly used symbols in automotive wiring diagrams, and for the wiring diagrams in this book.

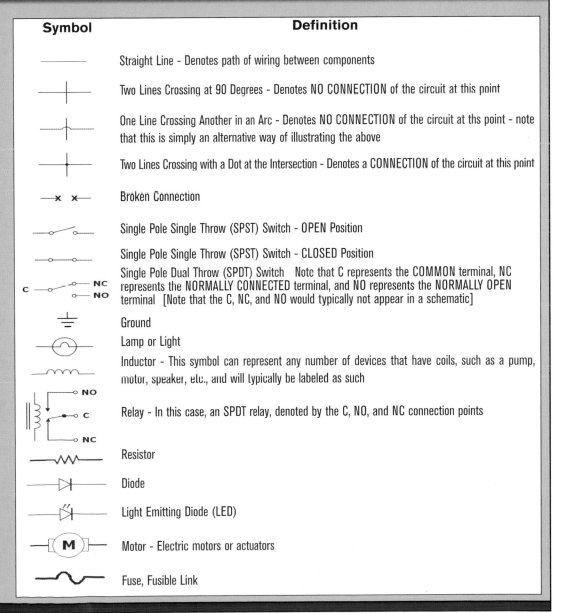

Symbol	Definition
	Straight Line - Denotes path of wiring between components
	Two Lines Crossing at 90 Degrees - Denotes NO CONNECTION of the circuit at this point
	One Line Crossing Another in an Arc - Denotes NO CONNECTION of the circuit at ths point - note that this is simply an alternative way of illustrating the above
	Two Lines Crossing with a Dot at the Intersection - Denotes a CONNECTION of the circuit at this point
	Broken Connection
	Single Pole Single Throw (SPST) Switch - OPEN Position
	Single Pole Single Throw (SPST) Switch - CLOSED Position
	Single Pole Dual Throw (SPDT) Switch Note that C represents the COMMON terminal, NC represents the NORMALLY CONNECTED terminal, and NO represents the NORMALLY OPEN terminal [Note that the C, NC, and NO would typically not appear in a schematic]
	Ground
	Lamp or Light
	Inductor - This symbol can represent any number of devices that have coils, such as a pump, motor, speaker, etc., and will typically be labeled as such
	Relay - In this case, an SPDT relay, denoted by the C, NO, and NC connection points
	Resistor
	Diode
	Light Emitting Diode (LED)
	Motor - Electric motors or actuators
	Fuse, Fusible Link

Combinations

Many times, you need to solve problems that neither Ohm's Law or The Power Formula addresses directly. However, they can provide the solution when you combine them via substitution. For example:

$$P = E^2 / R$$

This formula would allow us to solve for power if we know voltage and resistance, but not current. How did we determine this? Simple, Ohm's Law tells us that $I = E / R$, so we can substitute E/R for I in the Power Formula:

$P = I \times E$ (Recall that $I = E / R$)
$P = (E / R) \times E$
$P = E^2 / R$

Likewise, we can solve for power if we know current and resistance but not voltage the same way:

$P = I \times E$ (Recall that $E = I \times R$)
$P = I \times (I \times R)$
$P = I^2 R$

Kirchhoff's Law

If you were to Google this, you'd find the full explanation (and formulae)—quite a mouthful! Fortunately, this book sticks to what applies here. To explain Kirchhoff's Law, I'll separate it into the two different parts—one applies to voltage and the other to current.

Kirchhoff's Voltage Law

Kirchhoff's Voltage Law states that the sum of the voltages applied in a given circuit are equal to the sum of the voltage drops across the

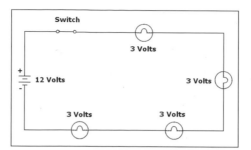

Figure 1-5: A simple lighting circuit illustrates Kirchhoff's Voltage Law. Note that the sum of the voltages across each of the lights is the same as the total voltage applied to them.

various components in said circuit. Figure 1-5 is an example of a simple lighting circuit with voltage drops specified.

Kirchhoff's Current Law

Kirchhoff's Current Law states that the current entering a junction in a circuit is equal to the current leaving said junction. Figure 1-6 is an example of a different kind of lighting circuit with current flow specified. (Note that this is a different kind of circuit than Figure 1-5—more on that briefly.)

Recall from your junior high school physical science class when you learned that energy can neither be created nor destroyed. This is

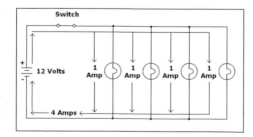

Figure 1-6: This simple lighting circuit helps explain Kirchhoff's Current Law. Note that the sum of the currents through each of the lights is the same as the total current flowing through the circuit.

called the conservation of energy. Kirchhoff's Law helps us to apply the conservation of energy to basic electronic circuits. In the example I gave above for the 60-watt bulb, it should be clear that the power the filament consumed was divided between light and heat—none was destroyed.

Understanding Ohm's Law and Kirchhoff's Law are paramount in grasping the basics of automotive electronics. Learn them and don't forget them!

Circuit Basics

See, that wasn't too bad! Now that you've gotten your Laws down, it's important to understand the difference between the different types of circuits—specifically the series circuit, parallel circuit, and series-parallel circuit. Furthermore, it's important to understand how Ohm's Law and Kirchhoff's Law govern these basic circuits.

Series Circuits

A series circuit is one that has all components connected in an end-to-end (or daisy chained) fashion. Operation of the circuit is dependant on all of the individual components of the circuit being in working order. A series circuit is only as good as its weakest link—if one component fails, so does the entire circuit. This is how strings of Christmas lights were once made. Problem was, when one bulb failed the entire string wouldn't light.

In a series circuit, the following apply:

- The sum of voltages across the individual components is equal to the total voltage applied.

• The current flowing through the individual components is the same throughout the circuit. (Note the tie to Kirchhoff's Law!)

Parallel Circuits

A parallel circuit is one that has all the components connected in a parallel fashion. Operation of the circuit is not dependant on the individual components of the circuit—one or more components could fail and the remaining components will still work. The typical parking light circuit is a good example of a parallel circuit.

In a parallel circuit, the following apply:

• The voltage flowing across the individual components is the same throughout the circuit.

• The sum of the currents across the individual components is equal to the total current flowing through the circuit. (Again, Kirchhoff's Law.)

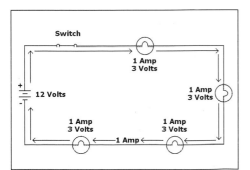

Figure 1-7: Series lighting circuit current specifications for all components. Note that this is the same circuit pictured in Figure 1-5.

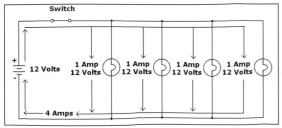

Figures 1-7 and 1-8 illustrate the differences between these two circuits. Both are simple lighting circuits. Note that in both, I've outlined voltage and current across the various components as well as totals in the circuits so that you can see how Kirchhoff's Law governs them.

Series-Parallel Circuits

You guessed it; there can be combinations of series and parallel circuits. These types of circuits, although not very common in automobiles, are referred to as

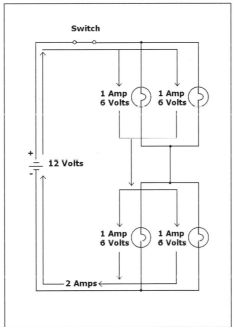

Figure 1-9: A series-parallel lighting circuit has voltage and current specified for all components. Note how Kirchhoff's Law governs the Series part of the circuit and the Parallel part of the circuit differently.

Figure 1-8: This shows you a simple parallel lighting circuit with voltage and current specified for all components. Note that this is the same circuit pictured in Figure 1-6.

series-parallel circuits. The rules above apply to the individual parts of the circuit. Figure 1-9 is an example of a series-parallel lighting circuit. Again, note how Kirchhoff's Law governs this as well.

It is important to understand the differences between series, parallel, and series-parallel circuits. Examples of each of them are found in nearly every vehicle on the road.

Short Circuit

For such a simple idea, this is one of the most misunderstood circuits that I know of. Quite simply, a short circuit is any circuit that has a circuit path between the battery (+) and battery (-). Certainly, these are not intentional and can be quite hazardous. Figure 1-10 shows a short circuit. Note that it is the same circuit as pictured in Figure 1-6, but the bulbs cannot illuminate as the circuit bypasses them.

How exactly does this happen? Any number of reasons. Let's say that you were mounting something under the vehicle's hood and you unintentionally pinched the parking light wire or pierced it with a screw in the process. All would be fine until you turned on the parking light switch, at which point, the parking light circuit fuse would blow as the switch just connected 12 volts directly to the vehicle's chassis. The blown fuse just protected the wiring and vehicle from any serious damage. (The value of a fuse should be fairly clear at this point!) Of course, you would now have to determine what caused this and fix the problem. This process is called troubleshooting, and you'll learn more about how to do this later in the book.

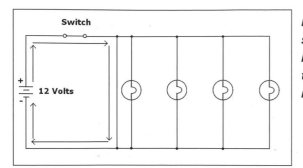

Figure 1-10: A short circuit, such as this, bypasses the lights altogether. Even though they are connected, they will not light.

Open Circuit

Now, this is the one that eludes folks—after all, any vehicle wiring problem is referred to as a short! In many cases, that just isn't true. An open circuit is a break in the circuit that does not allow the circuit to operate. Recall the example I gave above in the series circuit explanation of the way strings of Christmas lights used to be manufactured. Should a bulb fail, and the string go out, this is an open circuit condition. Now, we don't install many of these in vehicles, so let's look at Figure 11—note that it is also based on Figure 6.

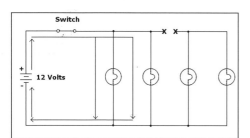

Figure 1-11: This open circuit is open in-between the two lights on the left and the two on the right. The two on the left work; the two on the right do not.

Again, there are any number of reasons for this to happen. Let's say that you were installing new carpeting in your vehicle and you used a razor knife to cut an opening along the sill plate for the big Torx bolt that holds your seat belt down. If you're not careful, you could cut through the wiring harness in this

area, thereby removing the parking lights in the rear of the vehicle from the circuit. The front lights would still work fine because they are still connected to the circuit. Obviously, this is a simple fix, and it's covered later in the book.

Wire Resistance Chart

We all know there is no such thing as a free lunch. Stranded copper wiring, which is what is typically specified for automotive use, has a certain amount of resistance per foot. This resistance per foot decreases as the gauge of wire increases (indicated by a smaller number; confusing, I know).

Figure 1-12 is the American Wire Gauge (AWG) standard for resistance of copper wire by the foot.

AWG Gauge	Resistance Per 1000 Foot	Resistance Per Foot
20	10.3600 ohms	0.010360 ohms
18	6.5200 ohms	0.006520 ohms
16	4.0800 ohms	0.004080 ohms
14	2.5800 ohms	0.002580 ohms
12	1.6200 ohms	0.001620 ohms
10	1.0200 ohms	0.001020 ohms
8	0.6400 ohms	0.000640 ohms
6	0.4020 ohms	0.000402 ohms
4	0.2530 ohms	0.000253 ohms
2	0.1590 ohms	0.000159 ohms
1	0.1260 ohms	0.000126 ohms
0	0.1000 ohms	0.000100 ohms

Example: Installing an Electric Fuel Pump

OK, now that you know your Laws and how they apply to basic circuits, it's time to give you a real-world example. Let's say that you just purchased an electric fuel pump and wanted to determine what gauge of wire to use to connect it.

Here's what you should know:

- Current requirements of the pump at 12 VDC (this should be provided by the manufacturer). For the sake of this example, let's say that it's 10 amps.
- Length of wire from the ignition switch to the fuel pump—let's assume this is 20 feet since it is typically located near the fuel tank.
- Length of return path from pump ground to charging system ground—let's assume this is 5 feet (more on this later).
- Resistance of different gauges of wiring via the supplied AWG wire resistance chart.

Figure 1-12: This chart outlines the resistance of stranded copper wire according to length and gauge. All gauges are according to the American Wire Gauge.

Stranded or Solid?

Why stranded wiring for automotive use? Simple: stranded wiring is used for its reliability. Stranded wiring offers greater overall resistance to breaks from the kinds of harmonics and vibrations that it is subjected to daily in the automotive environment. Solid wiring is just quite simply not up to this task—nor was it designed to be.

Another area of concern is the connection points of solid wire. Not only would traditional methods of connecting solid wires be unsuitable in an automotive environment, but the expansion and contraction of the wire itself from the temperature extremes it can be subjected to would put undue stress on these connections. This could make them high in resistance, unsafe, and possibly a fire hazard.

Finally, stranded wire designed for automotive use typically has a plastic insulator that is designed to stand up to extremely high temperatures and petroleum-based products, such as gasoline and oil. The wiring found within the walls of your home doesn't require this, so it isn't constructed that way.

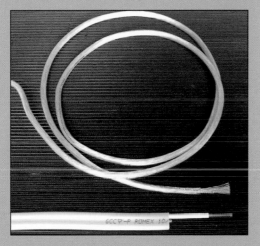

This compares 10 AWG stranded cable to 10 AWG solid wire, which is typically found in the walls of your home.

mine how much voltage drop is incurred in our 25-foot run of wire with the 10-amp current requirements of our pump. Finally, use Kirchhoff's Law to find out how much voltage is left to operate our fuel pump.

Let's start with 18 gauge because this is exactly how the high-output fuel pump in my Oldsmobile was wired when I purchased it. The chart tells us that 18-gauge stranded copper wiring has .00652 Ω of resistance per foot. Use Ohm's Law to calculate the voltage drop through the wiring:

$$E = I \times R$$
$$E = 10 \text{ amps} \times (25 \times .00652 \text{ Ω})$$
$$E = 10 \text{ amps} \times .163 \text{ Ω}$$
$$E = 1.6 \text{ volts}$$

Kirchhoff's Law says that if you lose 1.6 volts in the wiring, you only have 11.4 volts across the pump itself as 13.0 volts – 1.6 volts = 11.4 volts. This voltage loss nets the voltage across the pump below the manufacturer's specification of 12 volts. Not good! Especially for a fuel pump that needs to deliver the right amount of fuel to our engine at all times. We sure don't want to ever run lean.

This voltage drop in the wiring is converted into heat, which causes the wire to be warm or even hot. See the sidebar "A Quick Exercise" for a further explanation.

Just by looking at the chart, you can guess that 16-gauge wire won't cut it either. But, for argument's sake, let's do the calculation:

$$E = I \times R$$
$$E = 10 \text{ amps} \times (25 \times .00408 \text{ Ω})$$
$$E = 10 \text{ amps} \times (.102 \text{ Ω})$$
$$E = 1.02 \text{ volts}$$

We need to assume that the pump will only be running when the engine is running, so you should have 13.0 volts DC present at the ignition switch. For now, ignore the effect on available voltage other accessories will have. How do we determine this? Hint: Let's put Ohms Law and Kirchhoff's Law to work to solve this problem.

First, look at the circuit. Obviously, it's a simple series circuit as shown in Figure 1-13.

Now refer to the AWG Wire Resistance Chart in Figure 1-10 to determine the resistance per foot of different gauges of stranded copper wire. Then use Ohm's Law to deter-

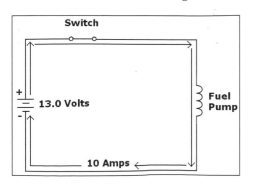

Figure 1-13: The sample electronic fuel pump circuit has a nominal voltage of 13.0 volts per the example.

Benefits of the American Wire Gauge

Unfortunately, we live in the day and age of over promising and under delivering. Over the last several years, the price of raw copper has sky rocketed. With the cost increase in raw materials, some wire companies have chosen to remove copper to be competitive—insane, but true. Last I checked, copper is the very thing you buy wire for! Fortunately, there is a way for you to tell—purchase only wire that is labeled as AWG, per the American Wire Gauge.

Illustrated are two different pieces of 4-gauge wire from different manufacturers. On the bottom is a piece that meets the specifications of the American Wire Gauge, and it has AWG printed right on the jacket. This is commonly referred to as "full spec." Second from the bottom is a piece that sells for much less per foot—labeled "4 gauge" but no mention on the jacket of AWG. Notice that it is roughly the same external diameter, but the copper within it is a fraction of the wire gauge on the bottom.

From the top, 10 AWG cable, 8 AWG cable, cheap 4 "gauge" cable, and 4 AWG cable are shown.

For comparison purposes, second from the top is a piece of full-spec 8 AWG cable. On the top is a piece of full-spec 10 AWG cable. Note that the cheap 4-gauge cable actually has slightly more copper than the 10 AWG, but not quite as much as the 8 AWG cable. I sure wouldn't want to rely on this to deliver current to my starter on a hot summer day.

Avoid the problem altogether and be sure you only purchase wire that is rated via the American Wire Gauge! And yes, it's more expensive because it contains the copper you need to get the job done right the first time.

13.0 volts − 1.02 volts = 11.98 volts. With just over a volt lost in the wiring, the net voltage across the pump is again short of the manufacturer's specification. This makes 16-gauge wire unsuitable for use.

Do the same math on 14-gauge wire:

$E = I \times R$
$E = 10$ amps $\times$ (25 $\times$ .00258 Ω)
$E = 10$ amps $\times$ .0645 Ω
$E = .65$ volts

13.0 volts − .65 volts = 12.35 volts. Better, but still not good enough. This nets just 35 hundredths of a volt over the manufacturer's specification of 12 volts across the pump. I don't know about you, but I'd rather spend a few extra bucks on bigger wire so that I don't risk the chance of starving the fuel pump for voltage when I've got my A/C on, radio jamming, and both electric fans at full tilt on a hot summer day!

Do the same math on 12-gauge wire:

$E = I \times R$
$E = 10$ amps $\times$ (25 $\times$ .00162 Ω)
$E = 10$ amps $\times$ .0405 Ω
$E = .41$ volts

13.0 volts − .41 volts = 12.59 volts. Better still, but now look at 10-gauge wire and see if the extra cost warrants its use:

$E = I \times R$
$E = 10$ amps $\times$ (25 $\times$ .00102 Ω)
$E = 10$ amps $\times$ .02346 Ω
$E = .26$ volts

13.0 volts − .26 volts = 12.74 volts. This nets 12.74 volts across the pump, and it would continue to get closer to 13 Volts as you continue to increase the gauge of the wiring. However, you're getting to the point of diminishing returns. The 14-gauge is the bare minimum, but for the cost difference I'd use 12-gauge or even 10-gauge to be confident the fuel pump is receiving ample current.

Keep in mind this example does not take into consideration the voltage drop through the fuse holder or connections. This voltage drop is due to their resistance and the resistance in the connections to them.

A Quick Exercise

Let's determine how much power is lost in the wiring to heat in the first three examples. To do so, we put the Power Formula to work:

18 AWG	16 AWG	14 AWG
$P = I \times E$	$P = I \times E$	$P = I \times E$
P = 10 amps x 1.6 volts	P = 10 amps x 1.02 volts	P = 10 amps x .65 volts
P = 16 watts	P = 10.2 watts	P = 6.5 watts

Keep in mind, that these calculations do not take into consideration any resistance in connectors, fuse holders, and fuses. Chapter 3 shows you how to minimize that.

Two of the many modules and computers in the 2004 Nissan Frontier are shown: a convenience module, housing circuits that control the door locks, interior illumination circuits, etc; and the ECM. Both units are located above and to the right of the gas pedal and can be easily accessed.

Chapter 3 shows you several methods to make strong, solid connections that minimize voltage drop through them.

Congratulations! You're now versed in Ohm's Law and Kirchhoff's Law. In addition, you've learned the formulas and theory behind them to put them to work. You've also learned about basic types of automotive circuits. Finally, you've put all of this new information to work to solve real world problems. Now, how many of you intend to re-wire that electronic fuel pump in your vehicle immediately after you get done reading this book?

I'm sure you're eager to put your new knowledge to work. Half of the challenge in automotive electronics is understanding it. The other half is understanding how to apply what you know safely, which is addressed next.

Generally speaking, automobiles present a number of challenges when working on or adding to the electrical system. As I discussed earlier, extremely high currents are capable—anyone that has tightened a positive battery terminal with that shiny new long-handled ratchet can attest. In addition, accessing or routing wiring in many areas involves the ability to contort your body in the weirdest of positions.

More than a basic understanding and respect for the complexity of the electrical systems in today's vehicles is required to work on them competently. The complexity of the modern vehicle is outside of the scope of this book. When in doubt, seek the advice of a professional—even if that means paying them to do the work. After all, this is how they make their living. Making simple mistakes on the modern vehicle can have serious and very expensive consequences; I cannot stress this enough!

Hazards Presented by On-Board Computers

Modern vehicles have many luxuries that we now take for granted, such as fuel injection, fully electronic automatic transmissions, anti-lock brakes (ABS), variable valve timing, supplemental restraint systems (SRS), and others. Each of these requires lots of decision-making power—power found in the host of on-board computers. The main vehicle computer is often referred to as the ECM (electronic control module), or PCM (powertrain control module).

Working on a vehicle with on-board computers is a way of life for today's mechanics, and they've learned over the years that old school ways of troubleshooting problems are for old school vehicles. Case in point is the staple of many a mechanic's tool box—the incandescent test light.

The "test light" has very low resistance between its ground clip and probe tip—low enough to deploy an air bag in the event you're probing around in the wrong area by accident. A better choice is a computer-safe test light. A digital multi-meter

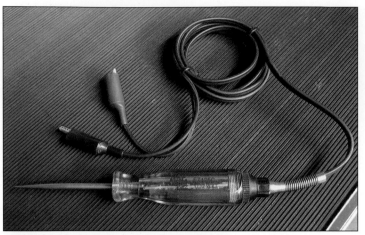

A Mac-computer-safe test light is radically different internally than a simple test light, although similar in appearance. The MAC Tools model ET125C is shown.

I bought my tried-and-true Fluke 87 in 1992, and it has served me well all these years. Although, it's not an inexpensive meter, it's loaded with many useful features.

(DMM) is even better. The correct use of test lights and DMMs is covered in Chapter 2.

Another topic worth mentioning is that of connecting 12 volts or ground to any wire that you're not 100 percent sure what it's connected to. I sure wouldn't do this in modern vehicles with electronic control units! Even the radio harness in today's vehicles can include numerous connections to on-board computers, such as the vehicle speed sensing (VSS) circuit or a data connection to a vehicle locator for example. Don't be a cowboy here! Only make connections to wiring you've verified. Fortunately, this is easy to do.

There are many sources on the Internet of wiring color codes and locations in vehicles. I can't tell you how many times I've seen damage from somebody taking this info as gospel without verifying it. Connecting to the "brown wire in the driver-side kick panel" isn't as easy as it sounds, especially if you look carefully and see that there might be numerous such wires in this area!

Finally, many of the connections between computers in the modern vehicle are of a new variety. Different BUS systems, such as CAN (controller area network) bus and MOST (media oriented systems transport) bus, are used in some vehicles. These BUS systems pass digital information to other components. Fiber optic cables are also becoming more common, and they also digitally pass information between components. Incidentally, we first saw widespread use of fiber optic cables in GM vehicles in the 1980s, and they were used for illumination.

Again, if in doubt, I recommend contacting a professional. It's less expensive to swallow your pride than to pay for a costly mistake.

Disconnecting the Battery–When?

ADVISORY: When working on or servicing automotive batteries, it is advisable to wear eye protection. Many automotive batteries have sulfuric acid within them—this is extremely caustic and can cause irreversible damage to your eyes!

CAUTION: When working on or servicing automotive batteries, it is advisable to remove jewelry, such as rings and watches as they can be great conductors. If they accidentally come between the positive battery post or terminal and the vehicle chassis, they could cause a short circuit. This results in extremely high current flowing through them and this creates heat that can cause severe burns to your fingers, hand, or wrist!

CAUTION: Never work on or around an automotive battery with a lit cigarette! In addition, be very conscious of the proximity of open flames near or around the battery, as they can cause a lead acid battery to explode!

I've always been perplexed when the first line in the instructions of any aftermarket product begins with "Step 1: Disconnect the Battery." Fact of the matter is, in many cases, this isn't necessary nor advisable. Now, I'm not suggesting that you not follow the manufacturer's instructions, but you should understand when to do this and when not to do this. Quite simply, the reason to disconnect the battery in the first place is to eliminate the risk of damaging the vehicle's electrical system when doing work to the vehicle—sound judgment indeed.

If you're working on a newer vehicle laden with computers,

disconnecting the battery can have a host of ill side effects. One such example is re-learning the idle. If the procedure outlined by the manufacturer is not followed after the battery is reconnected, the vehicle may not idle or even run correctly. In my years as an electronics installer, there were many cases that we used vise grips to ensure that the battery terminal did not come off when connecting an aftermarket accessory so that we didn't have to call the dealer in an effort to learn what those procedures were.

I recommend disconnecting the battery when:

- Making major changes or additions to the electrical system.
- Making extensive changes to the vehicle's drivetrain, exhaust, or suspension components.
- Working around a battery in tight quarters—as I mentioned earlier, the end of a wrench or ratchet between the positive battery terminal and the chassis is a good way to get in trouble fast!
- Unplugging a module or computer for any reason.
- Disconnecting any large power wires from anything—alternator, starter, fuse box, ignition switch, etc.
- Welding to the chassis, frame, or body.

These are simply common sense. If you're installing a piece of aftermarket electronics, it helps to understand whether disconnecting the battery is called for. Let's say that you were adding a tachometer. In most cases, its connection points to the vehicle's wiring are:

- Tach signal—typically found at the negative side of the coil.
- 12 volts when the ignition switch is in the run position.
- Dash lamp circuit, so that the tach is illuminated when the parking lights are on and its brightness varies with the dimmer control.
- Ground.

This is a good example for leaving the battery connected during its installation.

This is the proper way to loosen a battery terminal without allowing it to come loose from the battery post. In this case, I added the ground wire for an automotive security system without disconnecting the battery.

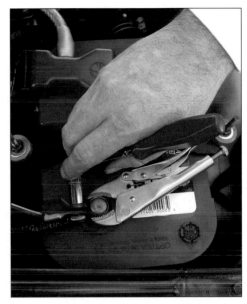

This is the correct way to add this ground wire. Slide the ring terminal under the head of the clamping screw on the side opposite the nut. In this fashion, the battery can be disconnected for any reason without accidentally disconnecting this ground wire from the terminal.

This is the finished connection. Note that this does not interfere in any way with the OEM battery terminals and would allow the battery to be disconnected or even swapped easily.

The Correct Way to Disconnect the Vehicle's Battery

Should you have to disconnect the battery for any reason, the correct way to do this is to:
1. Be sure all accessories in the vehicle are turned off and the ignition switch is in the off position.
2. Remove the negative battery terminal.

Loosen the negative battery terminal.

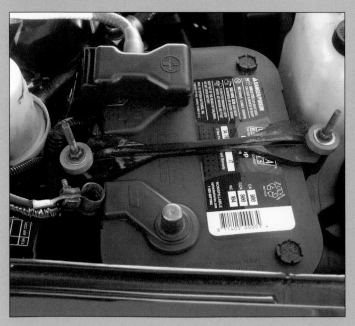

If, for any reason thereafter, you need to remove the positive battery terminal or connect anything to it, it has no reference to the vehicle's ground. Therefore, you are in no danger of accidentally short-circuiting the battery—even in the event that you accidentally connect a tool between it and the vehicle's chassis.

The correct way to reconnect the battery is to:
1. Be sure all accessories in the vehicle are turned off, and the ignition switch is in the off position.
2. Connect the positive battery terminal (assuming that it was removed at some point).
3. Connect the negative battery terminal.

In addition, refer to your vehicle's owner's manual to determine if there is anything special you need to do after reconnecting the battery to ensure proper operation of the vehicle. If in doubt, you can always contact the service department of your local dealership and ask.

CAUTION: Disconnecting or re-connecting battery cables while the battery has a load on it—such as with the ignition switch or any accessories on—is extremely dangerous and can cause sparks! Sparks can also cause a lead acid battery to explode.

CAUTION: Never disconnect the positive battery terminal from a running vehicle with on-board computers! The load the battery places on the alternator is typically factored into the design of the voltage regulator. This old-school way of determining if the alternator is functioning is a great way to see just how high its voltage regulator will allow the alternator's output voltage to climb. Within seconds, this voltage could climb to several times the safe input voltage level of the ECM or any number of other computers or modules, resulting in very expensive damage!

Finally, remove the negative battery terminal. Note that I located it far enough away from the negative battery post so that it does not become accidentally connected.

Installing the Tach

Here is the procedure for safely installing the tach with the battery connected.

1 Be sure the ignition switch is in the off position.

2 Mount the tach.

3 Run the wiring from the tach under the vehicle's dash.

4 Route the signal lead from the tach through a rubber grommet in the firewall to the coil and connect it to the negative side of the coil. (Note that since the ignition switch is off and the vehicle is not running, neither side of the coil has any voltage present on it.)

5 Route the ignition (+) lead from the tach to a source of + 12 volts when the ignition switch is in the run position. (Note that this lead needs to be fused at the source of power per the tach manufacturer's specification.)

6 Route the illumination (+) lead from the tach to the dash lamp circuit so that the light within the tach varies with the dimmer circuit, along with the rest of the lights on the vehicle's dashboard.

7 Connect the ground (-) lead from the tach to chassis ground.

8 Install the fuse in the fuse holder that you connected to the source of ignition (+) in Step 5.

9 Turn the dash lamps on and verify the correct operation of the illumination of the tach by rotating the dimmer to MAX and to MIN.

10 Start the vehicle and verify operation of the tach.

Computer Memory Savers

Several companies offer "computer memory savers." Such a device is designed to plug into the cigarette lighter of your vehicle and keep the computers powered up in the event that you have to remove the battery cable(s) for any reason. As they draw very little power when idling, this is possible to do with a very small power source. This would ensure that your vehicle would operate correctly after disconnecting and reconnecting the battery.

How do they work and are they necessary? Nothing more than a cigarette lighter plug is terminated with a pair of alligator clip leads. It is designed to allow one to have a source of power and ground for powering something up. In addition, if you were to clip the alligators to a 9-volt battery say, the 9-volt battery is the source of power for the on-board computers should the battery need be disconnected. Obviously, a 9-volt battery wouldn't be able to keep the computers powered very long, so this tool is intended for quick servicing needs.

Owning such a device certainly couldn't hurt; but in all my years, I never needed one. If you stick to the guidelines I've provided, nor will you.

As you can see, at no point during the installation of the tach did we make connections to a *live* circuit. In the event that we would have pinched or shorted any of the wiring to the tach during the installation, it would have had the same results as if we had done the installation with the battery negative disconnected, then reconnected it after the installation was complete. However, in steps 4, 5, and 6, it is necessary to verify the functionality of the wiring we're connecting to—this is not possible with the negative battery cable disconnected. Chapter 5 details step by step how to verify the wiring you're connecting to as you do the install.

DISCLAIMER: Connecting power to any piece of aftermarket electronics, whether to the battery directly or not, should be the last step you do and *not* the first. To simplify installation and provide an added measure of safety, I prefer to run wiring from the device to the connection point(s) and not the other way around. This power connection should be fused near the connection point to protect the wiring and circuit you've tied into. Note that in the previous example, the last step before verifying correct operation of the tach was to install the fuse in the fuse holder that supplied power to the tach. Without the fuse installed, no power can flow to the tach from the ignition circuit, even with the ignition switch in the RUN position.

OK, take a much-deserved deep breath and cue up your favorite car show from the DVR—you've just gotten through the most difficult part of this book. It's all downhill from here!

THE RIGHT TOOLS FOR THE JOB

This chapter explains which tools are needed in your tool arsenal to be ready to tackle the most common automotive electrical tasks. Furthermore, this chapter explains the differences between various types of measurement tools and how to properly use each of them. I don't know about you, but any time I learn new ways to do something, that gives me an excuse to buy the right tools!

Nowadays, specialized tools are more readily available than ever before. Obviously, the tool department at your local Sears is a great source. Your local hardware or home improvement stores can also be a great source. Professional tools, such as Snap-On and Matco, are sold from the tool trucks. These are best quality tools, but they are expensive. If you're in a rural area, most of the tool companies have great websites at which you can purchase directly from them. Regardless of where you buy your tools, if I cover anything unique, I'll tell you where I got it from to save you the time of looking for it.

Required Tools

OK, now you're ready to dig in with both hands. What tools do you need to get started? At the minimum, I recommend the following:

- Diagonal Cutters
- Wire Strippers
- Razor Blade
- Wire Crimpers
- Electrical Tape
- Soldering Equipment
- Electrical Measurement Device

Diagonal Cutters

I use diagonal cutters often—from cutting the end of cable ties flush to cutting wire. What's most important to me is that they fit my hand comfortably—not too big and not too small. Three common sizes are shown in the photo below, and all are available from Sears. I prefer the size in the middle. You may already own at least one pair of these.

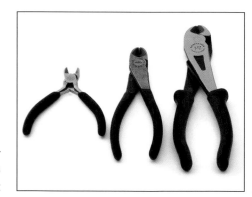

Diagonal cutters are available in numerous sizes from nearly every tool company on the planet. I reach for the size in the middle most, but the other two certainly have their place.

Here are the tools needed, at minimum, to tackle your wiring projects. You probably already own most of these.

Wire Strippers

This is probably the most personal tool I own. Ask any five mechanics what they prefer for stripping the insulation off of wires and you'll likely see five different tools. Not that I recommend this, but I've even seen wires stripped with a cigarette lighter! Shown are the most common types; I prefer the ones on the lower right-hand side.

Razor Blades

Now this is a trick that saves you time and effort trying to remove insulation from larger gauge wire. Since wire strippers for 8 AWG and larger wire really don't exist, I always use a razor blade to:

- Score around the insulation of the wire, being careful not to cut too deep.
- Run from the score to the end of the wire lengthwise—no worries on going too deep this way, as the blade is parallel with the wire strands.
- Tear the insulation off by

Wire strippers are the most commonly used wiring tools. The black pair at the top are Blue Point model PWC-22; they strip the ends of wires from 12 AWG to about 18 AWG. The red-handled pair are Ideal T-strippers and for wires 18 AWG and smaller. The blue-handled pair is from Klein and for wires from 10 AWG to 18 AWG.

hand—if you scored it deep enough, it tears perfectly, right at the score.

Wire Crimpers

A crimping tool is any tool that is designed to "crimp" a connector onto the end of a length of wire. There are numerous offerings in the

The red/black-handled crimping tool from Klein on the right is my all-time favorite and is good with both insulated connectors up to 14 AWG and non-insulated connectors up to 10 AWG. The yellow-handled Ideal crimping tool is good for insulated connectors up to 8 AWG and non-insulated connectors up to 4 AWG. Finally, the First Forever tool is a compound-action crimping tool good for insulated connectors up to 8 AWG and non-insulated connectors up to 4 AWG.

This mack-daddy crimping tool from Hex Crimp easily crimps connectors up to 4/0 AWG. The compound action gives the user the leverage needed to crimp even thick-walled connectors with ease.

marketplace. Buy the right pair of crimpers for the job—that one-size-fits-all pair won't work well for crimping a 4-gauge ring terminal on the end of the charge lead from your high-output alternator. As a result, wire crimping tools are readily available to crimp connectors on wiring up to 4/0 AWG—*really big stuff!*

Ironically, the least effective kind of crimpers is also the most commonly found in tool boxes across the nation. Those are the "squeezy" kind that have crimpers, wire cutters, and bolt cutters all built into a single tool. And, just as you'd expect, none of them work very well.

I would say the tool's operaation is equally important as the tool itself. I could fill an entire chapter (or even a whole book) with photos of incorrectly crimped connectors. Chapter 3 covers how to correctly choose and use each of the pictured tools for the task at hand and how to make ideal crimp connections with them.

Hammers, pliers, and bench vises are all great tools, but crimpers, they are not. Never rely on them to get the job done of a properly designed pair of wire crimpers, because they can't. Properly crimped connections have extremely low resistance and offer a solid reliable connection for years. Improperly crimped connections are high in resistance and pose numerous hazards—the least of which is the voltage drop through them.

Electrical Tape

A tool you say? You bet! In my opinion, this is one of the most important tools in your tool box. I've used Scotch Super 33+ Vinyl Electrical Tape for more than twenty years now and I've never had a problem with it—not one single problem. It's very pliable, stretchy, easy to tear, and it sticks! I only recommend one kind of electrical tape.

Here's an excellent tip when it comes to taping: Be sure that your hands are clean of dirt, oils, food, etc. As you invariably make contact with the sticky side of the tape in the process, clean hands help ensure that the tape sticks as it was intended to.

Soldering Equipment

Note that I am not listing soldering equipment as an option, as you really should have at the very least a soldering iron and a roll of rosin core solder in your tool box. The fact of the matter is that soldering is easy, and how to do it correctly is covered in the next chapter.

One of the oldest wives' tales is that soldering has no place in an automobile because the connections are subjected to vibrations. This is simply nonsense. In fact, a properly soldered connection likely outlasts the vehicle. In addition, I've seen thousands of problems from mechanical connections of all types—crimp connectors, Scotchlok connectors, and T-Taps are the most common. And guess what? In 99 percent of the cases, these were improperly chosen or installed to begin with.

Today, there are many different types of soldering equipment available. Many companies offer butane powered soldering irons. As they do not require electricity, they are totally portable and can be used anywhere. To be properly equipped for any automotive soldering job, consider purchasing:

- Soldering Iron—It should have at least a 25-watt capability for soldering wiring up to 14-gauge or so.
- Soldering Gun—This should have at least a 150-watt capability for soldering wiring up to 10-gauge or so.
- Propane or MAPP Gas Torch— This solders connectors on the end of the big stuff
- 60/40 Rosin Core Solder (in various sizes)—I use .040 diameter more often than any other size.
- Third Hand Device—A tool used to hold a connection in place, leaving both of your hands free to do the soldering.

Fortunately, all of the above are inexpensive and readily available. The third hand device is found only at your local Radio Shack, which also has all of the above with the exception of the torch.

Electrical Measurement Device

This is a must-have for any do-it-yourselfer. Prices, even on DMMs, are affordable for almost everyone. At the very least, buy a computer-safe test light, but understand that its light typically illuminates between 10 volts and 16 volts—so at best it's just a shot in the dark. Nod if you've actually got a meter of some type lurking in the bottom of your tool box but never use it...you are not alone. Soon, this will be as important a tool to you as it is to me.

The Test Light

As I mentioned in the Chapter 1, old-school incandescent test lights have no place in the modern automobile because they have very low impedance. I won't even check fuses with them—just too many horror stories that resulted in someone spending their hard-earned money to fix a problem that could have been easily avoided.

Detecting Voltage

This is simple enough and is the single most common use for a test light—you need to locate a source of power to power something up or need to verify the presence of voltage to be sure something is working properly. Just follow these steps:

1 Connect the clip of the test light to chassis ground.

2 Touch the tip of the test light to the connection point in question; in this case I've connected it to the headlight connector.

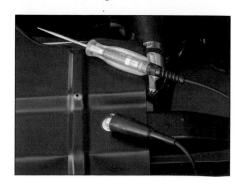

3 Turn on the circuit to be measured; the test light lights, indicating the presence of voltage.

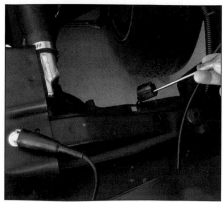

Another problem with a test light is that you really can't tell much other than the presence of voltage or ground or detection of current flow; you certainly cannot equate the brightness of the bulb to an actual figure. You need to know how to use one. Following is how to correctly use one in a non-computer equipped vehicle, such as my 1972 Olds Cutlass, for example.

All measurements have been taken with a Snap-On CT4G test light.

Detecting Ground

Let's say that you wanted to find a suitable place to ground an aftermarket device or electronic component. You would use this procedure to determine if the chosen spot has ground present or not:

1 Connect the clip to 12 volts.

2 Touch the tip to the proposed grounding spot of the vehicle's chassis.

3 If the test light lights, the spot provides ground, if not continue probing, until you find a spot that causes the test light to light.

Detecting Current

I know this one sounds kind of silly, but for years mechanics have used test lights to track down drains on the battery. Here's how to do it. Since the Olds has dual batteries, I've disconnected the front one to simplify the explanation. In addition, it doesn't have any low current items, such as under-dash lighting or a glove box light, so I've connected a small light bulb to the circuit breaker next to the batteries for this example.

For this example, I rigged up a small light. Note the connections via the blue alligator lead to both the main circuit breaker and the chassis.

1 Be sure all accessories in the vehicle are turned off, especially the ignition switch! The bulb within the test light can't pass much current through it—try to pass too much and it will burn out.

2 Disconnect the negative battery terminal.

3 Disconnect the positive battery terminal.

4 Re-connect the negative battery terminal.

5 Connect the clip of the test light to the positive battery post.

6 Connect the tip of the test light to the positive battery clamp—notice that the bulb in the test light is illuminated slightly—this indicates current flowing through the test light.

7 Disconnecting the small light bulb causes the light to go out entirely which eliminated the source of the current draw—if only it were that easy!

Impedance

What does impedance really mean? In Chapter 1 you learned that resistance impedes the flow of current. Sometimes the word resistance and impedance are interchanged with the same intended meaning, but they are quite different. Resistance is just one component of impedance. Impedance is:

- A measure of the overall "imped"ance of the flow of current in an AC (alternating current) circuit.
- A function of resistance, capacitive reactance, and inductive reactance.
- Measured in Ohms (interchangeable with the Ω symbol).
- Typically expressed as Z in mathematical formula.

The formula for impedance is a complex one and not introduced here because it really isn't relevant as this book deals with DC circuits. But, I will explain the concept as I've used the term in my description of measuring devices.

A low-impedance measuring device, such as a test light, would provide a moderate load on the circuit we connect it to—kind of like a light bulb. The circuit we're probing with the test light may not be designed to accommodate this additional load and could be damaged as a result.

A high-impedance measuring device, such as a computer-safe test light or DMM, would provide an easy load on the circuit we connect it to. This would allow the circuit to function normally with a negligible amount of current required to actually take the measurement.

In the case of a quality DMM, the circuit wouldn't even know the DMM was connected to it—a good thing. According to the manual that came with my Fluke 87 meter, it is specified to have an input impedance of 10 MΩ when taking voltage measurements, which is 10,000,000 ohms. Let's use Ohm's Law to determine how much current this meter would require when taking measurements in a typical 12-volt DC circuit:

$I = E / R$

$I = 12 \text{ volts} / 10,000,000 \text{ ohms}$

$I = .0000012 \text{ amps, or 1.2 millionths of an amp}$

Obviously, 1.2 millionths of an amp of current isn't going to cause damage to even the most fragile of circuits. (More correctly, this is stated as 1.2 µA and said 1.2 micro amps.) This is just one of the many reasons why I prefer a DMM over all other types of measuring devices.

Number Basics

When dealing with measurements and specifications, it is helpful to understand the correct verbiage that goes along with them. For example, .001 amp is 1 thousandth of an amp of current but wouldn't typically be said or expressed that way. Instead, this is expressed as 1 milliamp. Here are the simple pre-fixes and their meanings:

Prefix	Decimal Representation	Said As	Written As	Definition
mega	1,000,000	megamp	MA	one million amps
		megavolt	MV	one million volts
		megohm	MΩ	one million ohms
kilo	1,000	kiloamp	KA	one thousand amps
		kilovolt	KV	one thousand volts
		kiloohm	KΩ	one thousand ohms
	1	amp	A	one amp
		volt	V	one volt
		ohm	Ω	one ohm
milli	0.001	milliamp	mA	one thousandth of an amp
		millivolt	mV	one thousandth of a volt
		milliohm	mΩ	one thousandth of an ohm
micro	0.000001	micro amp	µA	one millionth of an amp
		micro volt	µA	one millionth of a volt
		micro ohm	µΩ	one millionth of an ohm

The Computer-Safe Test Light

A "computer-safe" test light is just that—a version of the test light that is safe to use in modern vehicles. Typically, they look and function similar to a traditional test light, but the similarities end there.

Computer-safe test lights have high internal impedance and two LEDs (light-emitting diodes) to indicate the presence of voltage or ground. Additionally, they require power, so they typically have alligators for power connections. They can also be designed to be plugged into a cigarette lighter. You can also purchase a complete kit, which typically includes:

- The computer-safe test light with a cigarette lighter plug.
- An adapter harness to allow the light to be powered by means of a positive and negative clip lead that can be clipped directly to the battery posts or power points.
- Different adapters or probe tips that can be affixed to the probe point for ease of probing just about any kind of circuit.

Computer-safe test lights are not designed to measure or detect the flow of current, so we cannot use them for such.

Let's do some of the same measurements as above with my MAC Tools Model ET125C computer-safe test light.

The Digital Multi-Meter

I like a DMM because it has high internal impedance, typically around

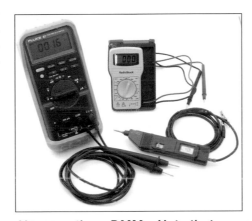

Here are three DMMs. Note that the small unit from Blue Point is quite handy as it fits in your hand like a test light, but is a basic DMM. Unfortunately, it is no longer available.

10MΩ, which makes it computer safe. In addition, the numeric display takes the guesswork out of your measurements. You know *exactly* what you're dealing with, not an approximate.

The VOM

There are other kinds of meters on the market, specifically volt ohm meters, or VOM. A typical VOM has an analog display with a needle pointer.

A VOM is able to capably measure voltage, current, and resistance. In addition, some mechanics prefer them over a DMM as you can readily observe fluctuations on the needle pointer that you cannot see on a basic DMM. A nicer DMM, such as my Fluke 87, has an analog bar graph display below the numeric display for just this reason. This allows a digital display to also have the functionality of an analog one, and thereby eliminate the need to own a VOM.

I don't recommend them for today's vehicles as they have low internal impedance due to their design, which is typically specified as a certain number of ohms per volt. According to the manual my Micronta VOM came with, it is specified at 30,000 ohms per volt for DC measurements. For a 12-VDC circuit, that's only 360,000 ohms—or 27.7 times the load that a 10MΩ DMM places on a circuit! Certainly not as low as a test light, but low enough to present a problem when probing delicate circuits.

Detecting Voltage and Ground

1 Connect the red clip to +12 VDC and the black clip to ground.

2 Touch the tip of the computer-safe test light to the headlight connector—notice the green LED is illuminated, indicating the presence of ground as the headlights are off

(the light is detecting ground through the filament of the passenger side headlight to the chassis, as both headlights are wired in parallel).

3 Turn *on* the headlight switch, the red light is illuminated, which indicates the presence of voltage.

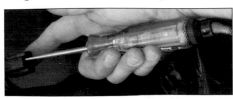

In addition, the cost of a DMM has come down to a point where you can get one at your local Sears or Radio Shack pretty cheap because they're available for as little as $25 or so.

DMM Basic Functionality

A DMM is quite a marvel, especially the nicer ones. Quite simply, it can measure voltage, resistance, and current. Personally, I've had my Fluke 87 since 1992, and it's a tool that I rely on often. While it wasn't an inexpensive investment, it's certainly paid for itself on many an occasion. Technology in DMMs has come a long way since then, and the

The Fluke 87 at a Glance

The following is reprinted from the owner's manual. It describes your meter and how to use it. For ease of reference, each description is numbered and keyed to the illustration.

Input Terminals and Input Alert

Items 1-4 describe the input terminals. If the test leads are connected to the Amperes input terminal, and the function selector switch is not in the Amp measurement position, the beeper will emit an Input Alert. An Input Alert will also sound if the test leads are connected to the mA uA terminal and the function switch is not in either Amp position. After an Input Alert sounds, the meter will attempt to take a reading from inputs applied to the xxx terminal. Input Alert can be disabled by pressing xxx while turning the rotary switch from OFF to any function position.

① **A — Amperes Input Terminal**
For current measurements (ac or dc) up to 10A continuous (20A for 30 seconds) when function selector switch is set to **mA⁼** **A~**

② **mA mA Milliamp/Microamp Input Terminal**
For current measurements up to 400 mA (ac or dc) when the function selector switch is set to **mA⁼** or **µA≊** **A~**

③ **COM — Common Terminal**
Return terminal for all measurements.

④ **VΩ→⊢ Volts, Ohms, Diode Test Input Terminal**

Function Selector Rotary Switch

⑤ Item 5 describes functions that are selected by setting the rotary switch. Each time the rotary switch is moved from OFF to a function setting, all LCD segments will turn on for one second as part of a selftest routine. (This selftest routine is also performed if the rotary switch is turned slowly from one position to another.) The meter is then ready for normal operations and will respond to the rotary switch and pushbuttons.

Off

Power to the meter is turned off.

ṽ **Volts ac** Autoranges to the 400 mV, 4V, 40V, 400V or 1000V range.

V̿ **Volts dc**
Autoranges to the 4V, 40V, 400V or 1000V range.

mV̄ **Millivolts dc**
Single 400 mV range.

⁾⁾⁾)Ω+⊢ **Resistance (Ω), conductance (1/Ω), capacitance or continuity ⁾⁾⁾) testing.**
Press BLUE button to toggle between the resistance and capacitance function. (The response of the display and the pushbuttons slows down in the capacitance mode.)
Autoranges to the 400Ω, 4 kΩ, 40 kΩ, 400 kΩ, 4 MΩ,or 40 MΩ resistance range.
In Manual Ranging mode, 40 nS conductance range (equal to a 25-100,000 MΩ range) is selectable. (See item 9.)

The Fluke 87 at a Glance CONTINUED

Autoranges to the 05.00 nF, .0500 μF, 0.500 μF, or 05.00 μF capacitance range.

When testing continuity, the beeper sounds if the resistance falls below the typical values indicated in Table 1.

Table 1. Beeper Response in Continuity Test	
Input Range	Beeper On If
400.0Ω	< 40Ω
4.000 kΩ	< 200 kΩ
40.00 kΩ	< 2 kΩ
400.0 kΩ	< 20 kΩ
4.000 kΩ	< 200 kΩ
40.00 kΩ	< 200 kΩ

━━┼ Diode Test

Measures forward voltage of semiconductor junction(s) at approximately 0.5 mA test current. Single 0-3V range.

mA⚏ Milliamps or amperes
A~

Defaults to dc. Press BLUE button to toggle between dc and ac.

Autoranges to the 40 mA or 400 mA range when using the mA mA input terminal, or to the 4000 mA or 10A range when using the [A] input terminal.

μA ≅ Microamps

Defaults to dc. Press BLUE button to toggle between dc and ac.

Autoranges to the 400 mA or 4000 mA range when using the mA mA input terminal.

Pushbuttons

Items 6-13 describe how to use the pushbuttons. These buttons are used (in conjunction with rotary switch) to select operating modes and set power-on options. When a button is pushed the beeper sounds (unless the beeper has been turned off or the Data Output mode has been selected). An annunciator is displayed to indicate that a mode or option has been selected. A quick way to reset all the pushbuttons to

their default state is to turn the rotary switch to an adjacent function and then back to the function you are using.

6 ⊚ Display Back-Light

Press the YELLOW button to turn on the back-light. Back-light turns off automatically after 68 seconds to extend battery life.

Power-On Option: 41/2-Digit Display Mode

The meter displays the readings at 10 times the resolution with a maximum display at 19,999 counts. The display is updated once per second. The 41/2-digit display mode works in all functions except capacitance, Peak MIN MAX and 100 millisecond MIN MAX. Use manual ranging for best performance.

7 ▬▬▬ AC or DC, Resistance or Capacitance

Press BLUE button to toggle between ac and dc when measuring current, or between capacitance and resistance when the rotary switch is set to ᵐ⁾⁾⁾Ω┤┣ .

Power-On Option: Disable Automatic Power-off

Automatic Power-off extends the life of the battery by turning part of the meter off if neither the rotary switch nor a pushbutton is operated for half an hour. (Automatic Power-off is not allowed in the MIN MAX Recording or Data Output modes.) The meter turns back on if either the rotary switch is turned or a pushbutton is pressed.

8 (MIN MAX) Minimum (MIN), Maximum (MAX), Average (AVG) Recording

Press (MIN MAX) enter the MIN MAX Recording mode (manual range only). Select the proper range before selecting MIN MAX to ensure that the MIN MAX reading will not exceed the measurement range. The minimum, maximum, and average values are then reset to the present input; the RECORD annunciator

The Fluke 87 at a Glance CONTINUED

turns on; the AUTO annunciator turns off; and the automatic power-off feature is disabled.

In the MIN MAX Recording mode, the minimum and maximum readings are stored in memory. The beeper emits a tone when a new minimum or maximum value is recorded. A continuous beeper tone is emitted when an overload is recorded. Push (MIN MAX) cycle through the maximum (MAX), minimum (MIN), average (AVG), and present readings. The MIN, MAX, or AVG annunciator turns on to indicate what value is being displayed. If an overload is recorded, the averaging function is stopped and the average value becomes OL (overload).

The true average of all the readings taken over at least a thirty-six hour period can be displayed. If this duration is exceeded, the actual minimum and maximum readings will continue to be captured and can be displayed. However, new averages are no longer calculated. The last average calculated is retained as the average reading.

At normal (default) record speed, changes to the voltage, current, or resistance inputs that last at least 100 milliseconds are recorded, and the "100 ms" annunciator turns on. Press and hold down the (MIN MAX) for 2 seconds to exit and erase recorded readings.

In the MIN MAX mode, press ( )))) to select the Peak MIN MAX mode ("1 ms", "RECORD", and "MAX" are displayed). Voltage or current inputs that last for 1 milliseconds or longer are captured. Press (MIN MAX) to select the minimum (MIN) reading. Press again to return to the maximum (MAX) reading. To reset the Peak MIN MAX mode press ( )))) twice: the first press exits the mode, and the second press re-enters the mode. To completely exit the MIN MAX mode, press (MIN MAX) for one second. In Peak MIN MAX mode, the present reading, average (AVG) readings, and analog display are not displayed. Before selecting Peak MIN MAX, select DC voltage or current to DC couple the input waveform; or AC voltage to capacitively couple the input waveform. Peak MIN MAX works in all functions except ohms, frequency and capacitance.

In the MIN MAX Recording mode, press (HOLD H) to stop the recording of readings; press again to restart recording. If recording is stopped, the minimum, maximum, average, and present values are frozen, but the analog display continues to be active. When recording is stopped, the stored readings are not erased and you can still scroll through these readings.

Power-On Option: Select High Accuracy MIN MAX Recording

The High Accuracy MIN MAX Recording mode has a response time of approximately 1 second. Changes of more than 1 second duration are recorded. The "1 s" annunciator is turned on. In the Frequency Counter mode, readings are always recorded at the high accuracy recording speed; the response time is not selectable.

9 (RANGE) Manual Ranging

Press (RANGE) to select the Manual Range mode and turn off the AUTO annunciator. (The meter remains in the range it was in when manual ranging was selected.)

In the Manual Range mode, each time you press (RANGE) button, the range (and the input range annunciator) increments, and a new value is displayed. If you are already in the highest range, the meter "wraps around" to the lowest range. (In the Frequency Counter mode, pressing (RANGE) manually selects the input voltage or current range.) To exit the Manual Range mode and return to autoranging, Press and hold down (RANGE) for 2 seconds. The AUTO annunciator turns back on. When the range is changed manually, the Touch Hold, MIN MAX Recording, and REL[ative] modes are disabled.

Power-On Option: Rotary Switch Test

The Rotary Switch Test is used only for servicing purposes. See the 80 Series Service Manual for details. In the Rotary Switch Test mode, normal meter functions are disabled. To exit the Rotary Switch mode, turn the rotary switch to OFF and back to any switch setting.

10 (HOLD H) Display Hold

⚠ Warning

Touch hold will not capture unstable or noisy readings. Do not use touch hold to determine that circuits with dangerous voltage are dead.

Press (HOLD H) to toggle in and out of the Touch Hold mode, except if you are already in the MIN MAX Recording or Frequency Counter mode.

In the Touch Hold mode, the H annunciator is displayed and the last reading is held on the display. When a new, stable reading is detected, the beeper emits a tone, and the display is automatically updated. Pressing (MIN MAX) when you are in the Touch Hold mode causes you to exit Touch Hold and enter the MIN MAX Recording mode.

In the MIN MAX Recording mode, press (HOLD H) to stop the recording of readings; press (HOLD H) again to resume recording. (Previously recorded readings are not erased.)

In the Frequency Counter mode (Hz), press (HOLD H) to stop the display; press (HOLD H) again to start it.

11 (🕪) **Continuity Beeper/Peak MIN MAX**

Press (🕪) to toggle the beeper on or off for continuity testing in the ohms function.

In the Frequency Counter mode, press (🕪) to change the trigger slope from positive-going edges to negative-going edges. The slope selected is indicated by the analog display polarity annunciator (±).

In the MIN MAX mode, press (🕪) to toggle in and out of the Peak MIN MAX mode. See item 8.

Power-On Option: Disable Beeper

When the beeper has been disabled, all beeper functions are turned off. The beeper is automatically disabled if the meter is in the Data Output mode.

12 (REL △) **Relative Readings**

Press (REL △) to enter the Relative mode, zero the display, and store the displayed reading as a reference value. The relative mode annunciator (D) is displayed. Press (REL △) again to exit the relative mode.

In the Relative mode, the value shown on the LCD is always the difference between the stored reference value and the present reading. For example, if the reference value is 15.00V and the present reading is 14.10V, the display will indicate -0.90V. If the new reading is the same as the reference value, the display will be zero.

13 (Hz) **Frequency Counter Mode and Duty Cycle**

Press the (Hz) to select the Frequency Counter mode; press again to select duty cycle (the alternate counter function); press again to exit. The analog display does not operate in either the Frequency Counter mode or duty cycle.

In Frequency Counter mode, the Hz annunciator is displayed. The frequency function autoranges over five ranges: 199.99 Hz, 1999.9 Hz, 19.999 kHz, 199.99 kHz, and greater than 200 kHz. The RANGE button manually selects the voltage or current input range. If duty cycle is selected, readings from 0.1 through 99.9 are displayed. The "Hz" annunciator turns off and "%" turns on.

Power-On Option: High Input Impedance Mode

The input impedance of the $\overline{mV}$ function (400 mV range) is changed from 10 megohms to greater than 4000 megohms.

Summary of Power-On Options

You can select a number of options each time you turn the meter on. These power-on options (also listed on the rear of the meter) are selected b holding down one or more of the pushbuttons for approximately 2 second while turning the function switch to any ON position. All power-on option are only disabled when the rotary switch is turned to OFF. Each power-on option is discussed in detail under "Pushbuttons" and summarized in Table 2.

Digital and Analog Displays

Items 14-19 describe the digital and analog displays and LCD annunciators.

14 **Digital Display**

Digital readings are displayed on a 4000-count display with polarity (±) indication and automatic decimal point

The Fluke 87 at a Glance *CONTINUED*

Table 2. Options Available at Power-on		
Option	**Pushbutton**	**Function**
Automatic Power-off	Blue	Disable Automatic Power-off
4½ Digit Mode	Yellow	Select 4½ digit display. Full scale 19,999 counts.
MIN MAX Record Speed	MIN MAX	Select High Accuracy record speed. (Response time approximately 1 second)
Rotary Switch Test	Range	For servicing purposes only. See 80 Series Service Manual
Data Output	Hold H	Enable ultrasonic data transmission. (For use in factory testing only, cannot be modified for customer use. Beeper functions disabled.)
Disable Beeper	)))	Turns off all beeper functions
High Input Impedance in mV DC	Hz	Provides >4000 MΩ input impedance for 400 mV dc range

placement. When the meter is turned on, all display segments and annunciators appear briefly during a selftest. The display updates four times per second, except when frequency readings are taken. Then the update rate is 3 per second.

15 ||||||||||||||||||||||||||||| **Analog Display**

The analog display is a 32-segment pointer that updates at a 40 times per second rate and is the best display to use for readings that are changing. It does not operate in the Capacitance or Frequency Counter functions or in the Peak MIN MAX mode

For increased sensitivity, the analog pointer moves across the scale four times for each range. The pointer returns to 0 (wraps around) when the equivalent digital display reaches 1024, 2048, and 3072 counts. Select the next higher range if the pointer is too sensitive.

The analog pointer indicates a value lower than the digital display (up to 2.5% of range). Examples on the 40V range are:

Digital Display = 5.00V 15.00V 25.00V 35.00V
Analog Pointer = 4.8 4.5 4.5 4.2
Wrap = First Second Third Fourth
Indication = 4.8V 14.5V 24.5V 34.2V

With stable inputs, use the digital display for the best sensitivity and precision.

16 0 1 2 3 4 5 6 7 8 9 0 **Analog Display Scale**

Scale for each 1000 counts in the digital display.

17 ± **Analog Display Polarity**

Indicates the polarity of the input except in the Frequency Counter mode, when it indicates the polarity of the trigger slope (edge).

18 **4000 Input Range Annunciator mV**

Displays 4, 40, 400, or 4,000 input range for volts, amps, or ohms, and 400 mV.

19 OL **Overload Indication**

Displayed on digital display when input (or math calculation in REL mode) is too large to display. If you are taking duty cycle readings, OL is displayed if the input signal stays high or low. All segments are illuminated on analog display.

Items 20-23 describe annunciators that indicate the mode or state in which the meter is operating:

20 **AUTO Autorange**

Meter is in the autorange mode and will automatically select the range with the best resolution. Meter powers-on in autorange mode.

In the autorange mode, the meter ranges up at 4096 counts and ranges down at 360. When the meter is in the Manual Range mode, the overrange arrow is displayed until you manually select a range appropriate for the input value.

See item 9 for manual ranging

21 ⊟+ **Low Battery**

Meter is powered by a single 9V battery, with a typical life of 400 hours with an alkaline battery. At least 8 hours of battery life remain when U is first displayed. A battery check is taken between measurements.

22 ▬ **Negative Polarity**

Automatically indicates negative inputs. When REL is enabled, indicates negative results of math calculations.

23)))) **Beeper**

Continuity test is enabled. See item 11 and Table 2. Items 24 through 31 describe math function annunciators and the annunciators that indicate the units of the value displayed.

24 Δ **Relative Mode**

The value displayed is the difference between the present measurement and the previously stored reading. See item 12.

25 **100 ms Normal Recording Speed in MIN MAX Recording Mode**

Input changes of 100 milliseconds or longer will be recorded. In the 1 s High Accuracy MIN MAX Recording Mode, the recording speed is 1 second.

26 **1 ms Peak MIN MAX Recording Mode**

Input changes of 1 millisecond or longer will be recorded.

27 **RECORD Minimum, Maximum, and Average Recording**

Readings are being recorded in the MIN MAX Recording mode. A maximum (MAX), minimum (MIN), or average (AVG) reading can be displayed.

28 **MIN Minimum Value in MIN MAX Recording Mode**

The value displayed is the maximum reading taken since the MIN MAX Recording mode was entered

29 **MIN Minimum Value in MIN MAX Recording Mode**

The value displayed is the minimum reading taken since the MIN MAX Recording mode was entered.

30 **AVG Average Value in MIN MAX Recording Mode**

The value displayed is the true average of all readings taken since the MIN MAX Recording mode was entered.

30 **H Hold**

The meter is operating in a Display Hold mode. See item 10 for Display Holds.

31 The following annunciators indicate the unit of the value displayed:

AC	Alternating current or voltage
DC	Direct current or voltage
V	Volts
mV	Millivolts (1×10^{-3} volts)
A	Ampere (amps). Current
mA	Milliampere (1×10^{-3} amps)
	Microampere (1×10^{-6} amps)
nS	Nanosiemens (1×10^{-9} siemens)
	Conductance (1/ohms)
%	Percent Annunciator (for duty cycle
μF	readings only)
Ω	Ohms. Resistance
kΩ	Kilohm (1×10^{3} ohms). Resistance
MΩ	Megohm (1×10^{6} ohms). Resistance
Hz	Hertz (1 cycle/sec). Frequency
kHz	Kilohertz (1×10^{3} cycles/sec). Frequency
	Microfarads (1×10^{-6} Farads). Capacitance
nF	Nanofarads (1×10^{-9} Farads). Capacitance

32 ☼ – Not Used

Duty – Not Used

The special fuses found inside the Fluke 87. One has to remove the back of the DMM to access the fuses, and they sell for around $5 for the small one and $10 for the big one.

current model Fluke 115 has many of the features that were once only available in more expensive meters, at a much lower price. A *really* nice DMM, like the Fluke 115, can be had nowadays for less than $200 and can be obtained locally at most Sears tool departments.

Be sure the DMM you select *can measure current*, as some manufacturers offer some really nice meters that do not. This is easy to tell because the selector switch lacks an A or mA setting. Furthermore, you should select a DMM that can measure *at least* 10 amps of current safely, or it really won't do you much good for troubleshooting current draw problems. No need to get carried away here as you'll not be using your DMM to measure how much current the starter motor on your big-block Chevy draws on a cold winter day. (Although, if you did need to know that, a clamp-on style Ammeter is the ideal tool for that job.)

Before using your new DMM, I have a few cautions:

- Always be sure that the probes are in the correct position given what you're trying to measure. Measuring current is

the only time the Red Probe is connected to the mA or A terminal!

- Familiarize yourself with the type of fusing your meter has. Most DMMs have an internal fuse (or two) that you can't find on a Sunday at your corner grocery store. It will pay off in spades to have spares on hand—trust me, you'll need them when you least expect it.
- Never loan your DMM to a buddy. Why? Simple—they don't know how to use it anyhow. Anyone that knows how to use a DMM owns one. They'll invariably put the probes in the wrong spots and blow the internal fuse(s)— unbeknownst to them—and return it to you that way. You'll find out when you use it next...on Sunday.

Using a DMM

Selector Switch: Right smack dab in the middle of any DMM is a switch or dial that allows you to set it according to the measurement you

are taking. Set it incorrectly, and you could damage the circuit you're measuring or even the meter itself, although this is quite uncommon. In most cases, the settings are not written out, but rather abbreviated. The sidebar on pages 26 to 32 illustrates the meaning of the abbreviations on my Fluke 87 DMM. This meter is used throughout the book, as it is still quite current in looks and functionality when compared to meters in the marketplace today.

Range Switch: Some inexpensive DMMs combine the selector switch and range switch into a single switch with numerous setting locations. They are typically labeled clearly and are self explanatory.

Most higher-end DMMs have a separate range button that allows you to manually adjust the range. As pictured, the range button in the upper row of buttons on the Fluke 87 allows for that. Most premium meters also have auto-ranging capability, as does the Fluke 87. Whether the meter does it automatically or you do it manually, setting the range is designed to maximize the display

The inexpensive Radio Shack DMM combines the range and selector switch into a single control. This makes the meter far less versatile than the Fluke 87, but it can be owned for a fraction of the price.

reading corresponding to the measurement being taken. Equally important is the accuracy of the measurement you're taking—do you need to know what you're measuring to the hundredth of a volt? No problem.

The Fluke 87, like most good DMMs, has a four-digit readout. The range can be set manually as follows for taking voltage measurements. This is how the display looks as you change the range (by pressing the range button):

- 0.000—Max range of 9 volts, with maximum accuracy of 999 thousandths of a volt.
- 00.00—Max range of 99 volts, with maximum accuracy of 99 hundredths of a volt.
- 000.0—Max range of 999 volts, with maximum accuracy of 9 tenths of a volt.
- 0000—Max range of 9999 volts with no further accuracy — Note that the meter is clearly labeled "1000V MAX."

In most cases, I set the meter for auto-range. This is the default mode when turning on most DMMs. If you're taking a measurement that exceeds the auto-range setting with this meter, the display typically reads OL—this means overload and is an indication that you need to manually range UP the DMM. (I've seen some that read OUCH—same difference.) This does not damage the meter—no worries if you see this!

Note that you should not attempt to make resistance measurements with a DMM on live circuits. If you do so by accident, most DMMs are internally protected from this, but this is a good rule to live by.

Probe Location: As I mentioned earlier, it is extremely important to have your probes in the correct location given what you're measuring. Even though you have the legend to refer to, I'm going to go over this just so that you're sure. Following are the four locations on the Fluke 87 and what they mean.

- A—amps
- mA A—milliamps, microamps
- COM—common
- VΩ—volt ohm

OK, now the black probe is *always* in the black COM location, but what about the red one? It can go in any of the other three locations and they are all red. Do not let this confuse you! This is how to determine this:

- A—Red probe goes here when measuring current of 10 amps or less. (Note that the meter says 10A MAX FUSED between this location and the COM. This means that you can safely measure 10 amps of current, and the meter is internally fused to protect it from more than that.)
- mA A—Red probe goes here when measuring current of 400 milliamps or less. (Note that the meter says 400mA MAX FUSED between this location and the COM. This means that you can safely measure 400 milliamps of current, and the meter is internally fused to protect it from more than that.)
- VΩ—Red probe goes here when measuring voltage or resistance (Note that the meter says 1000V MAX between this location and the COM. This means that you can safely measure 1,000 Volts without risk of damage to the meter. You shouldn't have to worry about exceeding that in your '32 Ford.)

Measuring Voltage

Now that you know the basics of how a DMM ticks, let's put it to use by tackling the same three examples from the test light section with our DMM.

(Please note that the labeling of your meter may be slightly different, but the functionality is the same.)

1 Be sure the probes are inserted as follows:
 a. Red probe in VΩ
 b. Black probe in COM

2 Turn the selector on your DMM to measure DC Voltage.

3 Connect the black probe to chassis ground.

4 Connect the red probe to the connection point in question; in this case I've connected it again to the headlight connector.

Measuring Voltage *CONTINUED*

5 Turn on the circuit to be measured. The display indicates how many volts are present.

6 By pressing the range button, I can now see the actual voltage accurate to hundredths of a volt.

Measuring Continuity

In the above example, I called it "seeking ground." Identifying a *good* location to ground a piece of electronics is only one of a DMM's many functions in this arena. It can also measure resistance in ohms as well as check diodes for functionality to name a couple. This is how to find ground:

1 Be sure the probes are inserted as follows:
    a. Red probe in VΩ
    b. Black probe in COM

2 Turn the Selector on your DMM to read continuity—typically labeled with the Ohm symbol or Ω.

3 Connect the black probe to the negative battery terminal.

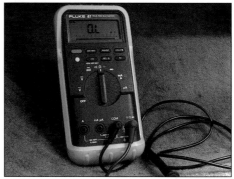

4 Use the red probe to find a low-resistance connection point, anything that reads less than

10 ohms is fine for any low-current device (more on this later).

A more common use of a DMM is measuring continuity when troubleshooting an inoperative circuit. This is explained in Chapter 7.

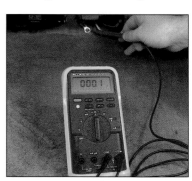

Measuring Current

This is the reason to own a DMM, and it dramatically helps you troubleshoot current draw problems quickly and easily without guesswork. I mean, who can really tell how much current is being passed through a test light given how bright it is? I know I can't.

1 Be sure all accessories in the vehicle are turned off, especially the ignition switch, so that you don't risk the chance of blowing the internal fuse within your DMM.

2 Disconnect the battery terminals as I outlined earlier and re-connect the negative terminal. (Note: I've re-connected my small light bulb.)

3 Be sure the probes are inserted as follows:
    a. Red probe in A
    b. Black probe in COM

4 Turn the selector on your DMM to read current—typically labeled as A. (Note: If your DMM has two current scales, start with the A scale so that you don't accidentally

blow the internal fuse on the scale with higher resolution by allowing too much current to flow through it.)

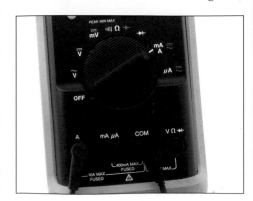

Measuring Current *CONTINUED*

5 Connect the red probe to the positive battery post.

6 Connect the black probe to the positive battery terminal.

7 Observe the reading on the DMM.

Note that this reading is well below .4 amps, which is 400mA. Therefore, I can change the selector to the mA scale on my DMM for the higher resolution setting. Additionally, I also have to move the red probe to mA because my meter has a purpose-built location for this scale. When measuring currents below 400mA, this setting is more accurate and gives the most accurate measurement possible with the Fluke 87. Again, this is spot on and not a guess—it is not possible to obtain such information with a test light.

Incidentally, you could then use this information to determine how long this draw takes to drain the battery; you only need to know the actual current draw and the amp hour (AH) rating of the battery to compute this. See the sidebar "Amp Hour Rating" for more details.

At this point you already know far more than any of your fellow car buddies in regards to electrical measuring tools. Continue on and you'll be able to charge them for your services!

Measuring Voltage Drops: Just as you can measure voltage, you can measure voltage drops. Actually, the practice of measuring voltage drops is measuring voltage across a component in a circuit. Recall, back in Chapter 1, when you learned

Amp Hour Rating

The amp hour rating of a typical automotive battery is sometimes printed right on the top of the battery. In other cases, you have to do a little research to find it. According to the Sears website, the AH rating is not specified for the Die Hard Gold batteries I use in the Olds, but the reserve capacity is at 115 minutes. You can take reserve capacity and multiply that by .4 for an approximate AH number.

This rating is a measure of how long a battery can deliver current over time. In reality, there can be times when this is not true. In fact, there is a law that addresses exactly this. That law is called Peukert's Law if you'd like to research it in an effort to learn more. But, for the sake of this example, it is close enough.

In the example, each battery in the Cutlass has an Amp Hour rating of 46 AH (115 x .4 = 46). Quite simply, this means that each battery can deliver 46 amps for one hour at a voltage above 10.5 volts. (Below 10.5 volts, said battery is considered dead.) This 46 AH rating can be any combination of current and time, such as 46 amps for 1 hour, 23 amps for two hours, or even

1 amp for 46 hours. Since the Cutlass has two identical batteries connected in parallel, the overall AH rating is doubled for the same period of time.

For the sake of this argument, let's assume the Cutlass has only a single battery like most vehicles on the road. To determine how long it would take a single one of these batteries to be drawn down by this light bulb, we can do some simple division:

$$\text{Time} = 46 \text{ AH} / .2505 \text{ amps } (250.5 \text{ mA})$$
$$\text{Time} = 183.6 \text{ hours}$$

The small drain of this little bulb would kill the battery in 7 days and 15 hours (although the two batteries in parallel would last twice as long). While that doesn't sound like much, consider that in a weekend driver. Like anything else, the AH rating of a battery decreases with its age. Even the relatively small current draw of this light bulb could draw down a weak battery overnight. Armed with your DMM, you can now determine this without guessing.

Specialized Probes and Kits

Most DMMs do not come with anything other than a set of the standard issue red and black probes. This book uncovers many uses for a DMM. If you decide to invest in one, purchasing a probe set of some kind is certainly a worthwhile complement to your investment. Pictured is one such kit.

Included in this kit are all kinds of probes and adapters that allow you to easily connect your DMM to any point in a vehicle you can conceive:

- Back Probes—These are used to easily probe in various types of pre-assembled plugs like Molex and Weatherpack connectors.
- Piercing Probes—These are used to easily probe into a wire without stripping its insulation.
- Alligator Clips—These are used to attach probes to various points, especially helpful to hold your black probe on a good ground while using the red probe.

A kit, such as this, makes it extremely easy to use your DMM to measure anything that you desire.

This kit from Pomona offers a host of DMM friendly probes, clips, and adapters. This allows you to quickly and easily connect your DMM to just about anything. Best of all, it comes with a nice roll-up pouch to keep it all in order.

about Kirchhoff's Law and Series Circuits (Fig. 1-7).

If this circuit really existed, and you were to take your DMM and measure voltage across any of the lamps, you would measure the voltage dropped through it—in this case 3 volts. Now, what if you really did need to determine why the starter motor on your big-block Chevy was sluggish, you've verified the solenoid trigger wire is not the problem, and you didn't have a DC clamp meter (more on this soon) on hand? Before pulling the starter and taking it to the store for testing, you can determine this the way most mechanics would. That way is to measure the voltage drop across the various components in the circuit to determine if the problem isn't really

the starter motor after all.

So what are those components? Since the starter circuit in most vehicles is incredibly simple, assume that it has the following components to it:

- Starter motor.
- Solenoid on motor excited by ignition switch in the start position.

- Length of cable between the battery (+) and starter motor.
- Length of cable between the battery (-) and the engine block.
- Starter mounted to the engine block.

Figure 2-1 is a diagram of such a circuit:

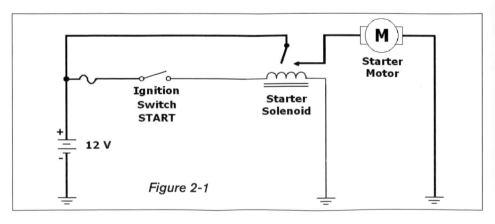

Figure 2-1

Finding Voltage Drops

Here's how you determine the problem:

(Note: Probe locations and selector switch settings are the same as for measuring DC voltage.)

1 Turn the headlights on for 30 seconds to 1 minute to dissipate any surface charge the battery might have on it.

2 Measure the voltage across the battery—for the sake of this example, let's say that was 12.6 VDC.

3 Disable the vehicle's ignition circuit—disconnect power to the coil or, better yet, disconnect the coil wire to the distributor.

4 Measure the voltage between the case of the starter motor and its (+) input terminal (the big wire!) while a helper cranks the motor—let's say that you measured 10.2 VDC.

Now that you've verified a voltage drop of 2.4 VDC, you need to determine the source of the voltage drop. Obviously, the starter pulls a bunch of current—how much exactly, is unsure. This explains some

of the voltage drop, but let's determine if we have a high-resistance cable or connection (or both) contributing to our problem. Figures 2-2 and 2-3 show how to do it:

First, measure the voltage between the positive battery terminal and the starter motor (+) input terminal as shown while a helper cranks the motor (A).

Next, measure the voltage between the negative battery terminal and the case of the starter motor—let's say you measured 1.8 volts (B).

The first place to look is the return path, as 1.8 volts seems quite high. Closely inspect the connection between the battery negative and the engine block because this is the return path for the starter motor in most vehicles on the road. (Obviously, you could also measure the voltage drop between the case of the starter motor and the battery (-) connection to the engine block and the voltage drop from that point to the battery (-) terminal to further narrow your search.) What you're looking for is evidence of resistance:

- Is the connection to the engine block tight?
- Has rust formed between the ring terminal and connection point?
- Has a star washer been used to ensure a good solid trouble-free connection?
- How is the integrity of the connection between the ring terminal and the wire itself?
- How is the integrity of the connection between the battery terminal and the wire itself?
- Is this connection tight?
- Is the wire corroded or oxidized at either end? (You will probably have to pull the insulation back from the connector or slit it with a razor blade to inspect it.)

If you find evidence of any of the above, make the appropriate repairs. This should restore the low resistance return path for the starter. Keep in mind, a complete negative battery cable assembly costs less than $10 at your local auto parts store. If this is your problem, you need to inspect the

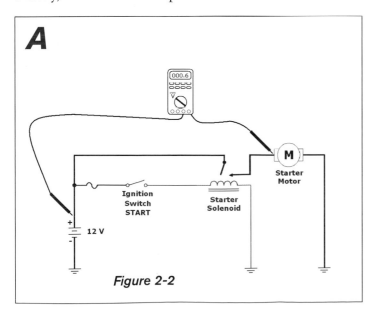

Figure 2-2

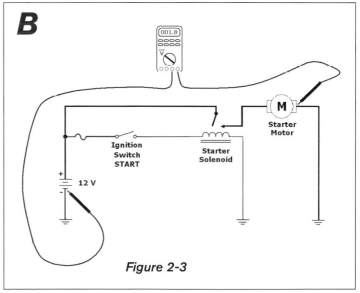

Figure 2-3

integrity of the other ground wires because they may have been damaged due to the starter seeking ground through them in the event that they offered a lower resistance return path to the battery negative. They are:

- Battery negative to chassis (typically 10–gauge or larger wire).
- Engine block or bell housing to firewall (typically a braided strap)—there can be many such straps from the engine block to the chassis and firewall in newer vehicles.

In some cases, I've seen one of these snapped in half from excessive current flowing through it from the above scenario. Although I've never personally seen it, I've heard stories of throttle cables or transmission kick-down cables burned in half or melted from exactly this.

This really is the only way to diagnose such problems. Even if you did know the current draw of your starter motor at 12 volts, it wouldn't do you much good, as only 10.2 volts is present at the starter. Recall, voltage is that which causes current to flow. When voltage is compromised, current flow is reduced.

Grounding problems can cause all kinds of maladies, and you can troubleshoot these issues the same way with a DMM. One accessory exhibiting erratic behavior when other accessories are operated is a tell tale sign of a grounding problem. Using your DMM to measure voltage drops helps you to easily determine the source of even the most difficult of grounding problems. Again, this is something you simply cannot do with a test light.

Advanced Uses of a DMM

Now that the basics are covered,

I'll show you the value of owning a really nice meter, such as my Fluke 87 for example. (At the time of the writing of this book, Fluke offers an updated version of this meter, the Fluke 87V.) Some of the additional functionality the really nice meters offer are:

- Making voltage and current measurements over time—minimums, maximums, and averages.
- Audible continuity checker.
- Measuring very high currents—optional accessory required.
- Diode checker.
- Capacitance checker.
- Measuring A/C frequency.
- Uploading measurements to a PC.
- Measuring temperature.

Obviously, the sky is the limit when it comes to what's available today, and I didn't even cover all the additional features that a combination scope (oscilloscope) meter offers! As usual, I'm going to stick to the applications that apply to typical automotive use.

Making Voltage and Current Measurements over Time: Since the idea is the same for both voltage and current, I'll just provide a single example. Let's say that I wanted to know the voltage drop caused when both of the 16-inch cooling fans in my Cutlass kick on. Even though they are wired with 10-gauge wiring, these fans consume so much current on turn on, they still cause the analog voltmeter on the dash to bounce radically for a split second. Although this causes no real harm (other than possibly pitting the contacts in the relays over time) it makes for an excellent example of how to record this minimum voltage. It also hap-

pens so quickly; the naked eye can't see the actual voltage drop on the dash-mounted voltmeter. Let's measure it.

Before starting, note that some DMMs have a MIN/MAX button that allows you to get into this mode. If this is not clearly labeled, you may have to refer to the manual of your DMM to see how to enter and use this mode.

Making Time Measurements

Make sure probe locations and selector switch settings are the same for measuring DC voltage.

1 Connect the red probe to the source of power for fans—not the wiring to the fans themselves.

2 Connect the black probe to the chassis of the vehicle.

3 Start the vehicle.

4 The DMM should display a reading in excess of 13.0 VDC at this point.

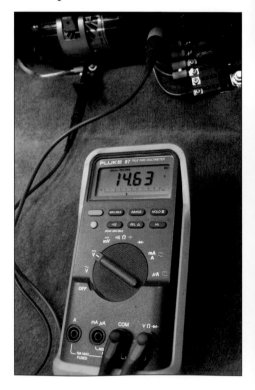

5 Press the MIN/MAX button to begin the recording process. (The Fluke 87 can log data over a time span of up to 36 hours!)

6 Wait for the vehicle to get to operating temperature and for the fans to kick on Immediately after the fans kick on, press and release the MIN/MAX button to stop the recording process.

7 Press the MIN/MAX button once to get to the MIN voltage recorded—the minimum voltage that occurred when the fans kicked on is displayed.

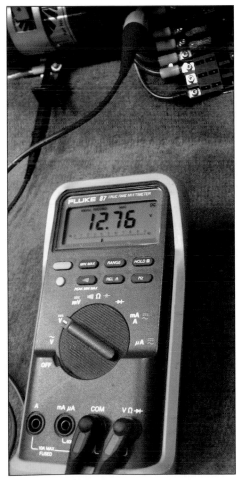

Audible Continuity Checker: This feature can be very handy when you're diagnosing an open circuit and you cannot easily see the DMM's display. Maybe your head is buried up in the dash or you have to troubleshoot an open circuit problem that spans the length of the vehicle. In this case, you probably have to extend one of the meter's probes. I have a pre-made 10-gauge wire that is terminated with alligators on both ends for just this reason. Simply clip one end to the black probe tip and you now have a *very* long black lead:

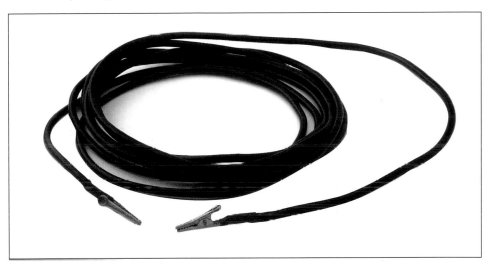

The mechanics of this are the same as outlined earlier in the chapter, but the meter emits a beep on detection of continuity. Imagine how handy this would be if you were trying to diagnose a problem with an inoperative tail light and the cause of it was a broken connection in the driver-side kick panel area. If you didn't know how to use a DMM to track this problem down, you could burn up an afternoon or even an entire day looking for the cause. Worse yet, you might not even find it.

Here's how you can go about it, the quick way:

- Be sure the circuit was turned off.
- Place the DMM in the trunk of the vehicle.
- Be sure the probes are inserted as follows: Red probe in VΩ; Black probe in COM.
- Turn the Selector on your DMM to measure continuity—typically labeled with the Ohm symbol or Ω.
- Connect the red probe to the power lead for the inoperative tail light
- Enable the audible continuity function.
- Probe with the black probe into the same color wire in the tail light harness, slowly working your way toward the front of the vehicle.

As long as you have continuity, the meter beeps with every step. It eventually gets to the point where the DMM no longer beeps when you probe the wire. This would pinpoint the source of the open connection between the current probing spot and the prior one, thereby greatly reducing the time necessary to track down this problem.

Measuring Very High Currents: Using a device called a Hall Effect current clamp is the simplest way to do this. Readily available for most of the premium DMMs, it allows you to measure DC current up to 1,000 amps.

Using Current Clamps

This example uses the Fluke Model i410 current clamp to determine how much current the starter motor in my Mustang consumes at start up:

1 Plug the clamp meter into the COM and VΩ terminals.

2 Turn the Selector on your DMM to the DC mV scale.

3 Power the current clamp on and zero the reading via the calibration dial.

4 Place the clamp around the power wire that goes directly from the battery (+) to the starter motor—be careful not to allow any other power wire to be within the jaws of the current clamp or this could skew the reading.

5 Have a helper start the vehicle, being sure that your DMM and wiring to the current clamp are out of the way of moving parts.

A Hall Effect current clamp is no meager investment. Although the above example was a quick and easy way to determine the maximum current draw of the starter motor, in this case 290.5 amps, you are able to discern more information about the overall state of the starting system by measuring voltage drops between the starter motor and battery as outlined previously. That being said, a current clamp allows you to quickly and easily measure the current draw of any accessory in the vehicle up to its current rating—and without having to disconnect it and place your meter in series with said accessory! Fluke claims the i410 current clamp is accurate from 1 amp to 400 amps.

Diode Checker: Diodes can be found in numerous locations in the modern vehicle. Most commonly, they are used in charging systems. The diode checker function of a DMM allows you to quickly determine if a diode is good or bad, but the diode has to be removed from the circuit to do so. This function allows the DMM to send voltage through the diode and the display indicates whether or not said voltage passed. When diodes fail, they most often fail open versus shorted. Since this procedure can be somewhat different from meter to meter, refer to your DMM's users manual for step-by-step instructions on how to proceed.

Congratulations—you're now the car guy who knows how to use a DMM! As you get more comfortable using the DMM, you'll find more uses for it.

THE FUNDAMENTALS OF AUTOMOTIVE WIRING

In my opinion, this is the single most important chapter of this book. Nothing is more telling of your wiring skill than the quality and integrity of your connections. In addition, your connectivity makes or breaks the reliability of the circuit you're adding, adding to, or repairing. If there is something that I'm overly picky about, this is it. Best of all, these skills are easy to learn and implement.

CAUTION: Obviously, making connections involves removing insulation from the wiring to do so. It goes without saying that you should not attempt to make connections to live circuits because you run the risk of shorting them in the connection making process. All of the methods in this chapter are written with the assumption that you are not connecting to a live circuit—turn it *off* before connecting to it!

Basic Connections

Basic connections are to wiring what knots are to rope. These are any connection between two wires that do not rely on a special connector or tool to establish. If you're at home in the comfort of your garage and walk-in-sized tool box, you'll typically elect to do things a better way. If you're on the side of the road making a quick repair, you need to know how to do it properly. Generally speaking, these types of connections are fine for circuits with 5 amps or less flowing through them and for wiring of 16 -gauge or smaller.

Twisting and Taping

Of the million different ways to make this rudimentary type of connection, I've only ever seen one that could stand the test of time. Now, before showing you how to do it, I have to give some credit to the person who showed me how to do it this way: B.J. Latting. He owns a business in Little Rock, Arkansas, called Arkansas Car Stereo. B.J. insists that this is the only way his staff can make these types of connections.

Here's the right way to do it:

1 Grab two pieces of 18-gauge wire and strip 3/4 inch of insulation from the ends of each wire.

2 Hold the two wires so that the bare wires cross at an angle.

3 Twist the two wires tightly together in a clockwise direction.

---

4 Bend the twisted connection into a U-shape.

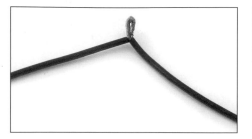

5 Lay the U-shape connection over one of the wires.

6 Tightly insulate the connection with Super 33+ tape.

The first time B.J. showed me this, he also showed me the strength of the connection by having me attempt to pull it apart by the wires. When properly done, the connection *will not break*. Rather, you will tear the wire in half. Go ahead, try it and see for yourself.

The Westinghouse Split

This connection is implemented when you need to tap into a wire without breaking it and don't have a soldering iron handy. Properly executed, this connection also stands the test of time. Here's the right way to do it:

1 Use a pair of wire strippers to cut through the insulation in the piece of wire that you intend to tap into.

2 Then, move about 1/2 inch forward of that cut and make a second identical cut into the insulation.

3 Use a razor blade to slice lengthwise from the first cut to the second cut.

4 Remove the section of insulation from the wire.

5 Insert a pick tool through the center of the copper wire and open a passage so that you can pass the second wire through.

6 Strip 3/4 inch of insulation from the end of the wire you are connecting to this one.

7 Insert the bare copper wire through the passage you made in Step 5.

8 Tightly wrap the wire around; be sure to get as much contact as you can between the two wires.

9 Tightly insulate the connection with Super 33+.

10 Use a small cable tie around the tape to keep the connection tight and a second small cable tie about 1 inch from the connection as a stress relief.

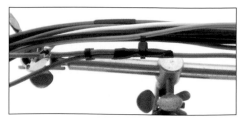

I've made thousands of both of these types of connections without a single problem. Like anything else, the key is knowing when to use them and how to do them properly. Note these connections are not suitable for 14-gauge and larger wire.

Crimp-Style Connections

This connection is simple to master, but before I show you the fundamentals of the connection itself, let's talk first about the different types of crimp connectors available. Crimp connectors are available in sizes to accommodate up to the largest gauge of wiring, including the really big stuff.

Seam versus Seamless Connectors

Although they may look similar from the outside, they are absolutely not. Quite simply, seamless crimp connectors are cut from round stock so they are tube-like in nature. Cheaper seam-type connectors are cut

On the right, I removed some of the insulation from the connector. A quick look to determine what kind of connector you're crimping ensures that you crimp it properly.

from flat stock and rolled into a tube-like shape, so they have a seam that runs the length of the connection. This can be hard to see through the insulation of the connector, but you can typically look at the ends to tell which type of connector you have.

This is especially important to know before you crimp the connector.

This is the right tool for a crimping job. Notice the seam is opposite the stake to prevent the stake from opening up the connector in the process of crimping, resulting in a questionable connection.

I typically only use seamless connectors for this very reason, but if you're crimping a seamed connector, be sure to crimp it in such a way that the seam isn't opened up in the process. This is easily accomplished by verifying the seam is perpendicular to the tool *and* opposite the stake if you're using a staking-type crimp tool.

Non-Insulated Connectors

Obviously, this type of connector has no insulation on it so it must be properly insulated after you've

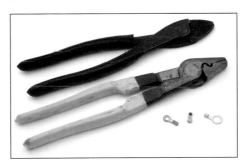

Either of these tools is suitable to properly crimp non-insulated connectors. I don't purchase non-insulated connectors, as one can simply remove the insulation from any insulated connector and have a non-insulated connector, should the need arise.

Yes, I think this is a lousy crimp tool. But, if this is all you have to use, it's even more important to orient the connector in the tool correctly.

crimped it in place—typically with heat shrink tubing. These types of connectors are available in a wide variety—from butt connectors to ring terminals, seam or scamless. The proper crimp tool for this type of connector is a staking-type crimp tool.

Insulated Connectors

This is the most common of all mechanical connectors. Like their non-insulated cousin, these are widely available in all different types and sizes and can also be seam

Insulated connectors are my connector of choice because it saves time when you don't have to insulate the connector after the crimping has been done. I have many different types of these on hand to accommodate any crimping job that I may come across.

Notice how the plastic insulation of the 8 AWG wire itself fits nicely into the insulation around this crimp connector. Some connectors have flared ends (such as this one), while others do not. I find that flared end connectors offer a higher likelihood of a perfect fit. This is equally as important as the wire fitting into the ferrule itself.

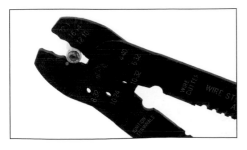

Insulated Connector Color Codes

Insulated connectors are color coded for easy identification. At a glance, you can tell the gauge of wiring they're intended for. Here are the color codes:

Red: 18 to 22 AWG
Blue: 14 to 16 AWG
Yellow: 10 to 12 AWG
Red: 8 AWG

For larger connectors, I've seen all different colors of insulation, but I don't necessarily assign a standard to them.

or seamless type. They can have vinyl or nylon insulation on them, and this insulation can be straight or flared at the ends. The trick here is to pick the connector that properly fits both the gauge and the insulation OD of the wire you are crimping it onto.

Heat Shrinkable Insulated Connectors

These are the nicest of all crimp connectors. Use them one time, and

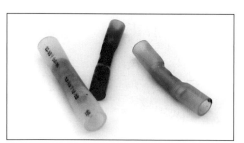

These connectors provide an exceptional connection and insulation. Think of them as a combination of a crimp connector with a heat shrinkable insulation surrounding them. Some, such as the 3M ones pictured, even have glue in them to provide a waterproof connection!

it's hard to go back to anything else. But, they're *very* expensive. The mechanics of using them are identical to typical insulated connectors, but the insulation is heat shrinkable to provide a weather-tight connection—perfect for under the hood, underneath the vehicle, or even marine use! Just crimp, and heat for a long-lasting waterproof connection.

Different Kinds of Crimp Connectors

One of the reasons that crimp connectors are so popular is the

As you can see, I keep a bunch of crimp connectors on hand. This represents about half of the various sizes and kinds that you'd find in my garage.

Look closely at the glue at each end. These connectors are suited for even the most arduous environments. The glue helps to encapsulate the electrical connection and protect it from the elements.

variety of connectors that are readily available. In addition, they're relatively inexpensive. This makes it easy to have a good selection of them on hand—I buy them in bulk so that I never run out. In addition, I like to "stock" all the various sizes available so that I always have what I need for the task at hand. I prefer insulated connectors over noninsulated.

I generally have butt connectors from 18 AWG to about 6 AWG on hand. As you can see, I have both flared and non-flared types that allow me to select the right connector for the job. Although this is a very basic connection, each connector requires two crimps so it's twice as important to install them correctly.

Butt Connectors: These are for making butt, or end-to-end, connections between two wires. This is one of the most common crimp connections, and these are readily available up to 8 AWG, with even larger sizes available on request.

Ring Terminals: The ring terminal is the second most common crimp connector. These are quite handy for terminating a wire to a connection point, such as a stud or bolt on the rear of a typical alternator. They're also used extensively to terminate a wire to a ground point. These are readily available with all different diameter rings and as large as wire is available.

Fork Terminals (Spade Terminals): These are popular because they allow termination of a wire to a connection point and provide easy connection to said point. A ring terminal requires that you totally remove the nut from the bolt or stud you're connecting to in order to establish the connection. A fork terminal allows you to simply loosen said bolt or stud and slide the terminal underneath. This is especially valuable when connecting to a barrier strip with multiple connections. These are readily available based on the diameter of the bolt that they need to fit around. I've been known to modify a ring into a fork on occasion!

A ring modified into a fork terminal. Simple and easy, this can be a real life saver if you don't have a fork large enough for the job at hand.

Quick Disconnect Connectors: I use these a lot because I try my best to keep serviceability in mind when adding a circuit to any vehicle. I use these wherever I need a simple connection to be easily disconnected. A good example is when mounting a switch or light in a dash panel that is removable. When removing the panel, a quick disconnect connection on the switch or light allows the panel to be quickly removed. This pays off in spades if your dealer services your vehicle, and they need to

The dash of my Mustang has two LEDs that monitor the operation of the installed water/methanol injection system. As they are mounted into the trim piece surrounding the cluster, quick disconnects allow a simple removal.

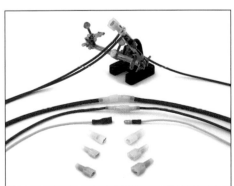

Quick disconnects are readily available for wire and cables of all sizes. I prefer the fully insulated push-on connector style over the bullet style.

remove said panel. Instead of cutting your wiring, they simply unplug it.

There are two types: bullet connectors and push-on connectors. Obviously, they're both available in male and female versions.

The push-on type makes a really good connection. I typically use this style of connector rather than a plug-type connector when dealing with fewer than four wires. With four or more wires, a male and female plug is really the correct way to do things. This connector is suitable for low-current use under the hood or vehicle as well. If you use them in this environment, I recommend that you fill them with white lithium grease before pushing them together. This helps keep the elements from affecting the electrical connection.

Filling the body of a quick disconnect with lithium grease is always a great idea with using these connectors under the hood or under the vehicle. This is an old favorite of mine.

Fundamentals of Crimping: The Right Way to Do It!

Choosing the Right Tool for the Job

First and foremost, you need the right tool for the job. Most professionals, including myself, prefer a good stake type crimp tool for *both* insulated and non-insulated connectors. When using high quality crimp connectors, the stake will not pierce or tear the insulation.

What more do you need to know about this tool? Super deluxe, it ain't.

Non-Staked Tools

This is any crimp tool that had a smooth radiused surface on both sides, such as the ones in the crimper/connector set available at your corner drug store.

These "squeeze-type" crimp tools just don't give you enough leverage to make good-quality crimps. In addition, their contact surface is typically quite narrow. If you insist on using this kind of tool, invest in one of the nicer models from Snap-On or Klein, to name a couple.

Traditional Staked Tools

This is any crimp tool that had a stake (or point) on one side of the jaw and a half-round surface on the other. These are what the pros use because they offer excellent leverage and make great crimps. In addition, they are available in a number of different sizes—handheld up to about 8 AWG. Most stake tools have at least two openings. You need to choose the opening that best fits the connector you're crimping. Properly chosen, this does not deform the connector, and the stake seats the connector fully on the wire without damaging the copper within it. I don't know of a "one size fits all" tool.

For general, all-around small-gauge crimping, I've always liked the Klein crimping tools because they have color-coded handles—the red handle identifies the side of the tool with the stake. Klein crimpers (shown on page 21) can easily crimp up to 14–16 AWG insulated connec-

tors and 10–12 AWG non-insulated connectors. The yellow-handled crimpers pictured are Ideal Model 30-425 and can crimp up to 8 AWG insulated or 4 AWG non-insulated connectors. (Snap-On offers a nearly identical set, P/N PWC30.)

Handheld Compound Action Tools

The red-handled crimpers (shown on page 21) are First Forever Model HD16L. These are a compound-type staking tool that provides increased leverage and can crimp up to 8 AWG insulated or 4 AWG non-insulated connectors. They are somewhat difficult to fit into tight places though. Another favorite is the compound crimping tools that have interchangeable dies like the one shown below from Paladin.

I originally bought this set for terminating RG-59 and RG-6 coaxial cable. As they're universal, the dies available from MSD (and others) screw right in. As pictured, mine have the spark plug crimping die from MSD attached but many different dies are available. One such avail-

A compound-action crimping tool, such as this one, has jaws that accept a wide variety of dies. By swapping out the dies, this tool can perform many different functions, such as insulated connectors, pin/plug assembly, spark plug wire, and so much more. The tool itself is somewhat big and bulky and can prove difficult to get in a tight spot under the dash though.

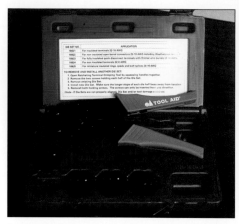

Included here are numerous dies that make all kinds of crimping tasks a snap.

able is a non-staked die for crimping non-insulated connectors the right way as you *can* get enough leverage—like shown in the Tool Aid set.

Crimping Non-Insulated Connectors

Now that you know the basics, let's tackle crimping a non-insulated ring terminal on the end of a piece of 16 AWG wire with the Klein crimp tool. Here's the right way to do it:

1 Strip about 1/4 inch of the insulation off of the end of the wire.

2 Twist the stripped end of the wire clockwise so that you can ensure that all strands of the wire can be inserted into the ferrule easily.

3 Push the ring terminal over the end of the bare wire making sure that all of the wire is inside the ferrule—there should be at least 1/16 inch of wire sticking out the other end.

4 Orient the crimp tool around the ring terminal so that the stake is opposite the seam.

5 Squeeze the tool fully, thereby making the crimp.

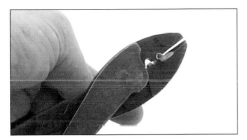

After crimping, grasp the connector and tug on it a little bit to be sure it's seated on the wire properly. If you didn't properly crimp it, it comes right off. This little check is good practice and is far better than having a connector come loose when you're driving down the road!

Crimping Insulated Connectors

This is not much different from the above. Let's tackle butt-connecting two 10-gauge wires together with a seamless butt connector using the Ideal crimp tool. Here's the right way to do it:

1 Strip 1/4 inch of insulation from both wires.

2 The two wires are properly prepared to be connected.

3 Twist the stripped ends of the wires clockwise.

4 Insert the first wire into the crimp connector so that the copper fits fully into the ferrule and the insulation fits fully into the nylon (or vinyl).

5 Orient the crimp tool around the butt connector on the half of the connector that the wire is within.

6 Squeeze the tool fully, thereby making the crimp.

7 Repeat this process for the other half of the connection.

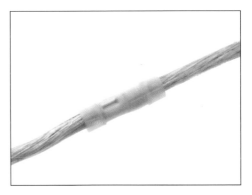

When crimping seamless butts, reverse the orientation of the crimp tool for each half of the crimp. That way, one stake is on each side of the connector. This keeps the butt connection nice and straight. If you stake both on the same side, the butt typically ends up slightly curved.

If you're crimping a seamed butt connector, be sure that the stake is always exactly opposite the seam. Both stakes are on the same side of the connector.

Crimping Heat Shrinkable Insulated Connectors

The method is the same as above with one extra step. Continue the example above as if you'd used this connector to begin with:

8 After the connector has been properly crimped, heat it with a heat gun until the shrinkable insulation encapsulates the connection

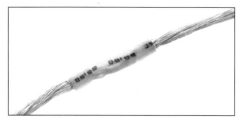

If you want the workmanship under the hood of your car to exude quality and to stand the test of time, then this is the connector for you. These are simply the best money can buy.

Crimping Large Gauge Wire Connections

There are really only two ways to do this properly, and both require a special tool to get the job done right. You're either going to

Most hammer crimp tools look like this. This inexpensive tool is an economical way to properly terminate connectors on the end of 4 AWG and larger wiring.

need a hammer-type crimping tool (inexpensive) or the mack-daddy hexagonal compound crimping tool (very expensive). Keep in mind, you cannot use the hammer-type tool to make terminations in the vehicle. Although you can use the hexagonal compound crimping tool for such, both tools are more easily used to make your connections outside of the vehicle so plan accordingly.

Using the Hammer Crimp Tool

Use of this tool is easy and who doesn't like to beat on stuff with a hammer occasionally? For this example, we crimp a ring terminal on the end of a piece of 4 AWG wire. Here's the right way to do it:

1 Strip the correct amount of insulation off of the wire with a razor blade; this varies per the connector you're crimping on to the wire, but you always want about 1/8 inch or so of wire sticking out the end of any big open ferrule connector (recall from last chapter—score and tear).

2 Push the ring terminal over the end of the bare wire making sure that all of the wire is inside the ferrule. There should be at least 1/8 inch of wire sticking out the other end.

3 With the crimp tool on a hard flat surface, insert the wire/connector into the crimp tool so that the stake is opposite the seam.

4 Use a hammer to drive the stake firmly into the ring terminal.

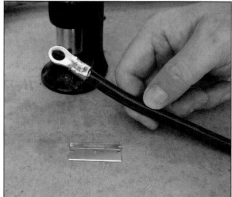

It typically takes only one or two good whacks from a big hammer to get the job done properly. If you hammer too much, the stake can tear through the bottom of the connector, which will damage the integrity of the crimp.

Using the Hexagonal Compound Crimping Tool

This tool is really no more difficult to use than a standard handheld crimping tool. However, if you're crimping big connectors, it takes a lot of force to get the job done.

For this example, crimp a ring terminal on the end of a piece of 1/0 AWG wire. Here's the right way to do it:

1 Set the dies on the jaws for the gauge of connector you're using—1/0 AWG in this case. (With this tool, the color-coded jaws correspond to a chart on the tool itself.)

2 Strip the correct amount of insulation off of the wire with a razor blade—this varies per the connector you're crimping on to the wire, but you always want about 1/8 inch or so of wire sticking out the end of any big open ferrule connector.

3 Open the jaws of the tool fully, hold the tool by one handle, resting the other handle on the shop floor. With the other hand, insert the cable/ring terminal

into the jaws of the tool, being sure to get the seam of the connector in the middle of one of the flat sides of the hex opening.

4 As you begin compressing the tool and the crimp, you should be able to let go of the cable and use both hands to to compress the tool fully.

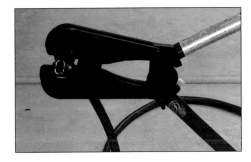

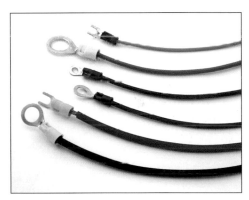

5 When finished, the termination should look like this:

Depending on how long the ferrule of the connector is that you've used, you may elect to do a second identical crimp directly next to the first crimp. Obviously, you should take this into consideration before making the first crimp.

Using the Hexagonal Compound Crimping Tool

If the basics of crimping seem pretty simple to you (and they should), then what are the pitfalls folks fall into when making bad crimp connections? Here are a few:

- Incorrect tool used—again, pliers and vises are not crimp tools!
- Right tool used, but incorrect size opening chosen to make crimp, which results in the connector being deformed or the wiring damaged.
- Poor-quality crimp connectors used.
- Seamed connectors crimped with no attention paid to the orientation of the seam come apart quite easily.

OK, admit it, you have a few connections that look like these lurking in your vehicle presently. Look closely at the errors in these terminations. Look closely under the hood at the next gathering and you'll see plenty of examples. From top to bottom, pliers were used to crimp a fork terminal, 10–12 AWG ring crimped to 16 AWG wire, connector was deformed by using an improper size crimp tool, a stake was driven into the seam of connector, connector is deformed by using improper size crimp tool and wiring exposed, stake was driven into the side of the connector.

- Too much of the insulation of the wire stripped off, making it impossible to get the insulation of the wire to fit into the insulator of the crimp connector properly and leaving the connection uninsulated.
- Wrong size connector used—if you don't have the right size connector on hand, the auto parts store just down the road will!

Soldering Irons and Guns How-To

If you want to make the best connection in an automobile, soldering is the ticket. Contrary to popular belief, soldering is very easy and can be mastered in no time at all. First, let's get the obvious out of the way and talk a little about safety.

Safety

CAUTION: A soldering iron or gun is a great tool indeed, but the heated end can cause severe burns if you come into contact with it. In addition, the only place in a vehicle that a soldering iron or gun belongs is in your hand. If you have to set it down, set it down on the floor outside of the vehicle. Be careful where you point it, as it can burn holes in anything that it comes into contact with—plastics, seats, door panels, carpet, etc.

WARNING: Butane-powered soldering irons are so handy you're tempted to use them anywhere. Don't forget that this iron has an open flame so KEEP IT AWAY FROM THE BATTERY!

CAUTION: Most solders contain lead. Anyone who hasn't lived under a rock for the last 30 years realizes the health hazards lead pose. Do your best to solder only in a well-ventilated place to avoid breathing solder fumes. You should also keep the solder out of your mouth—we've all used our teeth to pull a little more solder off the roll as we only had one free hand—bad idea! It is also a good idea to wash your hands thoroughly after handling solder or soldering.

Soldering Basics

Regardless of what kind of soldering tool you use, you're going to need some solder. As I mentioned in the last chapter, you need a 60/40 lead-based rosin-core solder that is for electronics use—which diameter you use is personal preference. In addition, you need to be sure your tip is properly dressed. This is called "tinning"—see the owners manual of your tool for specifics on how to do this.

The most fundamental thing about soldering is how you get the solder into the connection and that is the magic. The correct way to do this is to heat the connection from below and "flow" the solder into the connection from above. Like anything else, this takes a little bit of practice and patience.

The basics apply to both soldering irons and soldering guns. Soldering irons are great for wiring up to about 14 AWG before they typically cannot heat the connection enough to allow solder to flow into it. Soldering guns take over from there and can typically be used for wiring up to about 8 AWG. Soldering guns typically have two temperature settings, controlled by the trigger, and can get hot quite quickly making them handy for automotive use.

Soldering Two Wires Together End to End

This is pretty basic, and there are two ways of doing it. The first method is really only suitable for 18-gauge or larger wiring. For this example, we use a soldering iron to solder two 18 AWG wires together end to end. Here's the right way to do it:

1 Strip 1/2 inch of insulation from both wires and twist their ends tightly.

2 Tin the end of both wires by clamping them in your third hand jig and holding the iron under the wire and allowing solder to flow into the wire from above.

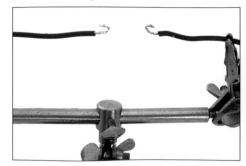

3 Bend the ends of both tinned wires into a U-shape with needle nose pliers.

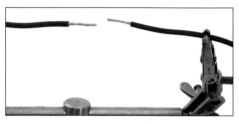

4 Hook them together end to end and flatten the Us with the pliers.

5 Use the iron to heat the connection from below, while feeding a small amount of solder in from above, thereby fusing the two wires together.

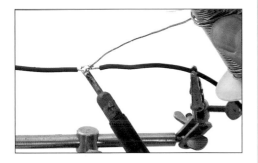

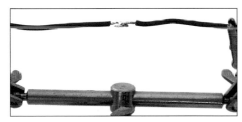

Cold Solder Connections

What is a cold solder connection anyway? After all, a soldering iron is *hot*! As I mentioned, the fundamental in soldering correctly is to allow the solder to flow into the connection. Any number of things can cause a poor solder connection—from an improperly dressed tip on the tool, to a lack of patience. The most common thing I see is not allowing the connection to become hot enough to allow solder to flow into it. It is also possible to get the connection *too hot* to allow the solder to flow into it.

Fortunately, a cold solder connection is easy to spot after the connection has been made. A good connection will look like that pictured above.

Notice that the connection is shiny and you can clearly see the strands of the wire through the solder. This is an indication of a nice, solid connection.

A poor connection could look like this:

Notice the solder is in blobs and is a dull gray color. Also notice that you cannot see the strands of the wire. This is a cold solder connection, as the connection was not heated to a temperature high enough to allow the solder to flow into it.

The second method is suitable for wiring up to about 12-gauge, although I have done this with 10-gauge wiring with a very high strand count and a high-powered soldering gun. For this example, we solder the same two 18 AWG wires together end to end. Here's the right way to do it:

1 Strip about 3/4 inch of insulation from both wires.

2 Hold them end-to-end with their bare copper ends crossing at a slight angle.

3 Twist the two wires together by wrapping them around each other in a clockwise fashion.

4 Hold the soldering iron under the connection and allow solder to flow into the connection from above.

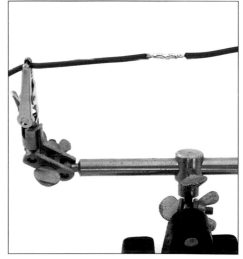

This is a bit tricky and takes some time to master, to get the wires twisted together properly. The benefit is that you do not have to tin the wires first. Either of these connections should provide a lifelong connection.

Soldering a Wire to a Pre-Existing Wire in the Vehicle

This is similar to the Westinghouse Split connection, but you solder the connection for better connectivity and reliability. For this example, connect a piece of 18 AWG wire to a pre-existing 18 AWG wire. Here's the right way to do it:

1 Use a pair of wire strippers to cut through the insulation in the piece of wire that you intend to tap into.

2 Then, move about 1/2 inch forward of the cut you just made and make a second identical cut into the insulation.

3 Use a razor blade to slice lengthwise from the first cut to the second cut.

4 Remove the section of insulation from the wire.

5 Strip 3/4 inch of insulation from the end of the wire you are connecting to this one.

6 Wrap this wire tightly around the pre-existing one.

7 Heat the connection from below while flowing solder in from the top.

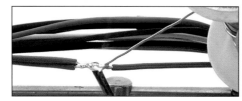

8 Tightly insulate the connection with Super 33+ tape.

Insulating Connections

Thus far, all of the connections except two have not been insulated. The two types of post connection insulators are electrical tape and heat shrink tubing.

Electrical Tape

Use Super 33+ and ensure your hands are clean. When taping connections, I typically:

- Tear off a piece that is the right length—tearing electrical tape takes practice—grab and snap! Done quickly, the tape does not stretch.
- Wrap the tape very tightly over the connection.
- Just as I come to the end, I ease up on the tension of the tape.

This provides a trouble-free insulator for many years and won't

Soldering Various Terminals

Soldering a terminal to the end of a piece of wire is no more difficult than soldering two wires together. Obviously, non-insulated connectors are the way to go here, and it's not uncommon for me to have what I need in an insulated connector—no problem, I just remove the insulation with a pair of pliers. For this example, we terminate a piece of 8 AWG wire with a ring terminal with a soldering gun. Here's the right way to do it:

1 Strip 3/8 inch of insulation from the end of the wire.

2 Twist the stripped end of the wire clockwise.

3 Push the ring terminal over the end of the bare wire making sure that all of the wire is inside the ferrule—there should be at least 1/16 inch of wire visible at either end.

4 Clamp the wire in the third hand jig and heat the connector from below with the soldering gun while flowing solder into the open end of the ferrule.

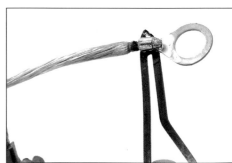

5 When you see solder in the wire on the other side of the ferrule, you know you have enough solder for the connection.

unravel itself as it would if the tape were pulled tightly all the way to the end. When taping soldered connections, let the connection cool for a few seconds and wrap it while it's still hot. The best thing about tape is that you can insulate any kind of connection after the connection has been made.

Nope, this isn't a pre-made plastic insulator. This is what a properly insulated connector looks like after you're done taping it. Just remember to ease up on the tension slightly as your finishing your tape job, so you keep the tape from pulling loose over time.

Heat Shrink Tubing

Unlike electrical tape, heat shrink tubing isn't "one size fits all." You also can't apply it to any connection after the connection has been made, as you can with tape—nope, this takes a bit of thinking ahead. I typically buy heat shrink tubing in 3-foot lengths and I have it

Heat shrink tubing is certainly handy. It comes in sizes from 1/8 inch to more than 3 inches in diameter. I use it for all kinds of stuff, so I keep plenty of it on hand in all different colors.

in all different diameters and colors, including white, which I use to label my wiring.

When using heat shrink tubing, slip it down the wire before making the connection. Also, keep it far enough away from the heat so that it doesn't shrink on the end nearest the connection as you're making it. It's always best to use slightly more than you need to insulate a connection, so on the off chance that does happen, you can cut that off with a razor blade and you're still in business. Slide the tubing over the completed connection and heat it with a heat gun until it shrinks tightly around the connection.

Heat shrink tubing gives your work a very professional look. Just remember to slide it down the wire before making your termination.

Heat shrink tubing yields the most professional looking results of any insulator. If you want folks to look at your work and think *wow*, then heat shrink tubing is the only way to go. Heat shrink tubing has many other uses, a few of which you'll learn later in the book.

Temporary Mechanical Connectors

This type of connector is all too common in automotive use. These refer to any connector that is designed to be installed over an insulated wire—like T-Taps or Scotchlok connectors. These are only suitable for low-current applications because they have quite a small contact area.

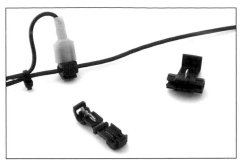

Temporary mechanical connectors are only suitable for short-term connections. If you do have to use a T-Tap for any reason, this is how your finished installation should look. The cable tie acts as a strain relief.

In addition, as they are not weather tight, you'd never see me use these under the hood or under a vehicle to connect, say, a trailer harness. I like to think of these as temporary connectors because they do not offer the reliability of a properly crimped or soldered connection.

Incidentally, I've repaired more "connections" made with these than any other—I can't tell you how many times I've solved major problems when fixing someone else's work by removing these entirely and using a different method of connection.

Scotchlok Connectors

These are the easiest connectors to install. Be sure that the connector you're using is properly sized for the wire you're putting in it. If you're using this connector to connect two different-size wires together, you'd be best advised to pick another connection method. These are color coded via the same scheme as insulated crimp connectors.

T-Tap Connectors

These remain a favorite among those who perform auto security

Electrolysis

Dissimilar metals in contact with one another cause a chemical reaction called electrolysis. Some car manufacturers, Nissan being one, use a steel battery clamp to connect the copper battery cables to the lead battery posts. Three different types of metal is the perfect recipe for electrolysis, and over time it causes gook to form over the connection. Without proper maintenance, this can cause all kinds of problems.

The same thing can happen with temporary mechanical connectors. Electrolysis between the copper wire and metal within the connector can cause a similar problem, especially in high-humidity environments. This can be further aggravated by heat caused by higher resistance due to the small contact area.

The net result is that the connection can fail. If you must use these kinds of connectors for any reason, use them inside the vehicle only.

Wire Nuts and Crimp Caps

I do not recommend wire nuts whatsoever for automotive use. There are many better connections. If you like the simplicity of a wire nut, use a crimp cap instead and rest assured it will not come loose! Simply twist the wires together to be connected, slide the cap over the connection and crimp. I don't use these too often because I don't like the look of the finished product.

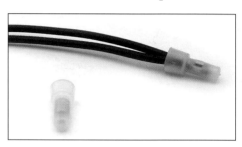

Wire nuts are great for home wiring jobs with solid wire, and that's about it. If you need to connect two wires that are side by side at their ends, use a crimp cap instead.

and remote starter installations because they pride themselves in speed. Their installation is slightly more complex—the T-Tap itself is closed around the wire that you're tapping into.

When using a T-Tap, it's important to use the one that properly fits the wire you're connecting to. Using a T-Tap or Scotchlok connector that is too small cuts through the copper in the wire that you're tapping into, and thereby the connector damages the integrity of wire and the circuit it's part of.

Then, crimp a male push-on connector onto the wire that you're connecting to the wire above. Slide the spade into the body of the T-Tap for a quick connection. Admittedly, this connector can be a life saver if you're

trying to tap into a wire that is in a very-difficult-to-reach spot. Even still, I've used fewer than 10 of them in my time working on autos. These are also color coded via the same scheme as insulated crimp connectors.

This is a T-tap connection at its most basic. Notice the connector and male push-on terminal are both sized properly for the 18 AWG wiring, in this example.

Between Scotchlok and T-Tap connectors, I've seen a range of problems. Typically, the wrong-size connector is used. Too small of a connector can cut into the wiring your connecting it to, thereby compromising its integrity. Too big of a connector doesn't get a good grasp on the wire.

Fuse Taps

Stay away from these! These connectors are designed to slide under the fuse in the fuse box of a vehicle and provide a push-on terminal tap for power.

Folks, fuse taps just aren't the way to do things properly. Read on to learn how easy it is to find a source of power, making this type of connection totally unnecessary.

I have numerous problems with this; here are my top three objections:

- Number 1: The manufacturer has a pretty good idea of the current capacity of the fuse panel in your car. Shoving wiring under a fuse in the panel is not a safe way to power up your new accessory, as you could exceed the safe current capability of the circuit.
- Number 2: Most people install these incorrectly! How so? Simple. A fuse tap should always be installed under the load side of the fuse and not the power side. Get it backward, and the length of wire from the fuse tap to your accessory will burn if it becomes pinched or shorted. I just witnessed this happen in a car.
- Number 3: If the fuse tap is removed for any reason, the fuse can no longer make good contact with the fuse box because the contact points have been spread out to allow the fuse tap to fit. The fix is to use a small flat blade screwdriver to bend the contacts back to where they were to begin with, but I can't tell you how many times I've had to charge someone two hours of labor to track down and repair this!

It's just too easy to find a source of power under the dash of a car with your DMM that doesn't involve tapping under a fuse. Just say *no* to these and be safe. You'll thank me in the long run.

Distribution-Type Connectors

These are commonly found on aftermarket electronics, such as ignition boxes and audio amplifiers, but you can also purchase them for wiring projects. I use them a lot because they give me a great place to terminate connections between different components. They're available in two types—barrier strips and cinch-type. Both are available at most auto parts stores as well as Radio Shack in different sizes and lengths.

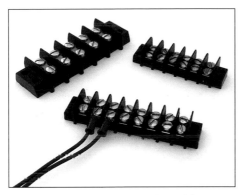

These barrier strips are found in numerous places in automotive use. Connecting to them requires the correctly dimensioned fork terminals in order to fit the barrier strip.

Connectors and Plugs

Work on vehicles long enough, and you come across all kinds of connectors and plugs. The number-one reason that manufacturers use them is to speed up assembly and disassembly when it comes to servicing the vehicle after it's been built. Imagine how difficult it would be to remove a console or dash from a vehicle without these. The nice thing is that you can purchase and install them as well. This gives your wiring project the same kind of serviceability the rest of the vehicle has.

Molex Plugs

The word Molex is to these types of connectors that Coca-Cola is to soft drinks. There are a bunch of different manufacturers of these kinds of plugs, and they're all similar in use. I bought a four-pin male and female set designed for 18 AWG wire at Radio Shack for this example. I've seen these available for up to 12 AWG wire at various electronics parts houses.

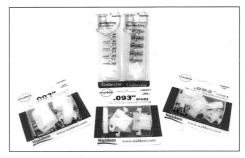

Radio shack is a great source for connectors of all types, including these. I picked up some Molex brand plugs at the local Fry's Electronics. The plugs come as kits with pins and the male/female connector bodies for many different configurations and wire sizes. Best of all, they were less than $5 a pack.

Tools Required

Really, the only tool you need is the crimping tool itself. Pictured is the one that works with this connector, but depending on the connector you purchase, it may call for a special crimp tool.

This is a run-of-the-mill pin-crimping tool. These are readily available at your local Radio Shack or your local electronics supply house.

If you have a set of compound crimpers with interchangeable dies, you can usually buy just the die for that tool versus buying a whole new crimp tool. It's also nice to have a pin extractor for the unlikely event that you have to remove a pin from a plug. They're inexpensive and typically sold at the same places you buy crimpers.

If you don't have the tool, you can use a pair of needle-nose pliers to do the crimping and a soldering iron to ensure the connection is solid. It's painfully slow but works equally well.

Assembly

The assembly of all types of connectors is similar—Molex, GM Weatherpack, or Deutsch, so I'm just going to cover one of them. First, let's take a look at the pin itself. Notice that there are two crimping points—on the right is where the pin is crimped to the copper wire and on the left is where the pin is crimped to the insulation of the wire as a strain relief.

Look closely. The strain relief on the far left is crimped around the insulation of the wire. The wire is connected to the pin electrically via the part of the pin just to the right. The crimp tool bends both in a U-shape to hold the pin on the wire firmly.

Note also that there are male and female pins as well as male and female plugs. It's important to keep these oriented correctly so that you can assemble them, so pay attention!

These are the pins available in the plug kits at Radio Shack. You have to cut them apart before you can use them. It's also necessary to leave some of the metal in place when you make your cut and keep the pin from pushing through the back of the connector.

Assembling Connectors

Assembly is easy. Here's the right way to do it:

1 Strip 1/8 inch of insulation off of the end of the wire and put the wire in the pin as shown.

2 Holding the two together, insert them into the crimp tool and crimp the pin to the insulation of the wire first. This provides the strain relief for the electrical connection itself.

3 Remove the pin from the tool and re-orient it in the correct spot to crimp the pin to the wire.

4 Correctly crimped, it looks like this.

5 Insert the pin into the body of the plug in the correct orientation. Make sure that it "snaps" or locks into place and confirm this by tugging on it gently to verify that it doesn't come out.

6 Repeat for the rest of the pins—male and female.

A completed assembly typically looks like this:

The fully assembled plug. Notice that this plug has a female body with male pins.

This is a very time consuming process, and it takes a bit of practice to get good at. I've actually gone to the trouble of soldering the pin to the copper *after* I've crimped them to ensure they don't ever come loose, but I'm sure that doesn't surprise you by now. Finally, some of the plugs allow you to orient the male/female *pins* into the male/female *plugs* any way you like. This is quite handy if you have multiple connectors with the same pin count and you don't want them to be accidentally plugged into one another.

Basics for AWG Wire 8 and Larger

When you have to work with *big* cables, and you often do when working on a vehicles charging system, there are some additional things you need to know.

Tools Required

- Battery cable cutters designed to cut large soft copper cable (OK, a hacksaw works nicely in a pinch).
- Large AWG crimp tool—be it the hammer type or hex crimp type, or cheaper yet...
- Propane or MAPP Gas Torch—I bet you already have one of these in your tool box anyhow!

When working with large-gauge wiring and connectors, you can get by with only a torch and pair of cable cutters. The Klein cable cutters here are their model number 63050 and available at your local home improvement store.

WARNING: Wielding torches is dangerous enough. Because they have an open flame, avoid using them near a battery. To be safe, I recommend using them at your workbench only.

Soldering Large AWG Connectors

Let's say that we need to solder connect the same 1/0 AWG ring terminal on the end of the same piece of wire that we did with the big-dollar hex crimp tool, only we didn't have that tool. No problem, equipped with an inexpensive torch, we can do the job—and better!

Here's the right way to do it:

1 Fill a small cup with cold water and set it nearby.

2 Strip the correct amount of insulation off of the wire with a razor blade as before.

3 Clamp the cable softly in a bench vise in a vertical fashion and slide the ring terminal over the wire so that 1/8 inch or so of wire is visible at each end of the ferrule.

4 Heat the ring terminal and wire with the blue end of the flame in your torch, being careful not to burn the insulation of the wire—a little won't hurt anything, but this isn't good to breathe, either.

5 As the wire and ring terminal get to temperature, you can now flow solder into the connection from the top. (Tip: To keep from burning up the solder with the torch, move the flame of the torch away from the connector.

6 Feed solder from the bottom up into the connector to complete the connection.

7 When your connection looks like this, remove the heat from the connection and turn off the torch.

8 Carefully remove the wire from the vise and dip the ring into the cup of water, being careful that it doesn't fall off, to cool and complete the connection.

This takes some practice to get it down to a science. Don't worry about burning up the insulation on the wire with the torch, as you're going to do it anyway the first few times you attempt this. Plus, it's easily covered with heat shrink tubing or the plastic insulator that came with the ring terminal, which you're going to use to insulate the connection anyhow.

Large AWG Distribution-Type Connectors

Working with large-gauge wire can be frustrating when connecting it together. Fortunately, there are more such products available today than ever before. Distribution blocks, battery clamps, and fused distribution blocks are just a few examples of what's available today. A great source of these is your local car stereo shop.

Large AWG Quick Disconnects

Think of these as giant-sized Molex plugs able to handle incredibly high currents. I've always known these as "Anderson" connectors and a Google search confirmed that.

These are available up to 4/0 AWG and are handy when you need a reliable high current disconnect. I've used these connectors for years and have not a single problem to report. They are used in *very* high current applications—like the biggest of winches and for connecting the battery packs on fork lifts to their respective chargers.

These are typically crimped on the ends of the cable, and they are same-sex connectors. In addition, the (+) and the (-) can only go one way, which eliminates the possibility of connecting them incorrectly.

These provide a fast connection between a battery charger and battery in a race car—just pop the trunk and plug the connectors together. No worries about getting the cables reversed—ever!

A termination like this is not difficult to perform, and it has the lowest resistance of any large-gauge termination. Rest assured this connection will not come apart. Be warned, it takes a bit of practice to master the assembly technique.

Large-gauge wire distribution products are now readily available thanks to the car stereo industry. The block on the left is an ANL fused distribution block that accepts up to 1/0 AWG wire for both its input and outputs. The block on the right is a MAXI fused distribution block. Its inputs accept up to 1/0 AWG wire, and up to 4 AWG wire for its outputs. These are also available without the fuses.

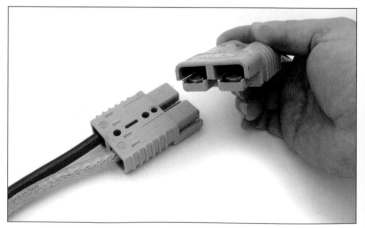

The Anderson Connector is a functional and practical high-current, quick-disconnect connector, and it's one of my all-time favorites. A pair of very high-current "pins" terminates the end of the wiring and then snaps into the plugs. The ferrules of these pins are typically 2 inches long so they allow dual crimps to ensure they won't come off.

Switch Panels

What if you don't want to use a traditional ignition switch in your hot rod or race car? You can use a panel, like one of those made by Moroso or Painless Wiring.

A typical aftermarket switch panel, like this one from Painless Wiring, allows the operator far more control than a simple ignition switch. As you can see, the switching for all accessories is manual. These types of panels are commonly found in vehicles built for racing.

As you can see, there are START, IGNITION, and ACCY switches, as well as switches to control up to two FUEL PUMPs, electric WATER PUMP, and LIGHTS.

The difference is that the operator has to manually trigger any and all accessories that they wish to use at any given time. This isn't possible with a traditional igni-tion switch. For example, maybe you need to adjust the valves and don't want the engine to turn over while a helper is bumping the starter for you. No problem, just leave the IGNITION switch OFF and have them quickly depress the START button. The engine bumps, but will not turn over, making your life so much easier.

You can also combine a panel like this with your standard ignition switch to prevent vehicle theft if you also drive the car on the street. Here is a simple diagram to do that:

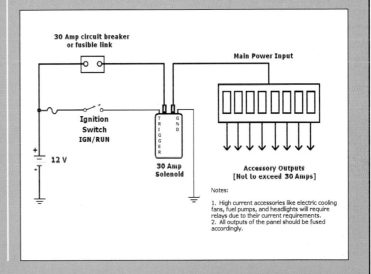

the form of pops, clicks, ticks, or even noise from the alternator. This noise can cause erratic operation of delicate or sensitive electronics if:
1. It travels up its own ground wire due to poor filtering.
2. It is picked up inductively by either its chassis or wiring—this is called induced noise.

Rest assured the engineers of the electronics on-board the modern vehicle have taken both of the above into consideration so they have high immunity to such noise. That may not be the case for the aftermarket CD player you're adding, though. Over the years I've experienced my fair share of troubleshooting time with such problems, and they can be extremely difficult to resolve. There is simply no substitute for experience in these cases.

Typical Routing

Since the beginning of auto manufacturing, automakers have gone out of their way to keep the wiring out of sight of the occupants. So, where is it all? The bulk of it has always been behind the dashboard. Runs from there to the following are common:

- Through the firewall to power the underhood accessories, such as the ignition system, headlights, parking lights, horn, etc.
- Down the kick panel(s), under the sill panels and carpet, to the rear of the vehicle to power accessories, such as brake lights, parking lights, back-up lights, fuel pump, etc.
- Through the doorjambs and into the doors to power accessories, such as power door locks, power mirrors, power windows, etc.

Again, as the number of on-board electronic features increases, so does the complexity of the wiring harness. If you're working on a late model vehicle, assume some of the vehicles harness, and even control modules, could be just about anywhere!

Designation of Harnesses for Safety Equipment: Thankfully, the wiring for any on-board safety equipment (SRS systems, ABS brakes, etc.) is typically clearly called out. Some harnesses are yellow, others orange, and others red or green. In other cases, such as my wife's Nissan truck, the harnesses are black, but the plug ends are bright yellow. This varies by vehicle, but assume these brightly colored harnesses and plugs are *verboten!*

This is the main computer for the SRS system in the 2004 Nissan Frontier. Take note of the bright yellow plugs on the right. The color designates the harnesses and module as part of the vehicle's on-board safety equipment.

CAUTION: Do not attempt to open, connect to, or otherwise service harnesses designated with brightly colored tape or split loom. To do so is to risk damaging the fragile and sensitive circuits that control the vehicle's on-board safety components and/or computers. Leave this to the pros!

If your hot rod is a late model one, then you may want to consider

purchasing a shop manual that has a diagram of the wiring harness. This certainly can't hurt to have around. On the other hand, if you're restoring a '50 Merc, rest assured it has a relatively simple wiring harness and most of it is self explanatory.

If you have to troubleshoot a problem in a vehicle with a complex wiring harness, then you're best advised to purchase a manual that shows an exploded view of this. You can buy a consumer manual at your local auto parts store from Haynes or Chilton that has the basics. You should also check with your local library because many of them have quite a selection of these on the shelf. A more advanced manual can sometimes be purchased directly from the manufacturer. When I was in the shop, we relied on manuals from Mitchell, and they were extremely accurate. Figure 4-1 is what you're likely to see when looking at such information today.

Controllers: the Basics

OK, now that you know about the ignition switch and the wiring harness, you should understand their roles. As I said earlier, I consider the ignition switch to be the gatekeeper. It is the master control switch in the vehicle and ultimately allows the passage of power to all of the vehicle's accessories—save for any that function with the key in the off position. A controller is considered anything that controls or governs the operation of an accessory—be it a simple switch or an on-board computer.

Switches

Switches are the simplest of all controllers. Most are manual, meaning that the operator of the vehicle has to operate them manually, such as a turn signal switch. Switches are typically used to control low- to medium-current accessories. Higher current switches are sometimes used for high-powered accessories, such as

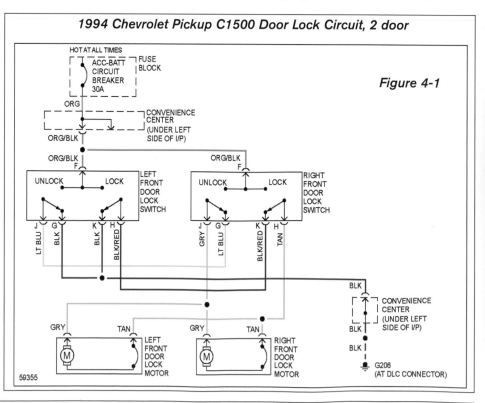

1994 Chevrolet Pickup C1500 Door Lock Circuit, 2 door

Figure 4-1

headlights or fog lights. When using a switch of any kind, it is important to match its current rating to that of the accessory it is controlling—a little bigger is never a bad idea.

Single Pole Single Throw: Commonly referred to as S.P.S.T., this is the simplest of all switches (Figure 4-2). As its name implies, it has a single pole (common) and a single electrical path that can be thrown open or closed. These switches are available in toggles, pushbutton, momentary, and many other styles.

In the *on* position, the switch allows current to flow from the pole to the accessory. In the *off* position, the switch interrupts the flow of current to the accessory. These switches are easily identified, as they have only two electrical terminals.

Single Pole Dual Throw: The single pole dual throw (Figure 4-3) is commonly referred to as S.P.D.T. This switch is simple in concept, but incredibly versatile as it can be used in a great many arrangements. This switch doesn't have traditional on or off positions.

All of the switches here are of the S.P.S.T. variety. Notice the one with the clear red toggle has three terminals—don't let that throw you for a loop. This third terminal is simply a ground input for the light. It is built into the toggle itself that goes on when the switch is closed.

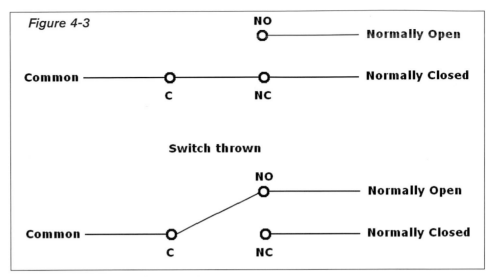

Figure 4-3

NO — Normally Open

Common — C — NC — Normally Closed

Switch thrown

NO — Normally Open

Common — C — NC — Normally Closed

Think of it like this—an S.P.D.T switch can be used to connect the pole (C) to *either of* two contacts—the normally closed (or N.C.) or the normally open (or N.O.), but not to both simultaneously. These switches are also easily identified, as they have three electrical terminals. (You may have grabbed one of these by accident for some project in the past and after wiring it up, realized that your accessory was *on* when you thought it should be *off*. After some head scratching, you swapped one of the connections and it all worked fine. Now, what you did should make sense to you.) The S.P.D.T. switch is my absolute favorite because I've found no end to what I can do with them, especially when they're of the electromagnetic variety called a relay—more on that soon.

Both of the above switches are available in multiple different varieties based on the needs of the vehicle designers. D.P.S.T., D.P.D.T., and many others exist. Now that you

S.P.D.T. switches can also come in a number of physical arrangements. Of special interest is the push-button switch on the right. Press the button once and the switch is thrown one way, press it again and the switch is thrown the other.

understand S.P.S.T. and S.P.D.T. switches, you should also understand the rest—including a D.P.D.T., for example. You can easily determine what kind of switch you're dealing with by checking for continuity between terminals with your DMM—remember, to do so, remove the switch from the circuit. (If you're buying one for a project, most switch manufacturers provide an electrical contact diagram on the back of the packaging or on the switch itself.)

Center OFF: Similar looking to a S.P.D.T., a Center OFF switch has three terminals, a C and two N.O. terminals. In the center position, the C is not connected to anything. In the up position, the C is connected to one of the N.O. terminals and in

Figure 4-2

Input — C — NO — To Accessory

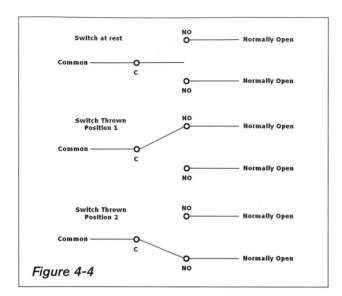

Figure 4-4

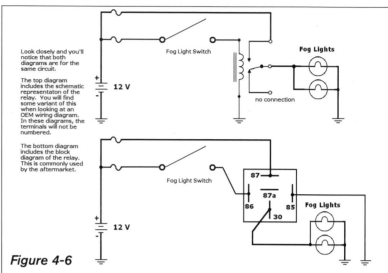

Look closely and you'll notice that both diagrams are for the same circuit.

The top diagram includes the schematic representaton of the relay. You will find some variant of this when looking at an OEM wiring diagram. In these diagrams, the terminals will not be numbered.

The bottom diagram includes the block diagram of the relay. This is commonly used by the aftermarket.

Figure 4-6

the down position, the C is connected to the other. A switch like this (Figure 4-4) is what automakers use to control the turn signals. Painless uses a Center OFF switch to control the headlights and parking lights in the panel I have in my Olds. By adding a simple diode to the switch, the up position allows the parking lights only to be on, and the down position allows both the headlights and the parking lights to be on—clever. (See the sidebar "Diodes" for an explanation.)

Rheostats: A rheostat (Figure 4-5) is a switch that allows one to vary how much voltage is applied to an accessory. In addition, a rheostat is typically designed to allow the passage of a considerable amount of current. The dim-

The rheostat is built into the light switch assembly, which is used to dim the dash lights in my Mustang. Look closely for the white ceramic part with the spring nearby; this is the rheostat itself.

mer switch controller for your dash lights is one such example.

A rheostat is really nothing more than a variable resistor. It has a wiper that rides along a carbon contact surface that has a varying level of resistance, which is linear by design. This

allows the switch to have any voltage between 0 VDC and 12 VDC available at its output, based on where the dial is manually set.

Current Ratings: Most switches have a specified current rating. This is the amount of current that the switch can safely pass through its contacts. This doesn't mean that a 15-amp switch is the perfect choice for a 15-amp load. In fact, OEMs typically use a switch with a higher current rating than the load connected to it, so that the switch provides many years of service. Exceeding the current specification can cause the switch's contacts to fail prematurely. In addition, this can be a fire hazard.

Relays

As I said earlier, this is my absolute favorite switch. Sometimes referred to as a "Bosch" relay, these are readily available with current ratings up to 40 amps. It's no secret; the typical automotive relay has been shrouded in a veil of confusion for as long as I can remember. A relay (Figure 4-6) is simply an electromagnetic switch, so you already know what it does. The difference between a simple

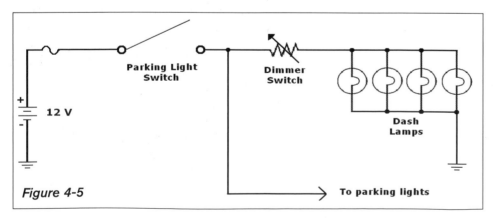

Figure 4-5

Resistors

A resistor is a non-polarized electrical component that converts electrical energy into thermal energy (heat). This can be quite useful to limit the amount of current available to an accessory—like when a light-emitting diode (or LED) is used in place of a standard light bulb. LEDs cannot accept more than about 2 volts and need very little current to light fully—on the order of 20 to 30 mA to be exact. Exceed that and they burn out.

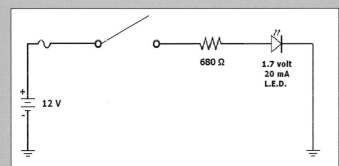

This is a great example of how to put Ohm's Law to work for you. I had a Radio Shack L.E.D. that was rated to handle up to 1.7 volts D.C. and 20mA of current. Since Kirchoff's Law tells us that current is the same across components in a series circuit, we know that 20mA will also flow across the resistor. Then, use Ohm's law to determine what value of resistor will be needed if we desire a 10.3 volt drop across it (12 - 1.7):

R = E / I
R = 10.3 Volts / 20 mA
R = 515 Ω

Since 515Ω resistors aren't readily available, we'll go to the next size up - 680 Ω . Incidentally, if we were going to put this in a running vehicle, the 680 Ω resistor would be good to about 15 volts.

Resistors are readily available in all different values, measured in ohms, and power ratings, measured in watts. If you're using them in a project like above, then you have to use a little Ohm's Law to determine the correct value. They can be used in any number of electrical circuits in the modern vehicle, and are most commonly found within the electronics of the controllers or modules. Various ignition circuits also rely on resistors—usually the higher powered sand cast (or ballast) type.

As resistors become hot in normal operation, their very purpose can be the cause of their demise over time. This can be further aggravated by other sources of heat. Fortunately, resistors are incredibly easy to test with your DMM. Remove them from the circuit first—disconnecting one end is all that is required. In many cases, the resistor has its specifications printed right on its side, like a sand cast resistor.

This tells you its:
- Resistance in ohms
- Power-handling capability in watts
- Tolerance as indicated by +/- some percentage

Higher wattage resistors are sand cast, such as the one here. These are also commonly referred to as ballast resistors. This one is clearly labeled as 6.8Ω with 5 percent tolerance. It has 10 watts of power handling capability.

In other cases, the resistor can have lines painted on it—typically four such lines, starting at one end. Here's how to decode them:

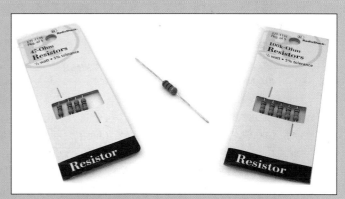

Smaller wattage resistors, like these, have a different labeling system due to their physical size. I get mine at the local Radio Shack.

- First line—First number in the value
- Second line—Second number in the value
- Third line—Multiplier
- Fourth line—Tolerance

Fortunately, this has been standardized, as shown in the chart at the top of page 66.

Resistors *CONTINUED*

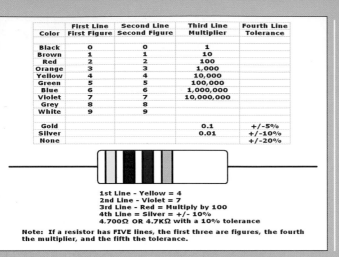

Color	First Line First Figure	Second Line Second Figure	Third Line Multiplier	Fourth Line Tolerance
Black	0	0	1	
Brown	1	1	10	
Red	2	2	100	
Orange	3	3	1,000	
Yellow	4	4	10,000	
Green	5	5	100,000	
Blue	6	6	1,000,000	
Violet	7	7	10,000,000	
Grey	8	8		
White	9	9		
Gold			0.1	+/-5%
Silver			0.01	+/-10%
None				+/-20%

1st Line - Yellow = 4
2nd Line - Violet = 7
3rd Line - Red = Multiply by 100
4th Line = Silver = +/- 10%
4.700Ω OR 4.7KΩ with a 10% tolerance

Note: If a resistor has FIVE lines, the first three are figures, the fourth the multiplier, and the fifth the tolerance.

The wattage isn't specified on these kinds of resistors, but 1/8 watt to 2 watts is the power range of such resistors. After a while, I've just come to know it by their overall size—close enough for government work anyhow.

When measuring a resistor, don't forget to take into consideration its tolerance. The sand cast resistor pictured above is a 6.8 Ω unit with a specified tolerance of 5 percent. This means that it could measure from 6.46–7.14 Ω and meet specification. In the unlikely event a tolerance is not specified, I typically assume it is bad if it falls more than 10 percent outside of its specified value.

Diodes

A diode is a semiconductor that allows current to flow in one direction only. One side of the diode is called the Anode, and the other side is called the cathode (denoted by the end with the white stripe).

Diodes come in many varieties. Simple diodes, such as the ones on the left, are sized based on their voltage ratings. LEDs, such as the ones on the right, emit light when current passes through them, hence the name.

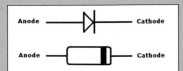

These are some of the many uses for diodes:

- Rectification: Used in the vehicle's alternator, diodes convert the AC voltage made by spinning

the alternator into DC voltage that can be used to charge the battery or power accessories.

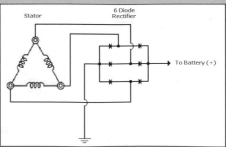

Note: the diodes are shown for illustrative purpose only and would not be visible as they are within the isolator.

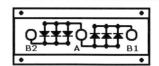

- Isolation: Used in many vehicle circuits, diodes can isolate devices or circuits from one another for whatever reason. Isolation diodes can have incredibly high current capability, like a battery isolator, which is really just two groups of very high current diodes housed in an aluminum heat sink. Within the isolator, the anodes are connected and tied to the A (alternator) terminal,

Diodes *CONTINUED*

the cathode of one diode connects to the B1 (battery 1) terminal, and the cathode of the second to the B2 (battery 2) terminal. A battery isolator like this allows a single alternator to charge both the starting battery and auxiliary battery(s) while keeping them electrically isolated from one another. These are commonly used in motor homes to this day.

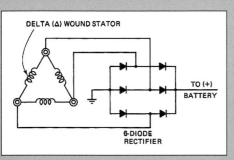

- Voltage spike prevention: Electromagnetic switches, such as relays or solenoids, use an electromagnetic field to move a switch from one position to another electrically via a coil of wire wound around an iron core. When power to the coil is removed, the electromagnetic field collapses. This can cause a voltage spike very high in voltage and if not directed to ground, could cause damage to the circuit that controls the relay or solenoid itself. A diode can be used to shunt this spike to ground, preventing damage. When used in this application, said diode is referred to as a clamping or quenching diode.

- Illumination: Special kinds of diodes, called LEDs, have been in use for many years. The OEMs commonly use these to illuminate various switches so that they can be easily seen at

night. Electrically, these diodes function like all others, but the passage of current through them causes them to illuminate. (These are especially neat to use in projects!)

A diode can be connected in one of two ways—forward bias or reverse bias. When a diode is installed in a series DC circuit, the diode allows current to pass through it when it is connected in forward bias, but not in reverse bias. A typical silicon diode consumes about 7 tenths of a volt (.7V) to turn it on, so voltage measured at the cathode will be 7 tenths of a volt less than present at the anode. This is something to take into consideration when troubleshooting circuits with them or using them for projects.

When used in a parallel DC circuit, such as in the prevention of voltage spikes as outlined above, the diode is connected in reverse bias. It has no function when the circuit is on, but when the circuit is off, the diode allows the spike created by the collapsed field to be shunted to ground as shown below.

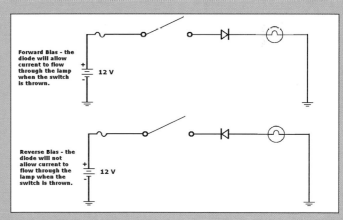

The clamping diode is installed in reverse bias across the coil of the relay. The collapse of the electromagnetic field caused when power is removed from the relay's coil. This diode prevents the voltage spike from damaging the device controlling the coil. Notice that the leads of the diode are fully insulated.

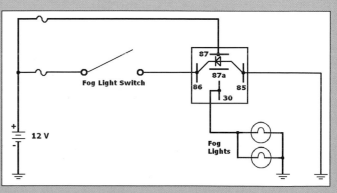

switch and a relay is how the switching is done. A switch is manual while a relay's switching occurs when voltage is applied across its coil.

Relays are available in all shapes and sizes. Shown are S.P.S.T., S.P.D.T., and D.P.D.T. versions.

There are three main reasons automakers choose to use relays:

- Reliability: The current requirements of the accessory are in excess of 10 amps or so. Relays are often used in this application instead of a high-current switch for reliability.
- Use a low-current controller to operate a high-current accessory. This allows the high current required by the accessory to be routed through the relay's contacts and the controller only has to power the coil. (Typical Bosch-style relays only require about 110 mA of current to power the coil. This makes relays friendly for the low-current outputs of the many ECMs, PCMs, and other controllers of the modern vehicle.)
- Serviceability: By locating the relays in a central spot, it is easy for a service technician to troubleshoot and diagnose a problem, then pull and replace a defective part. This is far less labor intensive than replacing

a switch and it's also a lot less likely to happen to begin with.

Unlocking the Mystery: OK, so why are relays typically regarded as black magic? Simple, if you don't understand the different types of switches, you don't have the foundation required to understand the relay. As a result, I've run into very few that actually understood what these little black boxes do and how they do it. Since you already know all about switches, the relay is simply an extension of that knowledge.

No different than switches, relays are also available in many different variations. Electrically speaking, they're identical to switches of the same type with one exception— the switching is done electrically. This means that a relay really has two electrically isolated parts:

- The switch.
- The coil—when powered, this causes the switch to be thrown.

S.P.S.T. relays are the simplest, just like the switch of the same name. They can have four or five terminals. Even though they may look similar from the bottom, not

all five terminal S.P.S.T. relays are identical.

S.P.D.T. relays are the most versatile and all have five terminals. I believe that this is where some of the confusion begins. After all, the five terminal S.P.S.T and the S.P.D.T. relays look identical, but electrically they aren't even close. Diagram 4-15 illustrates the differences between the four most commonly used automotive relays.

How do you know for sure what kind of relay you have or need to purchase when looking at them in the store? Easy—the body of the relay itself typically has an electrical diagram embossed or stamped on it; this is called the legend, and it is similar to the diagrams in Figure 4-7, allowing you to determine which relay you need. All relays that I've ever seen have numbers embossed on their bottoms in the plastic next to the electrical terminals themselves. Here's how to decode them:

- 85—Coil input
- 86—Coil input
- 30—Common
- 87—Normally Open
- 87a—Normally Closed

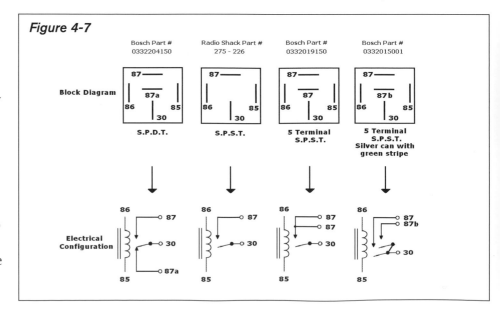

Figure 4-7

Only S.P.D.T. relays have a terminal labeled 87a. Five-terminal S.P.S.T. relays typically have two 87 terminals as pictured.

The numbers embossed in the plastic are the key to decoding the type of relay you're looking at. Terminal 30 is labeled, but is just above the terminal on the left and out of the shot.

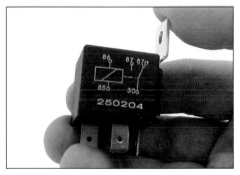

This same relay has the electrical diagram screened on the side of the body itself. Obviously, this is an S.P.D.T. relay given the style of switch shown in the diagram.

Although the Bosch relay looks identical to its S.P.D.T. cousin, the legend clearly shows that it is a simple S.P.S.T. relay with two 87 terminals.

The Bosch "silver can with green stripe" five-terminal S.P.S.T. relay has the following:
• 87b — Normally Open #2
The legends on the housings of this S.P.S.T. relay and their standard five terminal S.P.S.T. show that these relays are electrically different from one another—this is illustrated in Figure 4-7. This means that you cannot use one of these in a circuit that calls for the other.

To power the coil of a relay, voltage needs to be applied across terminals 85 and 86. This means that one terminal has to have +12VDC and the other side ground. Obviously, a coil of wire has no polarity, so it really doesn't matter which side is connected to which. That being said, some relays have built in quenching diodes (see the sidebar on diodes for an explanation) so polarity must be observed with these. This should also be clearly labeled in the relay's legend—remember, the stripe denotes the cathode of the diode and it is connected in reverse bias.

S.P.S.T. relays are simple. The coil is powered to establish an electrical connection between the common and normally open terminals. Note the electrical difference in the two five-terminal S.P.S.T. relays that I mentioned above—specifically, the Bosch silver can with green stripe relay allows the normally opens to be isolated from one another when the coil is at rest.

S.P.D.T. relays are just as simple as there are only two positions they can be in, electrically speaking:
1. Coil un-powered—terminal 30 connected to terminal 87a (C to N.C.)
2. Coil powered—terminal 30 connected to terminal 87 (C to N.O.)

See, I told you relays were simple. No different than an S.P.D.T. switch, S.P.D.T. relays can have numerous applications due to their versatility. (The next chapter explains how to use them in your own projects.)

Obviously, it's important to understand the difference between the various types of relays. If you had to replace one that went bad over time for whatever reason—you'd better replace it with a new unit that was electrically identical, otherwise the circuit does not work correctly.

Current Ratings: No different than switches, relays have current ratings as well. The current rating of a relay is the amount of current that can safely pass through the contacts and has nothing to do with the current the coil requires. A 30-amp relay does not require 30 amps of current to power it up. Rather, that means that the relay can power an accessory requiring up to 30 amps of current. Again, the OEMs choose to use higher current relays than necessary so that they last a long time.

There are different grades of relays. Hella, Potter & Brumfield, Tyco, and Bosch are but a few of the many manufacturers that make quality relays. Of course you know that I have a personal preference, and that has been the Bosch-branded relays.

To date, I've never pulled a properly installed defective Bosch relay out of a vehicle. That's a pretty impressive track record, especially considering that I've also used thousands of them over the years in projects of all types. (The current required to properly power the accessory determines which relay to choose and install. Using a 30-amp relay to power a 40-amp accessory causes its contacts to fail prematurely because they become pitted. In addition, a relay

Most of the relays in my Olds are located here. I made the mounting point for them from very thick strapping material and screwed that to the firewall. For each mounting point, I mounted a bolt to the strap. A single nut holds the relays in place for easy serviceability.

This is your basic Ford starting solenoid. The two silver terminals are for the coil, while the two copper terminals are the connections to the switch itself.

The underhood fuse box in the 2004 Nissan Frontier truck houses relays, fusible links, and fuses for those accessories that are tied to the battery directly. The box is located directly behind the battery.

should always be mounted with its terminals pointing down to avoid the possibility of water entering its case.)

Relay Centers: Most vehicles have a central location for all of the relays used for the high current accessories. Depending on the vehicle, this can be under the dash or under the hood. My wife's Nissan Frontier combines the underhood fuse panel and relay center as one.

In my Olds, I made my own relay center by locating all the relays on the firewall just above the transmission hump. This was done for serviceability because I know all the relays in the vehicle (except one) are in this location.

You should make a point to know if your vehicle has a relay center and more importantly where it is. The owner's manual of your vehicle should provide this information.

Chapter 5 offers gives several scenarios of how to use relays in your

The solenoid on the left is rated for 80 amps, and the one on the right is 200 amps. Both are continuous duty ratings. The terminal configurations are identical to the Ford solenoid.

Look under the dash of any vehicle and you'll typically spot at least a pair of these in the fuse box. The heavy-duty flasher in the middle is from Tridon and is rated for up to 25 amps of current.

own projects. By the time you're done with this book, the relay will be second nature to you.

Solenoids and Switching

Now that you know all about relays, you know about switching solenoids. Solenoids are used to do all kinds of things—electrical and non-electrical. As usual, I'll stick to the ones for electrical duty. An electrical automotive switching solenoid is really nothing more than a very high current relay.

Another example is the high-current aftermarket units shown. These are used for any number of things. One example is to disconnect an auxiliary battery from the vehicle's charging system when the Ignition switch is in the off position. (More on this in Chapter 7.)

Sometimes the case of the solenoid itself can be the negative connection to the coil. If so, it needs to be solidly mounted to a clean metal surface. When voltage is applied to the trigger terminal, its contacts close, thereby making the high-current electrical connection between the battery and load terminals.

Flashers

Flashers are typically found in the fuse panel and used in the turn signal and hazard circuits. Typically called LX flashers, they have two terminals only. One terminal connects to power, the other to the load.

As current flows through the flasher to the load, it has an element within it that is designed to break the electrical connection briefly and then restore it. Flashers are connected to the power input lead for the turn signal and hazard circuits. As the output of both to those circuits is typically directed to the same

filaments of the same bulbs, one flasher is required for the turn signal switch power input and a second for the hazard switch power input.

Circuit Protection

The Fuse Panel: In a given automobile, you have at least one central fuse panel. This panel is designed to protect the vehicle's wiring harness from damage if any of the connected accessories attempts to pull more current than it is rated for or if the wiring between the fuse panel and accessory(s) is damaged. Most vehicles nowadays have one fuse panel under the dash and one under the hood. The underhood panel typically contains the fuses for the high current (up to 100A) accessories and the main power to the ignition switch. The under dash panel typically contains all of the fusing and breakers for the vehicles lower current accessories—such as the radio, cigarette lighter, power windows, etc. 3-, 5-, 7.5-, 10-, 15-, 20-, 25-, and 30-amp fuses are common.

As I discussed in Chapter 3, it is important to understand that every fuse has two connections within the

The Mustang's interior fuse panel is located under the dash and to the left of the steering column. To the left of the fuse box is the G.E.M. module that I refer to later in the book.

panel. One side of the fuse is connected to the accessory; this is called the LOAD side. The other side of the fuse is connected to the source of power for the accessory; this is called the POWER side. The power side can be connected to the battery directly (such as a dome light circuit), the IGN/RUN circuit, the HEATER/AC circuit, or even the ACCY circuit. In some cases, you might run into fuses in the panel that are used to protect the output of a controller. Either

The underhood fuse panel of the Mustang houses relays, MAXI fuses, and those fuses that power accessories connected to the battery directly. The fuse holder in the foreground is an aftermarket kit available at your local auto parts store.

Most interior fuse panel covers have a built-in location for a fuse removal tool and spare fuses. The one pictured is from the Mustang.

way, the vehicle's owner's manual typically provides the legend to the panel.

I like to assume that the manufacturer of the vehicle has more knowledge of the wiring and accessories than I do. This means that I'm not going to replace a blown 20-amp fuse with a 30-amp fuse so it doesn't blow again, because that may be exactly what happens. Worst case, this could cause a fire by exceeding the current capability of the wiring within that circuit. Most fuse panels have a spare fuse of each size in the panel itself or the fuse panel cover.

If you replace a blown fuse with the same size fuse and it blows again, then the fuse is doing its job! Obviously, this is an indication that there is a problem causing the fuse to blow. Chapter 7 explains how to find and solve this kind of problem easily.

Fuses: A fuse is a device that has a metal strip (or wire) with a known current limit. Exceed this limit and the fuse blows. All fuses have a current rating and typically the fuse can pass this current rating for an extended period of time before its metal strip burns in half. In fact, a fuse typically passes many times its current rating for short periods of time before its metal strip is burned in half.

Over the years, I've seen a bunch of different fuse types for automotive use, and these can vary widely between domestic, Japanese, and European vehicles. This book covers the main ones (glass and blade types) and all have the same intended purpose and that is to protect the circuit from damage. Keep in mind that even though two fuses may look similar and have the same current rating, they may react differently

(slower/faster). These specifics can be determined via the three-digit alpha prefix that comes before the fuse's current rating itself. (If you require that information, refer to the manufacturer of the fuse.)

Glass Fuses: Glass fuses used to be the norm and were available in a number of different physical sizes and values. If you own an older vehicle with such a fuse panel, you'd be well advised to have at least two of every fuse in the panel in your tool box so you can avoid searching for them if one blows. Although AGC fuses were the most common, your vehicle may require something different—double check both the rating and prefix to be sure and get the right ones.

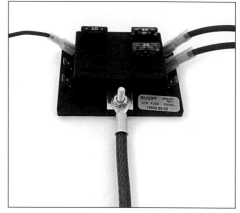

This is a simple six-circuit ATC fuse panel I picked up at the local auto parts store for less than $15. Many companies offer such fuse panels in all kinds of configurations, allowing you to upgrade an older glass fuse panel with a new Blade fuse panel.

This eight-circuit ATC fuse panel on the left is yet another example of an aftermarket fuse panel. This panel comes fully disassembled, so it is a much more complex installation. Unlike the fuse panel in the previous photo that has a common power input for all fuses, this panel allows the installer to configure the power side of the fuse to be any way they choose.

Blade fuses are available in sizes from 1 to 100 amps. ATC, Mini ATC, and MAXI fuses are shown.

The ANL fuse has proven popular with the aftermarket because it is ideal for very high current accessories. The fuse holder and fuses shown are available from Rockford Fosgate.

The fusible links that Ford uses on the stock charge lead of the Mustang are used in parallel to double the current carrying ability of a single link.

Cartridge-style fusible links are found in newer vehicles. Replacement of this style is much easier compared to a traditional fusible link.

These older style glass fuse panels can also have rust buildup on the contacts themselves. This causes resistance between the contact and fuse and can be a source of all kinds of problems. If you own a vehicle with this type of fuse panel and it has rusty contacts, you're best advised to swap it to a newer ATC (also called ATO) blade-type panel. Fortunately, these are readily available from any number of manufacturers.

Painless Wiring and others offer replacement fuse panels designed to make the task of upgrading an older glass fuse panel to a newer and more expansive ATC fuse panel a snap. In addition, these fuse panels can be purchased with or without the associated wiring harness, should your vehicle require a harness upgrade as well.

Blade Fuses: These are widely used in today's vehicles. In the 1980s, glass fuse panels gave way to ATC fuse panels, solving many problems in the process. These were used for 15 years or so, until the Mini ATC fuse and panel took over. Today's vehicles typically contain Mini ATC, and MAXI fuse panels. Unlike the glass fuse, blade fuses of all types are problem free and readily available! MAXI fuses are used both by the OEMs and by the aftermarket, as they can be reliably built up to 100 amps in size.

Blade fuses of any kind and their corresponding fuse holders and fuse boxes have a proven track record of reliability. This is the main reason why all the OEMs as well as the aftermarket fuse panel and wiring harness companies use them exclusively.

High-Current Fuses: Used mainly by the aftermarket, the most common types are the ANL and Mini ANL fuses. These are available in sizes up to 500 amps (or even larger) for the highest current applications. In addition, the ANL fuse holder is designed to accommodate these incredibly high currents across it

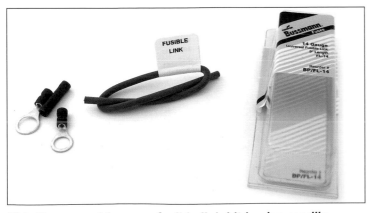

This Bussman 14-gauge fusible link kit is also readily available at your local auto parts store. Fusible links are installed in-line between the source of power and the accessory, no different than a fuse.

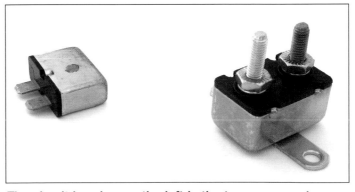

The circuit breaker on the left is the type commonly found in interior fuse panels for power windows and power seats. The breaker on the right is an aftermarket product. Both are auto-resetting and have the same intended purpose.

with minimal voltage drop because it securely holds the fuse in place.

As I said earlier, your local car stereo shop can be a great source for parts like this. In the past few years, ANL and Mini ANL fuses have become so common that many auto parts stores now stock them.

Fusible Links: Fusible links go back many years and are primarily used to protect high-current circuits. In the days of glass fuses, the highest rating available was about 30 amps. Fusible links were used to protect circuits with current flowing through them in excess of 30 amps. Currently, they've been replaced almost entirely with MAXI fuses, although my Mustang has both.

The fusible links pictured are on the stock alternator charge lead. Why would that be? Simple—if the alternator's voltage regulator failed, this could allow voltage "run-away." As voltage increases, so does current through the myriad of accessories in the vehicle that do not have over-voltage protection (like light bulbs) as well as the battery. If this occurs, the current from the alternator to the vehicle's electrical system would exceed that of the fusible links and snap them, thereby protecting the accessories and battery from damage.

A fusible link has the same purpose of a fuse, but they are constructed quite differently. Typically, a fusible link is 4 wire sizes smaller than the wiring the circuit calls for—a circuit with 10 AWG wiring would call for an 18 AWG fusible link to adequately protect it. In addition, the insulation of a fusible link is non-flammable and this makes them ideal for underhood use. Due to the nature of how they fail, fusible links are only recommended for underhood use. These are readily available in many sizes at your local auto parts store.

Fuse cartridges are used in some vehicles and act similarly to fusible links. They're smaller, more convenient, and much simpler to replace in the event of a failure.

Circuit Breakers: A circuit breaker is a device that is designed to open its contacts when the current flowing through it exceeds its rating. A simple bi-metal strip connects the contacts. As the current through this bi-metal strip exceeds its capacity, it changes shape and breaks the electrical connection between the two contacts.

Unlike a fuse, a circuit breaker does not need replacing in the event this occurs. There are two main types of circuit breakers:

- Auto resetting: These are the most commonly used by the OEMs. They are most commonly found in the interior fuse panel and can be used to protect circuits that have a very high current demand when first activated, such as power windows or power seats (or when they come to the end of their travel and the operator continues to hold the switch momentarily). In the event an auto resetting circuit breaker "trips," it automatically resets after a period of rest, restoring operation to the circuit.

- Manual resetting: These are most commonly used in the aftermarket, and I've seen them with current ratings up to 200 amps. In the event this kind of circuit breaker trips, its arm must be manually pushed back into position to restore operation of the circuit. Some of these have a "valet" feature which allows you to manually open the circuit breaker to intentionally interrupt power to the circuit—handy if you've got something you don't want people messing with in the event you had to leave your vehicle in someone's care.

Either of the above examples is considered to be thermally activated circuit breakers. Over time, the auto resetting breakers can wear out with heavy use. Circuit breakers have two terminals, sometimes labeled as BAT (battery) and AUX or LOAD. If that is the case, then this must be observed for the breaker to work correctly.

The aftermarket has used manual-resetting circuit breakers for a long time because of their current-carrying ability.

Shown are a pair of 140-amp breakers that have a built in "valet" mode. Pressing the red button opens the breaker's arm, thereby disconnecting power to the load.

POWER ACCESSORIES AND THE CHARGING SYSTEM

This chapter covers some fairly lengthy topics. Specifically, it gives the run-down on power door lock circuits, power window circuits, power sunroof and convertible top circuits, and an in-depth look at the charging system.

Before I get into the specifics of power door lock, power window, power sunroof, and convertible top circuits, I should mention that this chapter focuses on traditional analog circuits. No different than the evolution of the ignition switch that I discussed previously, many of these vehicle circuits have undergone similar changes with advancing technologies. Digital BUS systems bring about the opportunity to allow controllers to interface digitally between one another. Again, as these systems are the exception, rather than the norm, this chapter focuses on the norm.

Power Door Lock Circuits

When it comes to power door lock circuits, you need to understand that there are multiple types that all accomplish the same job. These can vary by manufacturer and can even vary among vehicles made by the same manufacturer. At the end of the day, the operation of the circuit is the same. Press the unlock switch and the doors unlock; press the lock switch and the doors lock.

Most of the door lock actuators are of the two-wire variety, no matter the manufacturer, OEM, or aftermarket supplier. Apply power to one wire and ground to the other and the actuator moves one way; reverse this and the actuator moves the other way. This is commonly referred to as "voltage reversal" and is the way things have been done in vehicles for a very long time. What varies is the way the switching is done to get voltage and ground to the motors. Here are four of the most common switching methods:

- Negative Pulse
- Positive Pulse (with and without relays)
- Voltage Reversal Rest at Ground
- Variable Voltage

Consider for a moment that the number of doors a vehicle has can be the determining factor as to what type of door lock circuit is most suitable. For two-door vehicles, it's safe to assume that a door lock switch is present in each door. Some four-door vehicles have door lock switches in the front doors only, while others include them in all four doors. In most cases, four-door vehicles are not wired via the voltage reversal rest at ground scheme because this would add unnecessary complexity, weight, and expense.

In the diagrams to follow, I've done my best to simplify each overall circuit for clarity. In addition, the diagrams simply show the door lock actuators wired in parallel—where exactly this occurs is vehicle specific.

Negative Pulse

This type of door lock circuit is my favorite because they're very simple and easy to interface to, as outlined in Chapter 8. This circuit (Figure 5-1) is very common in Japanese vehicles.

Note that a pair of parallel-connected switches (S.P.D.T. Center Off) are used to switch low-current ground to power the coil of either of the relays, which in turn powers the

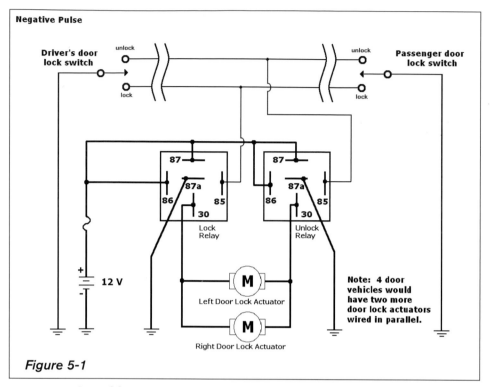

Figure 5-1

actuators. In addition, both relays rest at ground, so when a switch is depressed, it:

- Excites the coil of one of the relays, which causes
- the voltage reversal circuit to the actuators to be completed, which causes
- the actuators to move in the corresponding direction.

Four-door vehicles have two additional motors wired in parallel in the same fashion.

Positive Pulse—With Relays

Very similar to the negative pulse circuit, the switches just switch low-current +12VDC to power the coil of either of two relays, which in turn power the actuators. This is what Ford uses in my Mustang (Figure 5-2).

From the relays to the actuators, the circuit and operation is the same as the negative-pulse circuit. Four-door vehicles have two additional motors wired in parallel in the same fashion.

Voltage Reversal Rest at Ground

This circuit does not use relays (Figure 5-3). Instead, a pair of D.P.D.T. switches is wired in series and the overall circuit rests at ground. Note that one of the switches has four wires, and the other has five wires. The four-wire switch is the MASTER and the five-wire switch is the SLAVE. This overall circuit is easy as both actuator wires rest at ground as a result of the switches resting at ground. When one switch is depressed, it:

- Sends +12VDC to one of the lock/unlock wires, which causes the actuators to move in the corresponding direction.

In this circuit, the switches excite the actuators directly. As a result, they are of a higher current variety than either of the pulsing-type circuits and therefore require a larger gauge of wiring, which is typically 14- or even 12-gauge, depending on the vehicle. This large-gauge wiring and number of wires on the switches are a telltale sign of a voltage-reversal switching configuration.

This circuit was very common in two-door domestic cars and trucks

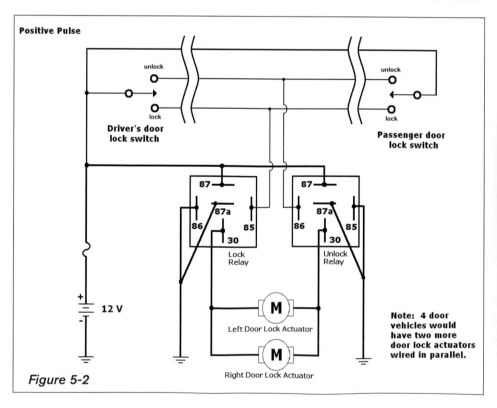

Figure 5-2

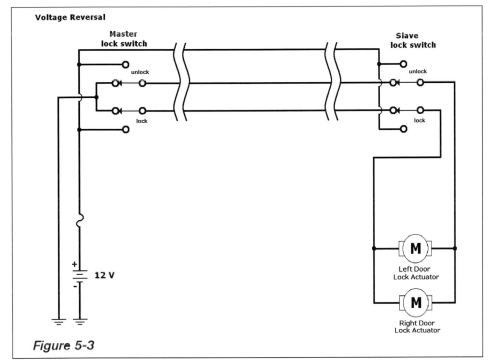

Figure 5-3

Positive Pulse—No Relays

In the early days of power door locks, GM built vehicles with three wire actuators. These actuators had two coils—one for lock and the other for unlock. Mounting the actuator to the metal door interior completed the circuit. At the end of the day, this is just a positive pulse circuit (Figure 5-5) that requires 5 to 10 amps per actuator to operate them, so the switches and wiring have to be up to the task. I remember the first time I came across this. I was looking at wiring diagrams in a Mitchell manual and I couldn't believe what I was looking at.

Other Types

There are a few other types of door lock circuits that are not covered in this book—like the one wire lock/unlock circuit used in Mercedes Benz vehicles for many years. In addition, some of the European and

for many years, as illustrated in the diagram at the beginning of Chapter 4. Keep in mind the master switch can be on either side of the vehicle. The master switch is often located on the same side of vehicle as the fuse box. A good example of this was the all-new 1997 Ford F150. Ford laid out the wiring harness in those trucks exactly backward and the fuse box was on the passenger side of the dash. The master lock switch is in the passenger door in these trucks.

Variable Voltage

Variable voltage (analog) configurations (Figure 5-4) use a single wire to send multiple signals to a controller and, as the name implies, these signals vary in voltage. The first vehicle I remember working on that used this type of door-lock circuit was the Ford Probe, which was actually built by Mazda. Today this is commonplace, especially in Chrysler vehicles for the last 10 years or so. A variable-voltage system requires

some kind of controller between the switch and actuators as shown. This controller decodes a voltage level as a command and takes the appropriate action.

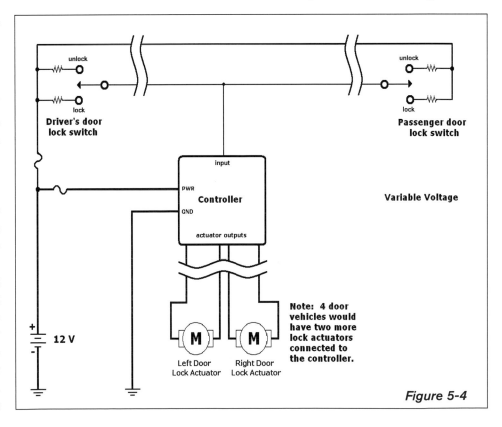

Figure 5-4

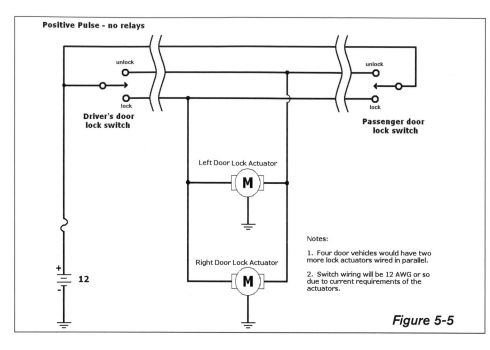

Positive Pulse - no relays

unlock

Driver's door lock switch

lock

unlock

Passenger door lock switch

lock

Left Door Lock Actuator

M

Right Door Lock Actuator

M

+
12
-

Notes:

1. Four door vehicles would have two more lock actuators wired in parallel.

2. Switch wiring will be 12 AWG or so due to current requirements of the actuators.

Figure 5-5

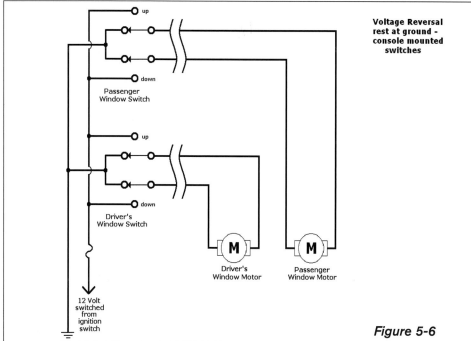

up

Voltage Reversal rest at ground - console mounted switches

down

Passenger Window Switch

up

down

Driver's Window Switch

Driver's Window Motor

M

Passenger Window Motor

M

12 Volt switched from ignition switch

Figure 5-6

British vehicles have "closure" wires—a single wire that when ground (or in some cases voltage) is applied to it, causes the door locks to be locked as well as all of the vehicles windows/sunroof to be closed. As the specifics of these circuits can vary by vehicle, get your hands on the wiring diagrams if you have to work on them.

Power Window Circuits

When it comes to power window circuits, there are also a couple types that accomplish the same job. These can vary by manufacturer and can even vary among vehicles made by the same manufacturer. At the end of the day, the operation of the circuit is the same: press up to raise the win-

dow and press down to lower the window.

The main difference between power window and power door lock circuits is that the windows are able to be operated independently of one another. Electrically, the overall circuits have many commonalities even though the power window circuits appear much more complex on paper.

Most of the power window motors are also of the two-wire variety, no matter what the manufacturer OEM or aftermarket and "voltage reversal" is the nature of the circuit. Like power door locks, this is also the way things have been done in vehicles for a very long time. Here are the most common switching methods:

- Voltage Reversal Rest at Ground.
- Voltage Reversal Rest at 12 volts Switched.
- Voltage Reversal Rest Open.

Before I go into the differences, we should consider that the location of the switches typically determines the kind of circuit employed.

Here are some common scenarios for two-door sedan with front power windows only:

- Switches in the center console—one switch per motor.
- Switches in the doors—one switch for the driver-side motor and two for the passenger motor.

Here are some common scenarios for two-door sedan/convertible with front and rear power windows:

- Switches in the doors and rear panels—one switch for the driver-side motor and two for all other motors.
- Four-door sedan with front and rear power windows.

- Switches in all four doors—one switch for the driver-side motor and two for all other motors.

In all of these circuits, the switches operate the motors directly. As a result, they are of the higher current variety. In addition, the wiring in these power window circuits is a minimum of 14-gauge, and in some cases 12-gauge.

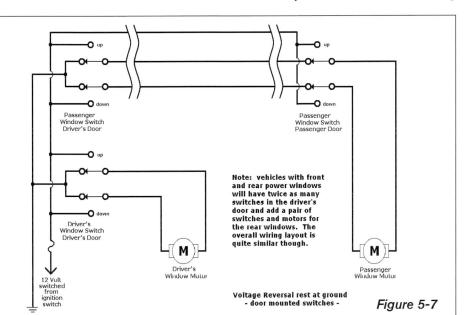

Passenger Window Switch Driver's Door

Passenger Window Switch Passenger Door

Note: vehicles with front and rear power windows will have twice as many switches in the driver's door and add a pair of switches and motors for the rear windows. The overall wiring layout is quite similar though.

Driver's Window Switch Driver's Door

12 Volt switched from ignition switch

Driver's Window Motor

Passenger Window Motor

Voltage Reversal rest at ground
- door mounted switches -

Figure 5-7

Voltage Reversal Rest at Ground
(two-door with switches in console)

This is the simplest power window circuit of all (Figure 5-6). A pair of D.P.D.T. switches is all that's required because the switches are centrally located. As shown, both switches rest at ground.

This circuit functions similarly to the voltage-reversal rest at ground power door lock circuit. That is, with the exception of being able to control the windows individually.

Voltage Reversal Rest at Ground
(two-/four-door with switches in doors)

- A single D.P.D.T. switch is used for the driver-side window and

One-Touch Convenience

Commonly found on the driver-side front window and sometimes referred to as the "express" feature on any car built from the mid 1990s on. Depress the switch fully and release, and the window fully opens. Some of the methods used to control this feature are incredibly archaic while others state of the art.

In most cases, a module of some type controls this feature. These modules can be located in the driver-side kick panel or even in the driver's door itself. In addition, the module can provide express up and down features to numerous windows. If you're working on such a circuit, get your hands on a service manual that clearly shows the specifics of it before digging in too deep.

Venting

This is the feature that when you first pull on the door handle to open the door, the window is vented about 1/2 inch to allow the door to be opened. This feature appears only on vehicles with frameless doors. It is intended to reduce wind noise by getting the window as far up into the gasket as possible. As such, it is not possible to close the door with the window fully up, necessitating this feature. Once found only on BMWs, this is now available on everyday vehicles, such as the new 2005-and-up Ford Mustang.

Add this to an express circuit for one or more windows (UP/DOWN or both) and this feature can mean that the power window circuit on a vehicle equipped with it is significantly more complex than the good ol' voltage-reversal types. Some vehicles that are so equipped use pulse or variable voltage switches, 5-volt DC motors and a sophisticated controller. Again, you're best served to seek out a service manual that clearly shows the specifics if you need to service such a circuit.

Regardless of the circuit used, have your DMM at your side for these. If nothing else, it points you in the path of obtaining the right information.

a pair of D.P.D.T. switches is used for each additional window—typically one in the driver's door at the main switch panel, and a second in each door.

- Paired switches are wired in series.
- All switches rest at ground.

Notice that in the case of the paired switches (Figure 5-7), one of the switches has four wires and the other has five. The four-wire switch is the MASTER and the five-wire switch is the SLAVE. This overall circuit is easy as both motor wires rest at ground as a result of the switches resting at ground. When one switch is depressed, it:

- Sends +12VDC to one of the up/down wires, which causes the window motor to move in the corresponding direction.

Voltage Reversal Rest at 12 Volt Switched

This circuit (Figure 5-8) is very similar to the voltage reversal rest at ground circuit, except, as the name implies, the switches rest at 12 volts when the ignition switch is on.

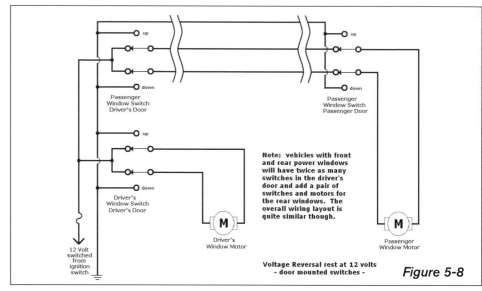

Note: vehicles with front and rear power windows will have twice as many switches in the driver's door and add a pair of switches and motors for the rear windows. The overall wiring layout is quite similar though.

Voltage Reversal rest at 12 volts - door mounted switches -

Figure 5-8

Which on position varies by vehicle, but rest assured the windows work with the ignition switch in the IGN/RUN position.

The specifics of this circuit's operation are the same as the voltage reversal rest at ground circuit, but as the switches rest at 12 volts when the ignition switch is on, depressing a switch with the ignition switch in the IGN/RUN position:

- Sends ground to one of the up/down wires, which causes the window motor to move in the corresponding direction.

Early Mercedes Benz vehicles used this circuit. I have also seen this used in some Chevrolet Corvettes.

Voltage Reversal Rest Open (two-door with switches in console)

Over the years, I've only seen this circuit in a handful of cars—Gen III Chevrolet Camaros being one of those vehicles. To be honest, I'm not sure why GM chose this type of circuit because it really doesn't save on wiring. As each of the switches rest open, so do both motor wires. When a switch is depressed, it sends both power and ground to the motors—weird.

The net result of this switching is identical to the voltage-reversal rest at ground example I gave for the two-door circuit with switches in the center console.

Variable Voltage

No different than power door lock circuits that employ this scheme, this can also be used for power windows. Although this is relatively uncommon, there are some late model vehicles that use a variable voltage scheme for the window and/or sunroof motors as well. How do you tell? Measure voltage at the switch wire(s) with your DMM.

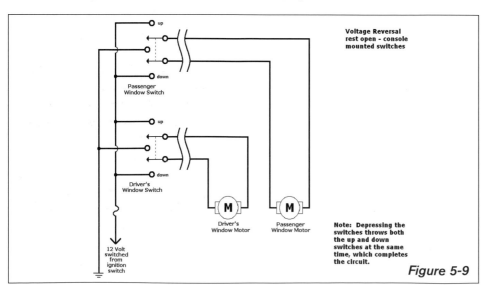

Voltage Reversal rest open - console mounted switches

Note: Depressing the switches throws both the up and down switches at the same time, which completes the circuit.

Figure 5-9

Other Types

Early GM vehicles also employed three wire window motors. Just like their three-wire door lock actuators, these motors have two coils—one for up and the other for down. The motors sourced ground via their mounting to the metal regulator, which is in turn mounted to the interior of the door. This is considered a positive pulse circuit that obviously requires high current to operate the motors.

Power Sunroof and Convertible Top Circuits

These circuits are really more similar to power door lock circuits as they have a single switch and single motor. As such, they can be switched via any of the following varieties:

- Negative Pulse
- Positive Pulse
- Voltage Reversal
- Variable Voltage

I've seen examples of each of them over the years. Circuit layouts for them are similar to power door lock circuits, so working on them is the same. Either of them consists of a two-wire motor that operates in a voltage-reversal fashion. Obviously, a convertible top requires much higher current to operate than a window or sunroof, so a pair of high-current relays mounted nearby is quite common.

Finally, many sunroofs have limit switches that are designed to limit their travel forward or rearward so that the mechanism isn't damaged. As their mechanisms are typically in a very confined space, this often determines what kind of motor and/or drive is used. As a result, some of these mechanisms can be quite fragile necessitating the limit switches. Remember, many sunroofs are a dealer-added feature at the time of the sale, so the OEM wiring may not apply to your particular unit.

The Charging System

The charging system consists of the battery, alternator, and return path. I've given many lectures on this topic over the years, and I've found that it is a topic of unbelievable controversy. Quite simply, there is a bunch of mis-information out there in regards to charging systems—more than any other topic I can think of in this book.

Let's get the obvious out of the way for any vehicle with a properly functioning charging system. When the vehicle is running, the alternator is the source of power for all electrical components. Furthermore, the battery is a load. How do I know this?

In Chapter 1 you learned that voltage causes current to flow. Ohms Law also implies that voltage flows from the place with the least resistance. And, guess what? In any circuit, that's always the place with the highest voltage potential. In a vehicle with a properly functioning charging system, that is the output stud of the alternator. Secondly, a typical battery requires between 7 to 10 amps of current to keep a surface charge on it when the vehicle is running so that it's ready to re-start the vehicle on a moments notice. Where does this current come from? You guessed it, the alternator. OK, now that you agree, let's move on.

The Battery

The battery's primary role is to start the vehicle. A good battery can do this on a very cold winter day—quite a feat indeed with a high-compression, dual quad tunnel-rammed setup that needs to be started at least five times to keep it running.

A typical lead acid battery has a chemical reaction that occurs when current is pulled from the battery. This chemical reaction occurs between the electrolyte (the mixture of water and sulfuric acid), and the lead plates that make up the individual cells of the battery itself. In

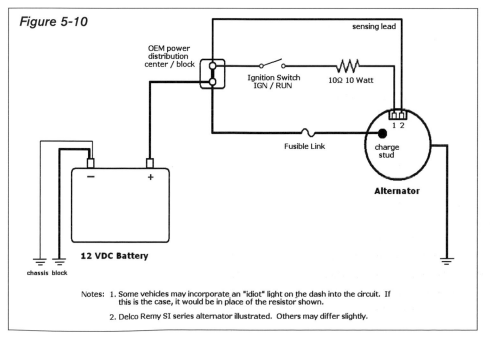

Figure 5-10

OEM power distribution center / block

sensing lead

Ignition Switch IGN / RUN

10Ω 10 Watt

1 2

charge stud

Fusible Link

Alternator

12 VDC Battery

chassis block

Notes: 1. Some vehicles may incorporate an "idiot" light on the dash into the circuit. If this is the case, it would be in place of the resistor shown.

2. Delco Remy SI series alternator illustrated. Others may differ slightly.

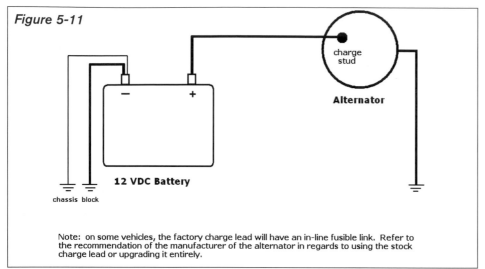

Figure 5-11

charge
stud

Alternator

12 VDC Battery

chassis block

Note: on some vehicles, the factory charge lead will have an in-line fusible link. Refer to
the recommendation of the manufacturer of the alternator in regards to using the stock
charge lead or upgrading it entirely.

addition, said battery has six 2.1-volt cells connected internally in a series arrangement. This nets a standard nominal voltage of between 12.6 and 12.7 VDC. When charge is flowing into the battery, such as from a spinning alternator, this chemical reaction is reversed, allowing the charge to be stored within the battery for future use. This chemical reaction can be enhanced by increasing the temperature of the battery, as is the case when it is located under the hood of the vehicle.

By nature of its design, the battery has an incredibly high amount of capacitance. This capacitance, coupled with the output of the alternator, has a filtering effect. A fresh battery does an incredibly good job of filtering any non-DC voltage present (i.e., ripple) at the output of an alternator. Unfortunately, this filtering benefit can be lessened as the distance between the battery and alternator increases. Worst case example are vehicles that have a trunk-mounted battery, as many of the German cars do. (Same net effect you can have when relocating your battery to the trunk—just goes to show you, there is no such thing as a free lunch.)

As the battery ages, its ability to release and store charge, as well as its ability to filter ripple, is lessened. This is why sometimes replacing an old, worn-out battery can solve all kinds of problems.

The Alternator

As I said above, the alternator is the primary source of power when the vehicle is running. An engine's spinning alternator generates AC voltage. This AC voltage is then

Capacitors

In the section about batteries, I discussed capacitance. Capacitance is obviously the function of a capacitor. What does a capacitor do? A capacitor does two things:

- Stores charge
- Opposes changes in voltage

Capacitors have many uses in both DC and AC circuits. In automotive use, one of their primary functions has always been filtration. Capacitance is:

- Measured in farads or F (more commonly as micro farads or F or MFD as a farad is a whole bunch!)
- Expressed as C in mathematical formulas.

The most common place you're likely to run across a capacitor is a points-type ignition system, in which case they're referred to as condensers.

Capacitors are made in all shapes and sizes. Pictured are a few traditional electrolytic capacitors (orange and dark blue), a non-polarized capacitor (light blue), and an extremely large 1 Farad capacitor. Such a capacitor is used to supplement the vehicle's charging system when adding a high powered audio system.

rectified into DC voltage. Any residual AC voltage present is considered ripple (or noise) and much of that is filtered off by the vehicle's battery.

There are two main types of alternators—one-wire and three-wire. Either can be internally or externally regulated. Most cars on the road come with a three-wire alternator while most hot rodders choose a one-wire because they're easier to install…or are they?

Three-Wire: A three-wire alternator has a distinct advantage over a one-wire alternator because one of its connections is made to a common power point in the vehicle to sample voltage. Consider this similar to the probe of your DMM as this wire can give the alternator more information about the actual operating voltage of the accessories in your vehicle. In addition, it can help the alternator to react more quickly in response to voltage dips caused by current draw of the accessories. Figure 5-10 is a simple diagram of a typical three-wire alternator installation.

Three-wire alternators typically have three connection points:
- Charge Stud
- Ignition Sense
- Battery Sense

The charge stud is typically connected to the battery (+), or nearby power distribution center, via heavy-gauge wiring. Some OEMs elect to protect this connection using fusible links, as is the stock charge lead on my Mustang that was pictured earlier. As mentioned previously, these links can protect the vehicle's battery and accessories from damage in the event of a failed voltage regulator causing a voltage runaway.

The ignition sense input is used to tell the alternator when the vehicle is running. This connects to the IGN/RUN output of the ignition switch. It is common for a ballast resistor to be used between this and the ignition sense input of the alternator, as the sensing circuit can be damaged by too much voltage. In other cases, an instrument-cluster-mounted "idiot light" may be wired in series between the ignition switch and this input. This can sometimes negate the use of the resistor.

The battery sense lead is the "probe-like" lead. It is connected to a point of commonality for power, such as a power distribution center. This gives the alternator feedback in real time to the power requirements of the vehicle's accessories.

One-Wire: A one-wire alternator has a distinct advantage over a three-wire in that it has fewer electrical connections. The alternator monitors voltage at its output stud, which isn't nearly as accurate as monitoring voltage the way a three-wire unit does. In addition, as a one-wire alternator does not have an Ignition input, you have to get it to some RPM to "turn it on"—typically over 1,200 rpm. Once it is turned on, it can charge even at lower RPM. Figure 5-11 is a simple diagram of a typical one-wire alternator installation.

Three-wire alternators are typically preferred over one-wire alternators because they can vary their output based on the actual needs of the vehicle. This is why the OEMs all use them. Finally, a one-wire alternator can drain a stored vehicle's battery over a month or two as it has a slight bleed-off between the output stud and its internal sensing due to its design.

The Return Path

The return path is the path of commonality between the accessory ground wires and the charging system ground. Remember that by nature of design, all of the accessories are grounded to the vehicle's chassis. For clarification, it's easiest to separate this into two separate parts—the return path for the starter motor and the return path for all other accessories.

Look at the battery under the hood of your vehicle. Notice that it typically has 4-gauge leads connected to both terminals. In addition, it may have an 8- or 10-gauge lead from both terminals. The 4-gauge leads are for the starter motor, and the smaller leads are for the accessories.

Return Path Starter: In Chapter 2, in the section on how to measure voltage drops, I described the return path for the starter motor in great detail.

Return Path Accessories: In most domestic vehicles, the small lead from the negative connects to the chassis of the vehicle and is the return path from the charging system negative to all accessory grounds in the vehicle. This can be different for import vehicles, as shown in the beginning of Chapter 1 in the Nissan Frontier. It is important to understand the difference between the two return paths.

Now, let's consider the return path of the accessories themselves to better understand it. Let's consider the return path for the tail lamps, brake lamps, and back-up lamps:
- From lamp negatives to chassis of the vehicle somewhere in the trunk (all typically tied together to a single grounding point).
- Through numerous different pieces of metal, typically spot welded and bolted together to the front clip.
- From the front clip (fender, inner fender, or front support)

The green 8-mm bolt at the top is the stock return path for the accessories in my Mustang as supplied by Ford. The wiring Ford used appears to be 12 AWG.

to the battery negative via the small lead.

As you can see, this certainly isn't ideal. In many cases, grounding problems can arise during the manufacturing process that can have all kinds of ill side effects. When this happens, a TSB (technical service bulletin) is typically issued to the dealer service departments so that the technicians can quickly repair these problems. Even if the vehicle was put together correctly, over time, this grounding scheme can lead to problems.

What if you're going to be adding all kinds of new electronics to your vehicle? How do you ensure that they function properly for years to come and that you don't place too much of a load on the stock return path? Simple—you upgrade the return path accordingly. The next chapter explains how to do this.

Tying it All Together

OK, now you know all the basics we've covered so far:

- The Ignition Switch
- The Wiring Harness
- Controllers
- Protection
- Power Door Lock Circuits
- Power Window Circuits
- Power Sunroof and Convertible Top Circuits
- The Charging System

What is the path of current flow to the accessories? For this example, let's assume we're talking about the radio in my Mustang:

- The ignition switch is turned into the ACCY position (so the vehicle is not running).
- This allows current to flow from the battery through the 40 amp MAXI fuse in the underhood fuse panel that supplies the power to the ignition switch itself.
- This current then continues through the ignition switch via its ACCY output lead to the interior fuse panel.
- This current then continues through fuse # 32 and on to the radio's power lead.
- The current travels through the power switch of the radio to the power supply of the radio .
- This current then exits the radio's power supply via the radio's ground lead, which is tied to the chassis of the vehicle.
- The current travels through the chassis of the vehicle, returning to the battery (-) by way of the jumper between the front support and battery, thereby completing the circuit path.

OK, it can be argued that current travels in the opposite direction from what I outlined, from negative to positive as free electrons are negatively charged. This is scientific theory versus electronic theory. Either way, the net result is the same.

And now you know. Regardless of how complex a vehicle is, the circuit paths are similar to what I outlined above. This is clearly outlined in the electrical diagrams available to you, which I spoke of in the last chapter.

Now, you have the knowledge you need to do anything and everything else in this book and you should have a feeling like you did when you first solved the Rubik's Cube (what—you haven't solve this?). The first five chapters in this book unlocked many a mystery to the topics I covered.

WIRING AFTERMARKET EQUIPMENT AND UPGRADING COMPONENTS

Now the fun begins! This is the time where we get to add things to the vehicle that improve it, add functionality, or customize it to our liking. This chapter puts to work all the new skills you've learned to this point.

When it comes to adding aftermarket electronics, there are really only two objectives:

- Add functionality—such as adding a tach to a vehicle that does not have one already.
- Duplicate the OEM controls— such as adding a keyless entry system to a vehicle that already has power door locks. Doing this simply adds functionality to an already existing circuit by allowing the user to control that circuit with a remote control.

Adding either of the above components can mean adding a new circuit, especially the first. In this chapter explains how to do it like the pros do every day.

Safety First

It should go without saying that when you're working on a vehicle, it's best to do so on a flat, level surface. If you need to raise the front or the rear of the vehicle in the course of the installation, then you should always support it with jack stands. In addition, you need to appropriately chock the wheels on the ground to prevent the vehicle from rolling off of the jack stands. In addition, set the emergency brake. Finally, make sure the vehicle is in park if it is an automatic and neutral if it is a stick shift.

You've already been educated on when and how to disconnect the vehicle's battery should the need arise. If you need to, refer to Chapter 1 for a refresher.

Passing Through a Metal Barrier

Invariably, the installation of aftermarket electronics requires passing wiring through metal barriers—like the firewall. In addition, these electronics need to be securely mounted in place. Either way, this can mean that drilling or screwing through something in the process.

CAUTION: Don't blindly drill holes or run screws through the firewall, floorboard, or even a center console without being sure that you know what's on the other side! To do so, you risk piercing or drilling through any number of things, such as brake lines, fuel lines, and the vehicle's wiring. Piercing a brake or fuel line creates a serious safety issue! Damage to the vehicle's wiring harness can run into the thousands to repair!

Tools Required

In addition to the tools I outlined extensively in Chapters 2 and 3, the following makes your job that much easier:

- Grommet Tool
- Drill
- Step Drill
- Hole Saw Kit

Grommet Tool: Another one of my favorite tools is the grommet tool. This tool has a hollow shaft that is quite pointy. It has been designed to pierce through a grommet and allow you to easily run wiring through it by pushing the wiring down through the shaft of the tool.

I bought this Thexton grommet tool from the Matco guy back in the day. Notice that the shaft is hollow—push it through a grommet, push your wire through the tool, remove the tool.

This is one of the coolest tools I own and eliminates the "straightened out" coat hanger or the car antenna that I use to use for this arduous job years ago. Plus, you no longer need to tape your wiring to the thing you stuck through the grommet, hoping it stayed while you pulled it through from the other side.

Drill: I'm not going to spend a lot of time on this because anyone reading this book likely has four or five of them lying about. For automotive use, I prefer the cordless or air powered variety. Pick your poison, just make sure it has a 1/2-inch chuck so that you can chuck up the big stuff.

Step Drill: The number one advantage a step drill offers over a standard drill bit I the ability to drill a hole in a metal barrier without the bit racing through said hole after the bit passes through the metal. This can be a life saver. Properly used, you will never run the risk of damaging

Unibit makes the step drills pictured here. The small one goes from 1/8 to 1/2 inch in 1/32-inch steps, and the big one goes from 1/2 to 1 inch in 1/16-inch steps.

something on the other side with a step drill. Note that the step drill also provides a nice center starting point for the drill bit in a hole saw arbor. Buy one!

Hole Saw Kit: Many times, you need to drill a hole through the firewall that allows the passage of a large-gauge wire, a large wiring harness, or even a drain tube like that of an aftermarket AC system. A hole saw kit with two arbors and numerous saws like the one pictured, which makes this job so much easier. The right size hole saw also makes the installation of aftermarket gauges a snap in a dashboard.

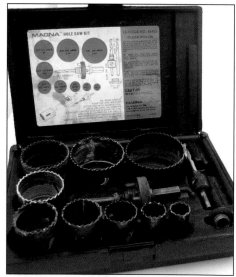

This is a Magna hole saw kit. A 2-5/8-inch hole saw is also available for installing gauges of the same size.

Installing a Tachometer

OK, now that the basics have been covered, it's time to get your hands dirty with one of the most common installations I can think of. Recall in Chapter 1, I discussed verifying wiring before simply connecting to it. The example I gave was that of installing a tach. This is an excellent example of how to use everything you've learned thus far to install a tach like a pro. In this case, we add functionality to the vehicle.

Pre-Installation

Before starting this job, let's give the following consideration:

- Turn the ignition switch to the off position. This is a good rule of thumb for a starting point of installing pretty much anything in your vehicle.
- Pay special attention to the routing of your wiring. It's always easier to follow the factory wiring harnesses when adding wiring, and this ensures that you keep it out of harm's way. Avoid moving objects, such as the pedals and steering column, at all costs and keep your wiring away from sharp edges to avoid damaging its insulation.
- Use an insulator to run wiring through the firewall. This protects the wiring and prevents chafing. A factory installed rubber grommet is ideal, but sometimes it is necessary for you to drill a hole and install one.
- Properly secure or anchor all wiring that you add to a vehicle.

Drilling Through the Firewall and Adding Your Own Grommet

This is an easy job and calls for only a rubber grommet or snap bushing. And no, never run your wiring from the engine compartment between the fender and door and through the jamb. In addition, avoid running your wiring between an existing grommet and the firewall. It looks horrible and creates a safety issue as the insulation of the wiring can be chafed over time, causing a short.

Running wiring through the doorjamb isn't safe because it can be easily chaffed and damaged. When running wiring from the engine compartment into the passenger compartment, always pass the wiring through the firewall.

Running wiring like this through the firewall is equally as unsafe as running it through the jamb. I can't tell you how many times I've seen this done, even on the expensive and exotic vehicles. Over time, the sheet metal can wear through the insulation of the wire. Do it right and route the wiring through the grommet!

This isn't nearly as difficult as most people think. The most difficult thing is actually finding a spot in the firewall that you can drill a hole without hitting an object on the other side. Here are the directions in short order:

1. Locate a suitable location for the hole to be drilled.
2. Use a step-drill to ensure that your bit doesn't pierce the firewall quickly and damage something on the other side.
3. Drill the first step with the step drill.
4. Shine a light in this general area and go around the other side and look for the hole you just drilled by using the light as a guide to be double sure that nothing is in the way. (A 3/4-inch hole drilled through the back of a brake booster can really dampen your spirits on an otherwise nice day.)
5. After verifying all is clear, finish drilling the hole to the appropriate size given the grommet or snap busing that you are installing.
6 Install the grommet or snap bushing in the hole.
7. Run the wiring through said grommet or snap bushing safely to the other side, being sure to keep it away from moving parts and sharp edges.

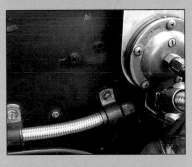

I should note that I like to think ahead when I'm doing this. What wiring will I pass through this today? Am I

Drilling Through the Firewall *CONTINUED*

planning on adding something else a month or two down the road that some of its wiring needs to pass through the firewall? If so, I typically install a bigger grommet or snap bushing than necessary so that it saves me the trouble of having to drill another hole or enlarge this one.

Whether you use a grommet or snap bushing, you need to prevent water getting through this and into the interior. Many times, I use a grommet with an "X"-type center that is kind of self sealing. In other cases, I try to match the snap bushing size as close as possible to the diameter of what I'm running through it, as I did in this example. Either way, sometimes it is necessary to use some silicone to ensure a water tight seal, especially if

Snap Bushings are handy and available in many sizes. Shown are 1/4 inch OD up to 1 inch OD. Just drill your hole and snap them in place. A step drill makes installation a breeze.

you use an oversize snap bushing or grommet to allow for additional wiring to pass through it down the road.

Installation

Now, let's get down to it. In this example, we install a tachometer in a 1970 Ford Torino using a DMM to verify all of the wiring. In addition, we are using a combination of soldering and crimping for our connections to ensure many years of trouble free operation of our tach.

Let's separate the installation into six different phases:
- Mounting the tach.
- Connecting to the tach signal lead under the hood at the coil.
- Connecting to the ignition lead at the ignition switch.
- Connecting to the dimmer lead at the parking light switch.
- Testing the tach for correct operation.
- Buttoning up the installation.

Mounting the Tach: (Note that it may be easier to install the tach by having access to the lower dash area.

This Auto Meter Sport Comp tachometer is representative of what's on the shelf at your local speed shop. Exactly what you need to install the tach, including brackets, mounting screws, a grommet, etc., comes with the tachometer. Incidentally, the length of wire Auto Meter included proved to be right on the money because I didn't have to extend a single wire.

This may require removing one or several panels to gain access. Do this prior to the start of the installation.)

1 Mount the tach.

2 Run the wiring from the tach under the vehicle's dash.

Connecting to the tach lead under the hood at the coil: I always like to do the most difficult part of any wiring job first. Without fail, passing through the firewall can be the most challenging part of a job. Let's get it done first.

1 Locate a rubber grommet in the firewall that is suitable to pass the tach signal wire through.

2 Route the signal lead from the tach through this rubber grommet in the firewall to the coil and connect it to the negative side of the coil.

3 Now how do we determine which side of the coil is negative? No problem...get your DMM ready.

4 Disconnect one of the coil wires (or the plug to the coil) and turn the ignition switch forward to the run position.

I routed the wiring along the factory wiring harness whenever possible. This gives the finished product a nice, clean look.

5 Use your DMM to determine which of the two wires reads + 12 VDC—this means the other wire is the coil (-).

6 Turn the Ignition switch OFF, make your connection to the coil wire, and reconnect the wiring to the coil.

Connecting to the Ignition Lead at the Ignition Switch: Many vehicles used to come from the factory with at least one spot in the fuse box that was intended to power a low- to medium-current accessory. GM used to provide connection points on the right side of the fuse box for a connection to constant power, labeled BAT, switched power, labeled IGN, and the dash lamps, labeled LPS. If your vehicle is so equipped, refer to the owner's manual to verify whether these outputs are fused or not and their current capability.

In addition, as mentioned in the last chapter, some later model vehicles do not use a traditional ignition switch. Some British vehicles have low-current negative outputs for all switch positions. There are also some 2008 model vehicles with two-wire ignition switches—an input and an output that varies in voltage or ground potential based on the key's position. As you'll not likely be adding a 5-inch tach to your 2008 BMW 7 series, the steps I outline cover 99 percent of the vehicles you're likely to own.

CAUTION: This step involves bumping the starter slightly, which could cause some vehicles to start. Be sure that the vehicle is not in gear, and the underhood area is clear of tools, wiring, or bystanders!

1 Bring your DMM inside the vehicle, and place it on the floor where you can easily read its display.

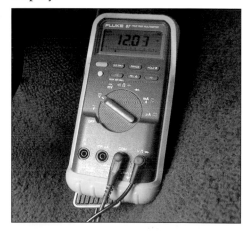

2 Locate the harness that comes from the ignition switch, and remove any tape or covering from it so that you can easily access the wiring to it.

3 Use the DMM to determine which of the BIG wires has +12 Volts on it is in the IGN/RUN position.

4 Verify that this wire also has + 12 Volts on it when in the START position. A quick turn to START is all that is required to verify that voltage remains during this step. This is the correct wire. (In the case of this Torino, I noticed a three position female bullet-style pigtail just above the ignition switch harness with the identical color wire and electrical properties as the ignition switch itself. It would appear that Ford included this to make adding an IGN powered accessory easier.)

5 Turn the ignition switch to the OFF position, and solder the in-line ATC fuse holder to the wire you determined in the last step. (In this case, I crimped a male bullet to the end of the fuse holder to allow it to be plugged directly into this IGN pigtail Ford provided.)

6 Crimp the Ignition (+) lead from the tach to the other end of the fuse holder. The fuse holder protects the wiring you've tied into in the event that the wiring to the tach gets pinched or damaged in some way.

Connecting to the Dimmer Lead at the Parking Light Switch: Access the wiring harness from your parking light switch (or dedicated dimmer switch if your vehicle has one).

1 With your DMM set up the same way as in the preceding step, use the red probe to determine which of the wires on the parking light switch has variable voltage on it with the parking lights turned on. That is, the correct wire should have voltage present on it, and it should vary from 0 to 12 VDC as you rotate the dimmer switch.

2 Turn off the parking light switch and solder a second in-line ATC fuse holder to this wire.

3 Route the illumination (+) lead from the tach and connect it to the other end of the fuse holder. (Note: on some vehicles, you can find a fused connection to this circuit in the fuse panel—although it may not be labeled. GM typically used LPS to denote this circuit.)

4 Connect ground (-) lead from the tach to chassis ground.

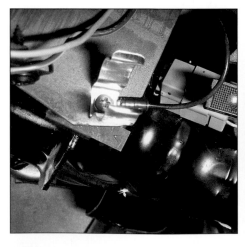

5 Per the tach manufacturer's installation instructions, install an ATC fuse in each of the fuse holders, and the tach is now ready for testing.

Testing the Tach for Correct Operation: Turn the dash lamps on. Rotate the dimmer to MAX and to MIN to verify the correct operation of the illumination of the tach. The light in the tach should follow the cue of the dash lights.

Start the vehicle and verify that the tach works correctly, and it certainly should!

Turn the ignition switch back to the OFF position and the tach should be off.

In the case of this Torino, the tach worked like a champ on the first go. In addition, the owner was pleasantly surprised to learn that the tach's back lighting would vary with the dash lights via the dimmer—just the way it should be!

Buttoning Up the Installation: Now that you've gotten everything working properly, it's time to button up the install:

1 Using cable ties, secure your wiring to the factory wiring in such a way that it is clear of moving parts and sharp edges.

2 Re-assemble any interior pieces you removed earlier.

You just used the skills you learned in the first four chapters to successfully and safely install a tach, just like the pros would! And you did it without having a mess of spaghetti under the dash that got tangled up in the steering column and a bunch of sub-par un-fused connections.

Adding a Remote Trunk Pop Circuit

Let's say that we had a vehicle that came equipped with an electronic trunk release button like my Mustang. Pressing this button opens the trunk of the vehicle electronically. The button is conveniently located in the glove compartment, so it is out of the way and it can be locked to prevent a would be thief from quickly accessing it.

The objective here is to interface with this circuit so that we could control it from the remote control of a generic auto security system. This is a great example of duplication the OEM controls to achieve the desired result. Here are our considerations:

- Output of auto security system provided for such.
- Said output is negative (-) on trigger and has 200 mA of output capability as specified by the manufacturer.
- Trunk release circuit powers a pull type solenoid that requires far more than 200 mA to operate it.

Here's what we need: a single Bosch relay, a few .250-inch female push-on terminals, some 18- and 16-gauge wire, and one quenching diode. Figure 6-1 is a diagram of the circuit interface to be made.

In this case, to access the wiring to the switch, it is necessary to remove the glove compartment to do so. Here's how to make the interface:

1 Use your DMM to determine which of the two wires on the rear of the trunk release button is the trigger wire to the solenoid (only has +12 VDC when the switch is depressed). The other wire is the power wire to the switch. (In some cars, this is only live with the gear selector in park.)

2 Determine a suitable mounting location for the relay

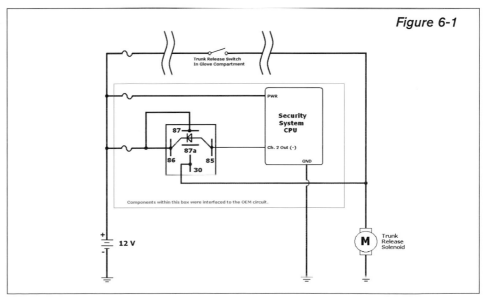

Figure 6-1

nearby—in this example, that's about 12 inches from the switch. Clamp the relay top down in a bench vise to pre-wire it.

3 Connect a short piece of 18-gauge red wire to the cathode of a diode and crimp a female push-on terminal to them both.

4 Connect this to terminal 86.

Connect the other end of the 18-gauge red wire to a 12-inch-long piece of red 16-gauge wire and crimp a female push-on terminal to them both.

5 Connect this to terminal 87.

6 Crimp another female push-on terminal to a 12-inch length of green 16-gauge wiring and connect this to terminal 30.

7 Connect both the output from the security system and the anode of the diode to terminal 85 of the relay.

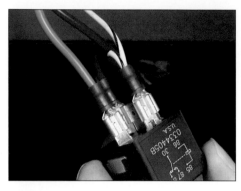

8 Tape around the body of the relay and the terminals to insulate the electrical connections from contacting any nearby metal surfaces via a push-on terminal crimped to both.

9 Mount the relay in the vehicle with its terminals pointing down—at an angle is OK.

10 Solder the red 16 AWG wire from Terminal 87 of the relay to the power wire of the switch (no fusing necessary as this is already done in the fuse panel) and insulate this connection with Super 33+ tape.

11 Solder the green 16 AWG wire from Terminal 30 of the relay to the solenoid wire (again, no fusing necessary) and insulate this connection with Super 33+ tape.

12 Test the circuit by depressing the trunk release button on the key fob—the trunk should pop.

13 Tie your wiring up and out of harm's way.

Now that you've verified the circuit works properly, you can reinstall the glove compartment. Congratulations—in this installation, you learned how to duplicate the OEM controls and installed a quenching diode. And all this time, you thought relays were a mystery. Well, mystery solved.

At this point, you really know how to install every piece of aftermarket electronics on the market. Remember, you're either adding functionality as we did by installing a tach *or* you're duplicating the OEM controls as we did by adding a remote trunk pop circuit. The logic is the same regardless of the complexity or scale of the project.

Adding A High-Current Accessory

Now let's say that you wanted to add a high powered audio amplifier, such as the 400 Watt RMS (the only number that means anything; pay no attention to PEAK or MAX numbers because they're meaningless) unit in my wife's Nissan Frontier. Most manufacturers specify the current requirements of their products. If not, you can look at the fusing or recommend fusing of the amplifier(s) to make this determination.

This amplifier calls for a 60-amp fuse on its main power lead. One of the main differences between audio systems and other high-current accessories is that the same powered audio system would draw roughly half as much current on average to play music at full volume, as music typically has a 50 percent duty cycle. This is because music is dynamic in nature—it has peaks and dips in the overall volume level so the amplifier does not draw current continuously like a headlight. Rather, it consumes it as it is required. Assume the

Using Relays for Projects

Relays can make any project easier. While they are fresh on your mind, this is a good time to dive in to the topic of using them in another project.

Let's say that you wanted to add the convenience of power door locks to your vehicle and control them via a traditional S.P.D.T. Lock/Unlock switch mounted in the center console. Here is a diagram of a pair of S.P.D.T. relays used to operate a pair of aftermarket power door lock actuators:

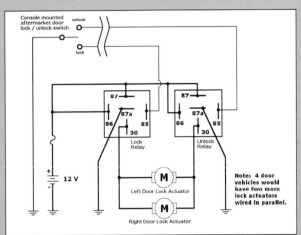

Note that the actuators need both power and ground to work. This is a classic example of the versatility of the S.P.D.T. relay as one relay supplies ground and the other power, and based on whether the lock or unlock switch is depressed, this reverses! Look closely at the diagram to see what I'm talking about. It should be clear to you now why terminals 30, 87, and 87a are not classified as inputs or outputs.

This is just one of many examples of how to put the Bosch-type relay to work for you. There are hundreds, even thousands, of applications.

Serviceability

Relay sockets are available for nearly all types of automotive relays. This greatly simplifies swapping a relay in the event one fails. I typically do not use them for Bosch-type relays. Instead, I crimp female push-on terminals on the ends of the wires terminating at the relay and push those directly on the terminals. Depending on the project, I use standard insulated or even fully insulated push-on terminals.

Regardless of your preference, be sure you use the ones that have a curved-style connector versus a flat-style connector as the flat style don't

On the left is a traditional relay socket. While these can make installation easy, you are limited by the gauge of the wiring that the socket is assembled with. On the right is a relay harness that I made using push-on terminals, allowing far more flexibility as demonstrated by the installation of a quenching diode across the coil.

Using Relays for Projects *CONTINUED*

grab the terminals tightly enough, which can create heat, and…well, you know by now.

When using push-on terminals to connect to the terminals of a relay, be sure and choose terminals that are curved like the two on the right. The one on the left does not grab the terminal tightly enough and results in a poor connection, creating heat as a byproduct.

I use relay sockets for any other relay with more than five terminals though, especially 4 P.D.T. relays because they have 14 tiny terminals that have to be soldered (I've used a lot of these in audio systems, headphone systems, etc.). Should the relay fail at some point down the road, I don't have to unsolder and re-solder all these connections; I can simply swap the relay.

Shown is a PC board-style D.P.D.T. relay. This could be used for any number of applications. When using such a relay, pay the few extra dollars to purchase the mating relay socket, which looks identical from the bottom to the relay itself. Then, solder your wiring to the socket. Should the relay fail at some point down the road, replacement is a simple as unplugging the bad one and plugging in the new one.

Using Quenching Diodes

The sidebar on diodes in Chapter 4 explains the problem and the solution clearly enough. But, how do you know when to use these? Simple—I use quenching diodes if I'm connecting the coil of a relay to a low-current output of any controller or module, like I chose to in the section, "Adding a Remote Trunk Pop Circuit."

I use IN4001 diodes for this as you don't need much current capability, you're dealing with a low-voltage circuit, and you can buy them in bulk quite cheaply. I get them at my local Radio Shack. A good tip when connecting a diode across the coil of the relay is to:

- Use 1/2 inch of insulation from a piece of 18 AWG wire to insulate each of the diode's leads.
- Twist its cathode lead to the wire you are connecting to the (+) coil terminal.
- Twist its anode lead to the wire you are connecting to the (-) coil terminal.
- Crimp the female push-on terminals on both the wire and diode simultaneously.
- Slide them on the contacts.

The end result is clean looking and protects the leads of the diode from being accidentally shorted.

Taking a few extra minutes to insulate the leads of quenching diodes ensures that the leads don't short to a nearby metal surface. Insulation from 18 AWG wiring fits over the leads nicely.

---

amplifier requires 50 percent of the fuse value to play music at full volume and 100 percent of the fuse value to reproduce test tones.

The manufacturer of this amplifier recommends 4 AWG wiring for the power and ground connections, which corresponds to the math you learned in Chapter 1. Let's double check by doing a quick calculation for voltage drop over this length of wire, assuming you had to use 17 foot of power wire and 3 foot of ground wire:

$$E = I \times R$$
$$E = 60 \text{ Amps} \times (20 \times .000253 \; \Omega)$$
$$E = 60 \text{ Amps} \times .00506 \; \Omega$$
$$E = .304 \text{ Volts}$$

This is more than acceptable. Keep in mind that you have to factor the maximum current draw from the amplifier to make this determination.

Now, suppose that you wanted to know how long you could play music with this amplifier at full volume with the key off with a typical 45 AH battery—in this case, you want to consider what the amplifier consumes on average when playing music. Simple, one and a half hours: 45 AH / 30 amps = 1.5 hours. If your objective was to be able to do this for 3 hours, for instance at the picnic in the park on Memorial Day weekend, you would need a second identical battery in parallel: 90 AH / 30 amps = 3 hours. (Obviously, you'd need to play the system at a little less than full volume for this period of time if you desired to start the vehicle and drive it away versus getting a jump.) Chapter 7 explains how to do this correctly (and safely).

It is possible that the addition of this amplifier could very well exceed the current capability of your stock alternator. To determine this, increase volume to loudest point you're likely to play it. Keep the vehicle running and measure voltage at the battery via the steps outlined in the "Upgrading the Alternator" section.

Sourcing Power for your High-Current Accessory

When you add a high current accessory, the best place to connect it is the positive post of the battery itself. I do this with any accessory that requires in excess of 15 amps of current. When connecting to the battery, observe all of the same safety considerations outlined in Chapter 1. When speaking of automotive batteries, there are two main types—top post and side post.

Connecting to a Top-Post Battery: The correct way is to make the connection to the battery clamp as I did in Chapter 1 with the ground wire to the security system in my wife's truck. For larger cables, you need the correct size ring terminal. In the case of the 4-gauge wire that supplies power to the amplifier in her truck, note that it connects to the positive battery terminal via way of the top bolt on the battery clamp. This provides an excellent connection.

This 4 AWG wiring terminated with a ring terminal connects to the stock top post connector on the Nissan Frontier. This provides a low-resistance connection that does not restrict current flow. To allow the plastic cover to fold back down over the terminal, I notched the side of it to allow the cable to exit neatly.

Connecting to a Side-Post Battery: Side-post batteries have been used in GM vehicles since the early 1990s. These are equally as simple to connect to, but the connection requires a GM side post battery adapter. These are available in short and long versions (for dual battery systems in diesel trucks) and readily available at your local auto parts store. One simply removes the 8 mm battery bolt from the cable entirely and replaces it with the adapter. The adapter has a bolt on its end that allows easy connection to an accessory power wire via way of a ring terminal.

Aftermarket Battery Clamps: Aftermarket battery clamps were designed to make adding high-current accessories, as well as upgrading the wiring in your charging system, a snap. These are typically available only for top post batteries, although there have been a handful of side post battery clamp offerings over the years as well. Sometimes, as was the case in my Mustang, the stock

Connecting an accessory power cable to a side-post battery has never been easier. The adapter on the bottom is a standard GM side post battery adapter. On the top left is a long version of the same adapter—handy for GM trucks with diesel engines and dual batteries. On the right is an adapter designed to screw into the side post of the battery directly and allow one to use a standard top-mount battery clamp. These are available in both (+) and (-) versions as the post diameters are different.

battery clamps have to be cut off the cables themselves to allow installation of aftermarket battery clamps. This is not a big deal, so don't worry!

Aftermarket battery clamps, such as the Lightning Audio clamps I use on the Mustang, allow you to easily connect multiple large cables to the battery. Although not visible, the set screws for each of the cables is on the bottom of the clamps. Not pictured are the plastic covers that these clamps come with.

Cautions When Connecting Accessories to the Battery Directly

This is widely accepted as common practice and in most vehicles is highly recommended when installing high-current accessories. Over the years, I've come across one vehicle that absolutely did not like this and I'd be remiss if I didn't point this out. That vehicle is the Ford Probe.

I've seen several examples where the alternator or even the battery in these vehicles would fail if this was done. This was such an issue that Ford issued a TSB on the vehicle in regards. If you own a Ford Probe and want to install a high-current accessory, you are well advised to ask your local Ford dealer for the specifics before attempting this.

The Charging System–Revisited

What if you wanted to add a high-current accessory that required more amperage than the stock charging system could support right out of the gate? Simple, you upgrade it! First, you need to determine what to upgrade. Remember, the charging system consists of three simple components:

- The Battery
- The Alternator
- The Return Path

Let's take them in reverse order.

Upgrading the Return Path

If I'm going to add any accessories to a vehicle, I make the assumption that the factory return path is not suitable for the additional load. At minimum, add a second lead of the same size for the additional current demands of the accessories being added.

If you're adding a high-current accessory, such as a power inverter or an audio amplifier (or a stack of 'em), look at the current requirements of these devices and the size of the cables that the manufacturer either includes with them or recommends. In addition, have the same-size cable between the battery (-) and the chassis as between the battery (+) and the unit.

It is always a good idea to upgrade the stock accessory return path. As shown, I connected a piece of 8 AWG from each of the 8 AWG outputs of the Lightning Audio battery clamps to each of the green 8-mm bolts.

Let's say that I was installing the 400 Watt RMS audio amplifier from the example above. Since I used 4 AWG wiring for the positive, this means, that I also need a return path between the amplifier (-) and the battery (-) with a minimum of 4 AWG equivalency. At the bare minimum, I would have to:

- Connect the amplifier (-) to the chassis with 4 AWG wire.
- Connect the battery (-) to the chassis with 4 AWG wire.

As pictured, the truck has a 4 AWG between the battery (-) and the chassis already, so this did not need to be upgraded. If I upgraded the sys-

tem further down the road, it would need to be.

In some cases, you can't reliably pass the high current required by such accessories through the chassis of the vehicle. For trucks and older cars, there is a simple solution—use the frame as the return path. This is what I chose to do with my wife's truck, even though it really wasn't necessary.

Even 1/0 AWG wire has far greater resistance per foot than the frame of a vehicle. For any vehicle that sits on a frame, I always use the frame for the return path when adding high-current accessories. This is easy.

If I'm installing a high-current accessory in any vehicle with a frame under it, I always use the frame for the return path for said accessory. As shown, white lithium grease can help to prevent such connections from corroding and/or rusting over time.

My Mustang has an audio system with 3,000 Watts RMS of power, so 4-gauge or even 2-gauge won't cut it. This is job for 1/0 AWG!

Go big or go home, right? An audio system with thousands of watts of power, such as this one, requires substantial upgrades to a charging system to supply it with power.

As I use a 1/0 AWG lead between the battery and audio amplifiers in the Mustang, follow along with the upgrades I did to the return path to ensure proper operation:

- Choose a connection point on the side of the frame closest to the vehicle's battery.
- Connect the same size cable from the battery (-) to the frame as the main power cable feeding your accessory—in this case that would be 1/0 AWG.
- Connect the same size cable from the case of the alternator as the alternator's charge lead to the frame at the same spot you connected the battery (-) to—in this case, that would be 4 AWG.
- In the rear of the vehicle, connect the same size cable as the main power lead to the same side of the frame to your accessories—1/0 AWG again.

Both the 1/0 AWG cable from the battery (-) and the 4 AWG cable from the case of the alternator are tied to the front sub-frame. This common connection point provides a low-resistance return path for the power-hungry amplifiers in the trunk.

Make sure to clean the paint or undercoatingwith a grinder or rotary tool to get a good electrical connection. I like to use star washers to get a good bite into the metal. Finally, use white lithium grease to protect these connections from rusting or corroding. This is just good practice to ensure good solid electrical connections for many years to come.

Many vehicles have unit-body construction, so they don't sit on a full frame. In the case of the Mustang, which I used in the above

All audio system electronics in the trunk are tied to a ground distribution block mounted in the driver's side of the trunk. In turn, this block is tied to the rear sub-frame on the driver's side (same side as the battery and alternator ground connections up front) with 1/0 AWG cable.

example, it has subframe connectors welded between the front and rear frames, so I chose to use the frame as a return path over the chassis. This is common practice. Even if it didn't have subframe connectors, I would have still done it this way, as experience has shown that this still offers a lower resistance return path than the chassis alone.

CAUTION: *Do not* drill holes in the frame of a vehicle, as it can be tempered for strength. Rather, locate a pre-existing bolt and connect your ground wire under it. If no pre-existing bolt is present, then locate a hole in the frame and tap it.

Upgrading the Alternator

If you add a hand-ful of low-current accessories, the stock alternator on your vehicle should be able to easily power them as it has some reserve capacity built in. How do you know when you've exceeded its ability? Simple—with your DMM:

- Connect it directly to the battery terminals so that you can observe its DC voltage.
- Have a helper start the engine and turn on your commonly used accessories such as the air conditioning, headlights, radio, defroster, etc.
- Raise the engine speed to around 2,000 rpm, which is typical when cruising around town or on the highway.

If voltage at the battery is below 13 VDC, then the battery will not receive sufficient charge to be recharged when you're driving and using these accessories. In addition, if your DMM indicates a voltage drop below 12.6 volts DC (great use for the MIN measuring mode), the battery acts as a buffer, supplying current to the accessories that

Upgrading the Return Path of a High-Performance Ignition System

Let's say that you've upgraded your ignition system to one of the high-performance variety. This may or may not be limited to an aftermarket distributor, wires, coil, and a capacitive discharge ignition box. Maybe you've got a newer vehicle and you've upgraded the coil-on-plug (C.O.P.) modules to some aftermarket units with much higher output voltage. Finally, you've purchased the best grade spark plugs money can buy.

What are you missing? You're missing a return path upgrade that allows you to take advantage of the increased power available to the spark plugs. Many ignition manufacturers, MSD included, recommend a low-resistance return path from each cylinder head to ground.

This is an easy upgrade as most cylinder heads have numerous threaded holes in them already. Just be sure to select a bolt that isn't too long that could bottom out in the head.

An 8 AWG wire runs from the cylinder head on the drivers side to the passenger side and down to the frame rail on the same side that the batteries and alternator are grounded to. This allows me to take full advantage of the MSD ignition system that lights the fire in this blown 454 V-8.

cannot be replenished by the alternator. This is a recipe for a dead battery—no, it isn't the battery's fault and, no, a bigger battery won't solve the problem!

You need to consider the additional current requirements of the accessories you've added and upgrade your alternator and its charge lead accordingly per the directions supplied by the manufacturer of the alternator you choose. In the case of the Mustang, this called for a 200-amp unit from Ohio Generator. A maximum of 4-gauge charge leads is recommended.

Upgrading the Battery

When is a good time to upgrade the battery? Notice that I left it for dead last—ironic, huh? Most folks upgrade the battery first because they have no idea of its real function. I typically upgrade the battery only when I need to.

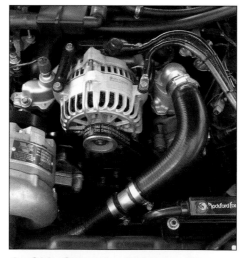

An Ohio Generator 200-amp alternator on the Mustang is a direct replacement for the factory unit. Per their recommendations, the stock charge lead is upgraded with 4 AWG. The 4 AWG silver wire connects the case of the alternator to the front sub-frame, as pictured on page 97. The insulation of these wires has turned black over time from heat due to their proximity to the thermostat housing.

A high-quality aftermarket battery typically has lower overall impedance than the OEM unit it's replacing. Therefore, it can store and release charge more effortlessly than a stock battery. There are many different types of high-quality batteries on the market, the most popular are the AGM (Absorbed glass mat) variety. When replacing or upgrading your battery, this is a good time to take into consideration the reserve capacity or AH rating. Often, you're limited only by the size of battery that fits in the stock location.

Replacing a Battery

As a battery ages, it can become increasingly difficult for the alternator to charge. In some cases, it can develop a dead cell, which causes the alternator to work overtime trying to charge. If you think your battery is in need of replacing, you can make a

Battery Maintenance

How simple is this? What if I told you that a dirty, filthy, nasty battery could lead to its demise? Well, it's true! A layer of dirt and grime can provide a high-resistance path for current to travel from the battery to the chassis. Over time, this can cause a good battery to fail. Every time I wash my car, I use a few wet paper towels to clean the top and sides of the battery. This simple maintenance has served me well over the years, and costs nothing. It also gives me the chance to inspect the battery cables and terminals for corrosion.

Chemical Maintenance

Another inexpensive trick for lead acid batteries with service-type tops is to keep an eye on the electrolyte within them. Admittedly, batteries have moved toward the maintenance-free type over the last few years, but the more inexpensive batteries still have these removable tops. A hydrometer can be used to tell you about the chemical makeup within the battery, as it is designed to measure the specific gravity of the electrolyte.

Hydrometers are readily available from any auto parts store and the instructions are simple and easy to follow. If you do have to add water to such a battery, follow the manufacturer's guidelines for such. This typically means that you have to use distilled water and fill it to where the meniscus just touches the bottom of the top. Don't stand there with the garden hose and top off your battery while chattin' on the phone to a buddy.

Trickle Charging

When a battery is in a poor state, before calling it a loss, you can try to revive it via a trickle charger. Use the lowest amperage setting and let the battery sit overnight. In the morning, disconnect the trickle charger from the battery and take a voltage reading. If the voltage begins to drop, even slightly, it will likely continue to drop over time, and you'll be able to observe this with your DMM. This indicates that the battery needs to be replaced. Most auto parts stores check a battery for you free of charge, but this obviously requires that you remove it. Do it yourself, and bring it to them for confirmation as you'll have it on hand for a core when you buy the new one.

---

more educated guess using the following steps:

1. Allow the vehicle to sit overnight.
2. With the Ignition switch in the off position, turn the headlights on for 30 seconds to bleed off any surface charge that may be present.
3. Turn the headlights off and connect your DMM across the battery to measure its voltage.
4. If you measure voltage below 12.4 VDC, let the battery sit for an hour or two and take a second measurement.
5. If you measure closer to 12 VDC on the second go around, it's safe to assume that your battery has seen better days and should be replaced.

Before yanking it out, you can try some of the things in the battery maintenance sidebar in an effort to bring it back to life.

Protecting Your Work

Adding a circuit of any type to a vehicle involves further considerations. Specifically, they are:
- Fusing.
- Suitable fuse locations.
- Routing of the wiring.
- Protection for the wiring itself.
- Anchoring the wiring.

This is the area most neglected by the do-it-yourselfer. Incidentally, overlook this part and your vehicle could be the next one on the side of the highway burning. (To this day, when I see that, it makes my stomach turn.)

Fusing

When adding an accessory that draws high enough current to have to be connected to the vehicle's battery directly, this wire has to be fused. This fuse value should be chosen according to:
- The manufacturer's specifications of the accessory(s).
- The current capability of the wire.

Again, there is a science here to work by and that science is math. The chart on page 100 shows the current capability of a gauge of wire versus its length.

Let's go back to the previous example of the amplifier in my wife's truck. The amplifier requires a maximum of 60 amps of current to be able to make full output. According

---

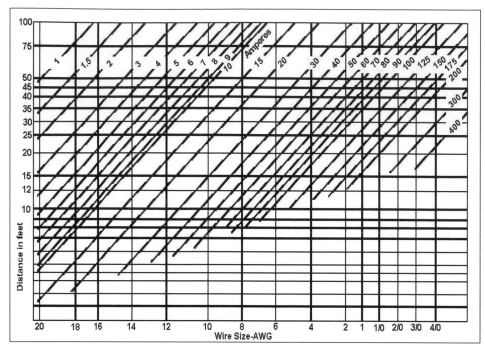

to the chart, this is well within the current carrying capabilities of 4-gauge wire over a 20-foot run.

Suitable Fuse Locations

More commonly, when we add a high-current circuit to a vehicle, we connect its power cable to the battery directly. This also necessitates that we fuse this lead within a short distance from the battery to protect it from a short circuit in its run. An example of such a short could be if the vehicle was involved in an accident and the power cable was pinched as a result. If this cable was not fused, it could start a fire, which would quickly turn a bad situation into a very bad situation. Common practice is to fuse a cable within 18 inches of the battery post. I typically install fuses closer than that, but certainly no farther apart.

A second consideration is where to mount the fuse holder under the hood of a vehicle so that it is within 18 inches of the battery and solidly mounted. You just have to look under the hood of any new car to notice that real estate is at a premium. This is the case in both the Nissan Frontier and the Mustang GT. Fortunately, it is simple enough to make a mounting bracket from metal or plastic, mount this to the vehicle, then mount the fuse holder to this.

It is *not* acceptable to leave a fuse holder unmounted or "mount" it to a wire harness with a cable tie. They have provisions for mounting for a reason—use them.

Routing of the Wiring

As I mentioned above, I follow factory wiring harnesses whenever possible. When it's not possible, I like to route my wiring as high as possible. Whether under the dash or

The Mustang's main power fuse for the audio system is located very close to the battery. The purpose of this fuse is to protect the run of wiring only. Each of the individual audio components in the vehicle is fused individually per their manufacturer's recommendations. I use a 250-amp ANL fuse to protect this run of 1/0 AWG wiring.

No place under the hood of your car to mount a fuse holder? Make one. Pictured here is a simple fuse holder mount that I made with 3/8-inch-thick plastic on a band saw. This took minutes, mounts to the overflow reservoir support, and provides a flat mounting location for the fuse holder itself.

under the hood, keeping your wiring up and out of the way of moving parts or sources of heat pays off in spades. Be aware of hood hinges as they're up and out of the way with the hood up!

If you have to run wiring in-between metal barriers, such as between the chassis and the door in the doorjamb, then you're best advised to think about how water travels. If you look closely at the harness installed by the OEM in a doorjamb, the hole in the body is always higher than the hole in the door itself. This allows water to flow downward when it rains. If water gets into the door, the door has drain holes in it to accommodate this, whereas the chassis inside the body does not.

Running wiring under the vehicle is totally acceptable and in many cases can be the only way to do it—especially with large-gauge power wiring. Be sure that you cover the wiring with one of the methods outlined in the next topic and that it is anchored properly. Inside or alongside the frame rail is an excellent location to run such wiring.

Protection for the Wiring Itself

There are many different types of wiring looms and sheathing avail-

able to protect the new wiring. In addition, this gives your work a clean and professional look. There are a seemingly endless selection nowadays; this book covers the three most common.

Split Loom Tubing: The most popular type of covering is split loom tubing and it is available in diameters ranging from 1/4 inch to more than 1 inch. This stuff is easy to slide over wiring, as it has a slit in one side.

Making Split Loom Tubing

I like to go the extra mile with split loom tubing and finish it off like the OEMs do. Here's how to do that with a wire terminated with a crimp connector like a ring terminal:

1 Cut the loom so that it is about 1/4 inch shorter than the insulation of the ring terminal.

2 Wrap Super 33+ Tape around the insulation of the ring terminal a turn and a half to two turns.

3 Slide the loom over the ring terminal so that the tape comes through the loom at the slice.

4 Continue wrapping the tape around the terminal and loom and go down the loom about an inch past the terminal, tear the tape and finish the wrap.

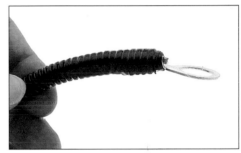

Heat Shrink Tubing: As stated in Chapter 3, this tubing is good to have on hand. I like to use it in conjunction with split loom tubing to provide an even better look than you can get with the method I showed you above. Just cut a piece about 2 inches long and heat it over the

Heat shrinking the ends of your split loom tubing is easy. You need to be sure to put it on the tubing first if you plan to terminate the cable with a big ring terminal like the one here. While heat shrink tubing takes a little extra time, the looks are sure worth it!

Split loom tubing is quite handy indeed. It's easy to install, looks just like what most OEM's use, and comes in sizes from 1/8- to 2-inch diameters.

If wire must be routed near sources of very high heat (such as the exhaust), consider using high-temperature sheathing for the wiring or looms of wiring. When I use this stuff, I typically loom my wiring as normal, then I slide the sheathing over the loom and heat shrink it to the loom to give it a nice finished look.

end of your split loom for a really great-looking finish.

High-Temperature Sheathing: When you have to run cables or wiring near areas of extreme heat, like the Hooker Super Comp headers in my Olds, you'd be well advised to cover it with this stuff. It's readily available at your local performance parts shop.

Consider the problem of a heat-soaked starter. We've all been there, and me just recently! You pull into the cruise, let your car sit for a while, then go to start it to leave and nada. No matter how hard you try, the starter just won't do anything. This meant that I had to wait another hour or so for it to cool down before I could leave—a favorite with the wife that just spent the last hour humoring me, looking at the same cars I saw the week before.

What really causes this? Is it a bad starter? In the case of the Oldsmobile, it was the following:

- The solenoid for the starter motor is on the top of the starter, so it is extremely close to the headers.
- The heat from the wrapped

2⅛-inch internal-diameter, thin-walled headers caused the copper within the solenoid trigger wire to become very hot after the car sat for a while, limiting its ability to pass current.

- The wiring going to the solenoid trigger couldn't pass the current the solenoid

required of it when subjected to this heat.

- The wiring to the solenoid trigger was 16 AWG (one of the few things that I left from the last guy's work)—the bare minimum to trigger the solenoid.

High resistance plus high heat is not a good combination. Fortunately, the solution was simple. I used the 16-gauge wire to trigger a Bosch relay mounted under the dash, which feeds 10-gauge wiring to the solenoid trigger input. As I installed an extra fuse panel in the Olds for circuit expansions, the source of power was easy. In addition, I sheathed this wire to the solenoid with high-temperature covering.

Problem solved! I've driven the vehicle for several months now and never had so much as a hesitation when starting it. I should have looked up the current requirement

Here is a great example of where and when to use high-temperature sheathing. I used it to protect the wiring for the trans-temp gauge, the trans-brake, and the starter in my Olds as all these cables pass within close proximity of the passenger-side header.

of the solenoid trigger wire versus assuming that it was like a Ford solenoid

Anchoring the Wiring

If this sounds so obvious, why then do I see so many examples of how not to do this when I'm looking under the hood or the dash of a car at the local gathering? Wiring is the one task that most people just *wanna get done*; once they get the circuit working, they tend to leave it that way. Finishing the wiring is always on a car guy's list—the list that never seems to get done because the turbo needs to be bigger, the suspension needs tweaking, etc.

When it comes to safety, this is one of the most important aspects of any wiring job. Second only to fusing, properly securing any added wiring is a really important thing to finish. Wiring hanging down below the dash is simply unacceptable as it can get tangled in the pedals, steering, etc. Wiring under the hood that isn't anchored can quickly find its way to the exhaust manifold or any number of other hot or moving parts. Even worse is wiring that isn't fused or anchored—this is simply a vehicle fire waiting to happen.

Again, this is easy stuff. The most common methods of anchoring are by use of cable ties and tie downs.

Cable Ties: These are available in both natural and black and in all different lengths up to about 3 feet. After I tie them and cut off the excess, I like to rotate the tie so that you can't see the cut end. This gives my work a really clean and professional look.

Do not use cable ties to tie anything to rubber vacuum lines or hard air-conditioning lines under the hood of the vehicle. Cable ties can damage these lines.

Tie Downs: These are available in both plastic and metal with rubber linings. You can get them at your local hardware or home supply store in bulk and save a few bucks over buying them in pairs at the auto parts supply store. These are handy for securing large-gauge cables or harnesses, especially when you have to run them under the vehicle.

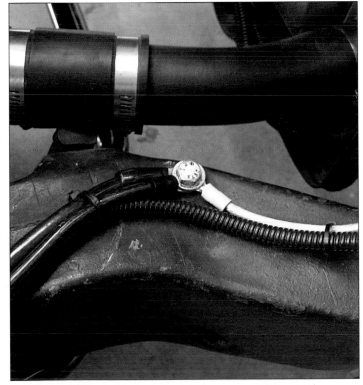

Cable ties keep your cable runs neat and tidy and out of the way of moving parts. Also shown is the connection from the alternator case and the return path for all the accessories in the front clip of the Olds. Note that I tapped an existing hole in the frame and used a 5/16–18 bolt for this connection.

Tie downs are great to anchor wiring and looms of wiring to a vehicles chassis or frame. The one used here has a rubber lining within a metal clamp assembly. Nice thing about these is that your local home improvement store typically stocks them up to about 2 inches in diameter.

TROUBLESHOOTING

Troubleshooting is the act of taking logical steps to solve a problem. In the case of automotive electronics troubleshooting, this is regarded as black magic. In reality, it's no more difficult than troubleshooting a problem of any kind. I'm betting if you didn't have the first six chapters under your belt, then maybe it would be.

This chapter starts out with an easy-to-solve problem and works up to the complex ones. What I hope to show you is the thought process that goes into solving each problem versus the actual steps involved, or even how difficult the problem is to solve. Afterward, you'll be prepared to dive in with both feet when something goes wrong.

First off, here are the tools you will need:

- Knowledge of the problem (or symptom) at hand.
- Some knowledge of the circuit you're diagnosing.
- Diagram of the circuit if possible.
- DMM.
- Wire probe kit for your DMM.

Understanding Flowcharts

One of the best things I ever learned in school was how to use and make flowcharts. I have many years of experience in troubleshooting and each time I do it, I go through the process as if it were a flowchart in my mind. I guess I should thank my computer science teachers for this ability!

Respective manufacturers can provide flowcharts to professional auto mechanics so the amount of time mechanics spend troubleshooting problems is reduced. As mechanics are paid by book hours, it cost the OEMs less money to develop this tool on the front side than to pay the mechanic the time the job would take if they didn't provide it. Unfortunately, these are not readily available to vehicle owners. I'll give one to you for two of the scenarios covered in this chapter. If you're troubleshooting a really complex problem, then a flow chart may be the only way to solve it in a timely fashion.

Typical Problems

Most of the examples assume that you do not have anything other than a basic understanding of the circuit and your DMM. A few of the examples have been recreated based on problems I've had to troubleshoot in real time. I hope you find them enlightening!

- Circuit inoperable
- Circuit works, but blows fuses
- Wiring burned up
- Battery is drained overnight
- Intermittent circuit operation

Circuit Inoperable

Example—Reverse light circuit, 1972 Olds Cutlass

Symptom—Driver-side reverse light not working

We have a bulb that doesn't work—how do we determine the problem? First, a basic understanding of the circuit is necessary. In order for the bulb to come on, the following have to occur:

- Ignition switch in IGN/RUN position.
- Shifter in REVERSE.

Before we start troubleshooting, let's be safe by following the safety outlines I gave you at the beginning of Chapter 5. Now:

- Move the ignition switch into the IGN/RUN position.
- Depress the brake pedal and move the gear selector in the REVERSE position.

Now, one reverse light is working and the other is not.

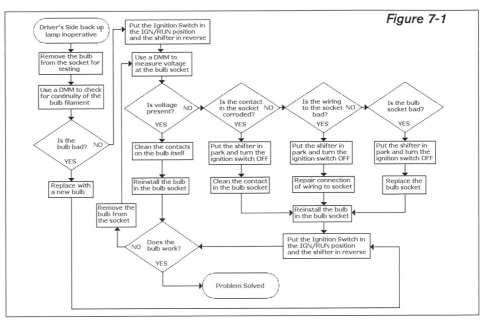

Figure 7-1

Simple problem, right? Let's dig in and find out ...

Since one of the lights is working, we know that overall the circuit is working properly. This means that there is an open circuit between the wiring and the non-working bulb. Possible causes are:

- A bad bulb.
- A bad connection between the bulb and the bulb socket.
- A bad connection between the connector and the bulb socket.
- A bad connection somewhere in the wiring harness to this connector.

Here are the correct steps in determining this. I always choose the most obvious problem first, that way I can eliminate extra work. In addi-

tion, it's always best to work from one end of the circuit to the other, don't start in the middle. In this case, we go to the very end and test the bulb first, as it's easy to remove. The flowchart above (Figure 7-1) shows the procedures:

Procedure
Checking the bulb itself.

Meter Settings
- Selector switch in the Ω Position
- Red probe in V/Ω
- Black probe in COM

Step-by-Step

1 Remove the bulb from the socket and connect the black probe to the metal bulb sleeve

2 Connect the red probe to the tip of the bulb (Note: Many automotive bulbs have two filaments and have two electrical contacts—one for each filament. This one does not.)

3 A reading of close to 0Ω shows continuity and means that the filament is good. No

reading means that the filament is burned out, and the bulb needs to be replaced.

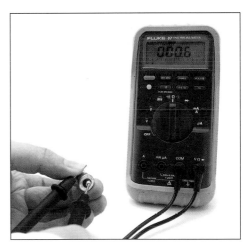

The bulb is good, as indicated by the 0.6Ω reading on my DMM, so we need to move on to the next step.

Procedures
Checking the connection between the bulb and the bulb socket.

Meter Settings
- Selector switch in the DCV Position
- Red probe in V/Ω
- Black probe in COM and connected to vehicle chassis ground

Step-by-Step

1 With the bulb out of the socket, the Ignition Switch in the IGN/RUN position, and the shifter in REVERSE, attempt to measure voltage at the brass (+) connection point within the bulb housing.

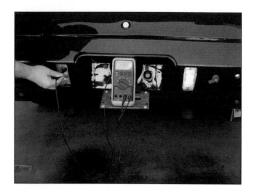

2 If voltage is present at the brass (+) connection point, we have a poor connection between the bulb and the bulb socket. In some cases, it may be necessary for me to use the tip of the DMM to get a good bite into this brass (+) connection point by scraping it back and forth across the brass contact.

That is the case here, but it isn't actually the brass (+) connection point within the bulb socket that is the problem. Rather, the bulb socket itself isn't getting a good bite into the ground lugs of the bulb as it is spent. In all fairness, it is 36 years

Both reverse lights are working now, but this is only a short-term fix. The long-term solution is to replace the bulb socket.

old! Although I can get the bulb to work as pictured, it is only be a temporary fix. The long-term fix is to replace the socket entirely.

If you determined that the brass (+) connection point was the source of the problem, then you'd need to clean it and the contact on the bulb itself to ensure a good connection. But, before cleaning either, put the shifter back in PARK and turn the ignition switch to the OFF position. Now you can clean the contact points, without danger of shorting the one in the socket, and re-install the bulb. (The tip of a small flat blade screwdriver works nicely for the socket contact and a file of any type or some sandpaper can be used to burnish the bulb contact.)

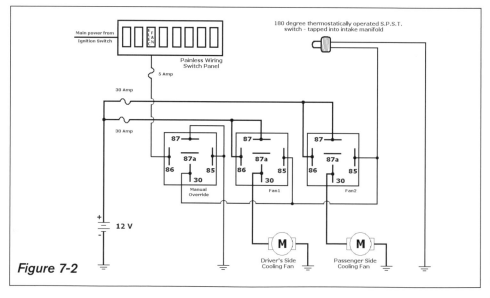

Figure 7-2

Since you narrowed the problem down to the socket itself, it is not necessary to check the integrity of the connection between the wiring and the bulb socket. This proved to be a good example as I thought the problem would be a little simpler than it actually was. Either way, it's the thought process that's important. Note that we didn't have to run to the auto parts store to get a new

bulb that wouldn't have solved the problem anyway. Now, let's move on to a more challenging problem.

Circuit Works, but Blows Fuses: Scenario 1

Example—Aftermarket electric fans in the same vehicle.

Symptom—The circuit works fine most of the time, but the driver-side side fan stops working occasionally when the vehicle is being driven. When this happens, the fuse that powers the relay for that fan is blown. I can replace it and restore operation to the circuit for a period of time before the fuse blows again. Before we begin, Figure 7-2 is a diagram of this circuit.

This problem is a little tougher to solve, but let's start with what we know:

- Spal 16-inch electric puller fans being used, and according to the manufacturer, each requires 22 amps at 12 VDC.
- 30 amp Tyco Relays for the fans are mounted under the dash and approximately 12 feet away.

- Relays are approximately 4 feet away from the fuse panel.
- Relays are fused with 30-amp fuses each.
- Ground wiring is about 3 feet long.
- 10-gauge wiring is used throughout.
- 10-gauge wiring has .00102 Ω of resistance per foot.

From Chapter 1, let's first calculate how much voltage is lost in the wiring:

$$E = I \times R$$
$$E = 22 \text{ amps} \times (19 \times .00102 \text{ }\Omega)$$
$$E = 22 \text{ amps} \times .01938 \text{ }\Omega$$
$$E = .43 \text{ volts of loss in the wiring}$$

That's certainly acceptable. Now that we've quickly ruled out that the wire gauge is insufficient for the task, let's get on with the troubleshooting.

Procedures

Since there are two identical circuits, we focus only on the one that is blowing the fuse. Possible causes of this problem are:

- A faulty fan.
- Intermittent short in the wiring between the fan and the relay.
- Intermittent short at the relay itself.
- Intermittent short in the wiring between the fuse block and the relay.

Notice how I basically just dissected this circuit into four different parts. Some of the wiring is within split loom tubing so it is naturally out of sight—again, out of sight out of mind... This can certainly be an obstacle to some, but if you follow my lead it won't be an obstacle for you.

Here are the correct steps in determining where the problem lies within the individual parts of the cir-

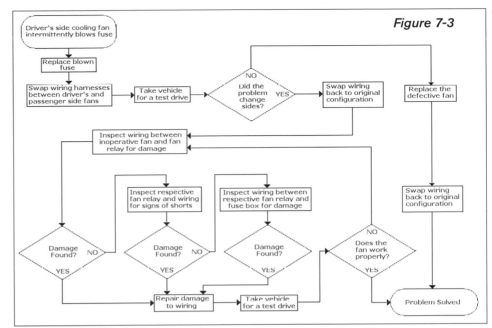

Figure 7-3

cuit. Again, I like to go the end of the circuit and work my way back. The flowchart (Figure 7-3) outlines the procedures:

Checking the Fan Itself—The Process of Substitution: The easiest way to determine if the fan on the driver's side is bad is to swap the wiring from this into the other fan and vice versa. This allows me to rule out a bad fan by the process of substitution. (Incidentally, if you were troubleshooting a circuit with only one fan, assume the fan is not

the problem and proceed to the next step. Remember, troubleshooting is not the act of replacing parts until you find the one that was at fault.) I don't need tools of any kind to do this, just a little common sense and one extension harness that I can easily fab up on the bench so that I can connect the driver-side fan to the passenger-side fan harness. (The driver-side harness is obviously long enough after I cut loose a few of the cable ties holding it in place.)

This is the fan harness as originally installed. The radiator in my Olds is a Ron Davis Racing unit, an optional fan wiring kit that has mating plugs to the ones on the fans is also available. As I elected to make my own wiring harness, I chose not to purchase the kit.

Swapping the fans from one side to the other is simple with a short extension harness. Note that I was careful to tie this up properly before taking the vehicle for a test drive.

After a quick test drive, the problem still exists, but now the fan on the driver's side works fine. Since the problem changed sides, I know it isn't the fan itself. We've now eliminated one of the four parts of the circuit as the source of the problem. I can now put the wiring back to normal and proceed to the other three parts.

Checking the Wiring Between the Fan and the Relay: Continuing to work our way down the circuit, this is the next step. Also, this step does not require any special tools other than your keen sense of observation. As the wiring is covered in split loom to protect it, the chances of it being damaged are pretty slim. Inspect it along its routing, paying particular attention for any screws that may have pierced the wiring or possibly chafing as it passes through the firewall. Yes, this means that you have to cut the ties that anchor it to the inner fender and open the tubing so that you can see the wiring itself. As the wiring passes through a rubber grommet in the firewall and is properly anchored, we did not find any damage to the wiring or its insulation in the run from the fans to the firewall. Now, we need to get under the dash and follow the run from the firewall to the relay. This run is clean.

When inspecting a run of wiring like this one, it's best to cut all the ties and open it up as best you can. This allows you to inspect the insulation of the wiring for signs of damage.

This run is for the electric fans. It contains the power wires from the fan relays to the fan motors as well as the trigger lead for the thermostatically controlled switch. Since the Olds has no innter fenders, I've anchored the harness (up high) to the bottom of the fender.

As you can see, the wiring passes through the firewall through a snap bushing. The wire insulation is protected from potential damage by the drilled hole's sharp edges in the firewall.

Follow the run through the firewall and to the relays to look for evidence of any place that the insulation of the wire could be damaged by.

In the event that this is an OEM-installed circuit, the wiring to the fan is not so easy to access. In fact, it may travel through any number of lengths of tubing or conduit alongside any number of other wires. This can make this step more challenging, but you need to spend the time to be sure that the wiring hasn't been damaged in the run. Pay special attention to areas where accessories (OEM or aftermarket) have been mounted that are in close proximity to the wiring harness—like horns, sirens, cruise control modules, etc. Over the years, I've seen a number of cases where a loomed harness was pinched by a mounting bracket, bolt, or screw and it just took time for the insulation of a wire within the harness to wear through. If the wiring passes through the firewall, you also need to pay close attention to its proximity to moving parts under the dash, etc. The more thorough your investigation, the quicker you'll solve the problem.

Checking the Wiring of the Relay Itself: This is a typical S.P.D.T. relay. As pictured, connections to it have been made with female push-on terminals and they have been insulated with Super 33+ tape.

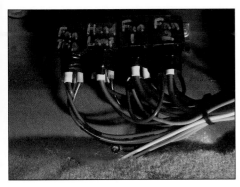

This brings us to the relays themselves. All looks good from the front. But you need to remove the relay specific to the driver-side fan and inspect it closely in hopes of finding and resolving this problem.

Even though the relay's electrical terminals have been insulated, let's remove the relay from its mounting position and inspect it more closely. When removing the relay, close inspection reveals that there is a puncture through the tape on the rear right next to terminal 30, which is the output to the fan itself. This could not be seen without removing the relay.

Well what do you know, the tape has been torn at the rear of the first relay removed. And terminal 30 is no longer fully insulated.

Further inspection reveals that a screw run through the firewall from the other side caused the short.

Look closely, see the screw coming through the firewall from the engine compartment? This screw came in contact with terminal 30 of the relay, causing our problem. This problem was intermittent because the screw was just far enough away from the terminal of the relay that the chassis had to flex a little bit for it to touch, thereby blowing the fuse.

This screw was just close enough to terminal 30 of the relay to cause it to become shorted only when the chassis flexed a little bit when driving. A shorter screw easily solves this problem. This is an excellent example of a simple, yet elusive, problem that was solved with simple and logical troubleshooting steps. (OK, rest assured that I'm more careful than that. I chose to replicate this based on how often I've seen a similar scenario occur!)

Circuit Works, but Blows Fuses: Scenario 2

Another more obvious case where a circuit works but blows the fuse is where some kind of aftermarket electronics has been added to an existing circuit and its current requirements, combined with the current requirements of the accessory(s) already connected to said circuit, exceeded the circuit's capability. This is where folks are tempted to

replace said fuse with a larger value fuse. In the example I gave, the gauge of wire, relay, and fuse were all selected based on the fans' current requirements, so this circuit is in harmony. This is exactly what the OEM does for every circuit in every vehicle they build. In such a case, the solution is to connect the aftermarket accessory to a different source of power, such as shown in Chapter 6 in the tach installation.

What if you removed a stock piece of electronics and replaced it with a better-performing aftermarket piece? For example, let's say that you upgraded your stock headlights to aftermarket units that consumed more current. If you simply connected them to the stock headlight harnesses, they might cause this exact same problem. This is where folks get into trouble—real trouble. Since it's easier to replace the fuse with one that's "only" 5 amps larger, this is commonly the next step. Next step is another 5 amps larger, right? Wrong! At this point, the circuit is no longer in harmony because the factory wiring isn't capable of the additional current. This may also be true for the contacts in the headlight switch or even the bright light switch. This creates problems of all kind, maybe even burning up some of the wiring in the process. (Chapter 8 shows how to do this the right way.)

Wiring is Burned Up

This is hopefully not something you've experienced recently. I've seen it happen many times over the years and it is typically caused by one of three things:

- Gauge of wiring insufficient for current demands of the circuit—as I just discussed.

- Wiring not fused/fused improperly, and pinched or shorted—this causes a short circuit, which causes an extremely high amount of current to flow through the wire, which results in the insulation being burned right off of it.
- A high resistance connection with high current flowing through it, such as a connector termination.

Burned cables and wiring can cause vehicle fires. Here are three examples of what can happen as a result of rushing things or poor planning.

Since I just covered the first bullet point above, let's look at the cause of each of the remaining two scenarios.

Wiring not Fused and Pinched or Shorted

CAUTION: Note that this is extremely dangerous and can cause a vehicle to burn to the ground! In the event that this occurs in a vehicle that is being driven down the road, the problem can escalate so quickly it can be nearly impossible to pull to the side of the road, find, and fix the problem before serious damage occurs.

Example—Simple short circuit
Symptom—Insulation burned off of the wiring

Pictured is a length of wire that came out from under the dash of the Olds. This piece of 10 AWG wiring wasn't fused between the positive connection and the accessory it powered. Somewhere along the way, it got pinched and the resulting short circuit burned the insulation off of the wire. Interestingly enough, the prior owner fixed the short, but chose to keep the burned length of wire in place just as you see it here. In addition, he chose to leave it unfused.

I forget exactly what this was connected to under the dash of my Olds, but it's a keeper. Notice that the ring terminal is crimped incorrectly and the insulation of the wiring is burned badly, even totally gone in spots. Nice!

More than likely, this damage took fractions of a second. Fortunately for the prior owner, the damage was limited to this cable. Imagine what damage this could have caused had it been laying across the plastic feed line for an oil-pressure gauge. Or even if it had been routed near or under carpet, plastics, or anything it was routed along side or anchored to.

If you're troubleshooting such a circuit, you have to assume that it wasn't protected or protected improperly (yeah, a 150-amp circuit breaker is too big for 10-gauge wiring.) and start at the very front of the circuit. If you happen to experience such a scenario first hand, the best thing that you can do is cut either of the battery cables as close to the battery as possible.

Obviously, you understand the value of protecting a circuit now that you've read Chapter 4, but you just never know when you might see this occur at a buddy's house, the local gathering, in the pits at the drags, etc. Thinking on your feet might save your (or somebody else's) vehicle.

Repairing such a problem typically requires removing the entire run of burned wiring, replacing it, and fusing it properly. Don't even think of trying to re-use it. In some cases, this is an extremely ambitious and time-consuming repair, especially if this wiring is routed inside loom with a factory harness or tied to one. Over the years, I've seen numerous cases in which large sections of the wiring harness required replacing because of damage created from such a simple oversight. In other cases, I've seen a burn in the carpet from the firewall to the rear of the vehicle, requiring its replacement. These guys got off easy and were luck they didn't have a fire!

High Resistance Connection

Example—Same fan circuit in the 1972 Olds
Symptom—Relay housing and wiring burned up

Interestingly enough, this really did happen to me. Remember when I told you earlier that I had a preference when it comes to relays? It just so happens that I didn't have any Bosch relays on hand when I built this circuit, but I had a few that came free with something I'd purchased over the years. I figured what the heck, and used them. Two weeks later, I noticed that the fan on the driver's side wasn't pulling as much air as the one on the passenger's side.

When I dug into the problem, using the same procedures I outlined above, I noticed that the body of one of the fan relays was melted slightly and so was the wiring and female push-on terminal connected to terminal 87.

The melted relay housing is a sure sign of a problem, but it will take some detective work to figure out what caused this.

Further investigation revealed that the relay was poorly manufactured and when I pushed the female connector on to terminal 87, the terminal itself pushed up into the body of the relay slightly. This was enough to break two-thirds of the electrical connection between the contacts within the relay itself when it was powered up. This caused high resistance, high heat, and subsequently damage to the relay and wiring.

Look closely at terminal 87 (front and center). Notice that the whole terminal is pushed up about 1/8 inch into the body of the relay.

The solution was to swap the free relays for some quality units (Tyco in this case, as the company I work for sells them and I thought I'd try them out) and this solved the problem long term. Although the problem I experienced was a problem within the relay itself, the same kind of thing could be experienced between a wire and connector or between a connector and accessory. This problem is magnified as current flowing through the circuit increases, which is why it is so important to make quality connections.

Example—Starter Circuit in same 1972 Olds
Symptom—Wiring burned up

Here is another example of a high-resistance connection. This length of 4 AWG cable went from the starter motor, between the header primaries, to the frame, and then finally to the battery in the rear of my Olds.

This is a jewel. Not only was the cable routed way too close to a source of high heat (and not protected in high-temperature sheathing), the ring terminal was improperly terminated on the cable.

As you can see, there are two problems:

- Close proximity to the headers, as evidenced by the solenoid trigger lead melted into both chunks of wire, as well as the burned insulation.
- Poor termination of the ring terminal to the cable, as evidenced by the hole burnt through the ferrule of the ring terminal itself.

Finally, when I removed this cable to replace it, I noticed that the electrical connection between the solenoid and armature itself was loose, further contributing to the heat generated at this connection point. Believe it or not, the motor actually started with the cable in this condition. However, the copper in the solenoid trigger lead and the copper in the 4 AWG starter cable have maybe 1/16 inch of plastic insulation left between them. Finally, the copper in the 4 AWG cable was nearly in contact with the frame due to the lack of insulation protecting it, which was totally melted by the heat from the headers.

Best case scenario would have been the starter getting stuck in "start" mode when the solenoid trigger lead finally fused to the starter cable. (You'd have a hard time fixing that if that occurred when you were backing into your parking spot at the cruise!) Worse case would have been the length of cable from the frame to the battery burning, and it was tied to the fuel line its entire length. It gets worse.

Notice the round contact point peeping up over the switch from behind (on the far left). This doesn't leave much of the contact left to mate with the switch when it is thrown. This resulted in a very high-resistance connection, and the associated heat melted the body of the relay as well as the push-on connector and wiring from terminal 87.

Fixing Burned-Up Cable

This is a classic example of what happens when you're in a hurry! I had the negative cable off of the battery within about 3 seconds of sizing this up. To fix this problem the correct way, here's what to do:

1 Remove the starter (which requires removing the passenger side header) so that you can clean and tighten the connection between the solenoid and armature. Use a lock washer to prevent this from occurring again.

2 Replace the entire run of 4 AWG cable from the batteries to the starter with new 1/0 AWG cable (to ensure the starter would never bog down).

3 Loom said cable to protect it the length of the run and anchored it along the frame rail so that it was secure.

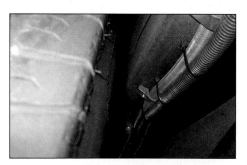

The cables and fuel line are properly anchored to the frame rail. Even though they are in close proximity to the exhaust and rear tires, a minimum of 2 inches is between them. The 1/0 AWG supply cable and the 4 AWG charge lead from the alternator to the batteries directly, as this vehicle has a bumper-mounted main power switch on the supply cable.

4 Install snap bushings in the tin surrounding the fuel cell to protect the insulation of the

cable itself (before, there were none) as it passes through the tin in three different spots.

As the charge lead passes through the tin that surrounds the fuel cell, it must pass through a snap bushing to protect its insulation. The 1/0 AWG supply cable is directly above this and out of the photo. It also passes through the tin-in the same fashion.

5 Install a distribution block on the firewall so that you can terminate the 1/0 AWG and have numerous 4 AWG and 8 AWG take-offs for anything you need—one such 4 AWG output goes directly to the starter.

The 1/0 AWG supply lead feeds this firewall-mounted distribution block. The 4 AWG red wire (top right) is the supply to the starter motor. The 4 AWG red wire and the two 8 AWG blue wires (bottom) supply power to the interior fuse panels.

6 Route the cable down the firewall and over the top of the starter to the solenoid, to get it

as far away from the headers as possible.

7 Sheathe about 3 feet of said cable within the high-temperature sheathing, just to be safe.

The wiring to the starter motor is protected in high-temperature sheathing. In addition, the ring terminal is soldered to the end of the cable, ensuring a good solid connection to the starter.

8 Add a pair of 200-amp circuit breakers wired in parallel. These breakers run between the battery and the ON/OFF switch mounted on the bumper. They protect the run of the cable from an unlikely short. (Admittedly, these breakers are large, but the pair of 140-amp units I installed originally would open on occasion during a cold start.)

A pair of paralleled Die Hard Golds ensure that the Olds starts right up, even on a cold morning. When locating your batteries in the trunk, it's a good idea to protect the run of wiring between them and the front of the vehicle with a circuit breaker, or a pair wired in parallel (shown here).

Servicing the Contacts of a Relay

There are times when your diagnosis leads to a troublesome relay. When you're talking about an easy-to-access OEM relay, replacements are typically just a trip away to the auto parts store. When you're talking about a relay that is located within a piece of electronics, this may be a different story.

Years ago, a friend brought a 1980s Lincoln Town Car into the shop and asked me to look at the power door lock circuit for him because it wasn't working. My diagnosis quickly led to this giant black box under the passenger side of the dash with three or four plugs on it.

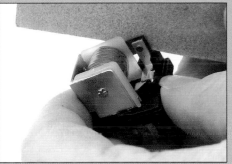

You can use sandpaper to burnish the contacts of a relay. Just slide the sandpaper down between the contacts and go to town.

Contact problems can be exacerbated by high currents running through them. Accessories that draw very high current on turn-on are the worst offenders.

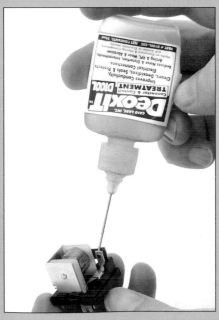

After burnishing the contacts, it's always good to treat them with a contact treatment, such as DeoxIT. This DeoxIT has seen better days, as its turned colors from the heat of the desert.

Specifically, I could hear the door lock and unlock relays clicking within this box by depressing the lock/unlock switches, but couldn't measure voltage at the output wires to the door lock actuators themselves. So, out this big black box came. A few phone calls later, it was determined that this box was about $250 from a salvage yard and three times that from the dealer. In about three minutes, I had it apart.

Within the box, I found numerous S.P.D.T. relays that were circuit board mounted. As they were inside this box, the manufacturer chose not to spend the money on the plastic housings around them so the contacts and coils were plainly visible. As I investigated the contact points of each of them, I noticed several were badly pitted and others simply corroded. I spent about an hour with a little file, some sandpaper, and some elbow grease and cleaned the contacts as best I could.

After cleaning the contacts, it's a good idea to use a chemical like Caig Laboratories, Inc's DeoxIT to keep the contacts free of oxidation for many years to come. This helps prevent this from reoccurring.

After I treated the contacts with DeoxIT, reassembled it, and reinstalled it, the power door locks worked correctly. This approach saved the owner a bunch of money, and as a result he was elated and gave me a nice tip.

Since then, I've dug similarly deep into any number of problems and I've been able to solve many of them with nothing more than a little know-how. I share this story with you because it isn't really hard to do and could help you to solve a similar problem, maybe even making you a hero as well. Incidentally, these same procedures can be used for anything with electrical contacts—from switches to rheostats. Finally, don't let the plastic housing cover around a relay deter you from servicing its contacts. In many cases, you can easily pry it off with nothing more than a screwdriver. If this had been the case in the Lincoln, it would have required unsoldering each of the relays from the board to do so. Although this sounds like a whole lot of work, it's really not that big of a deal. It just takes some careful work and time.

Remember when I said it gets worse? Well, imagine my surprise when I noticed that both batteries were wired in parallel with 4 AWG and grounded with a 5/16-18 bolt and nut to the tin surrounding the fuel cell. In addition, the tin was painted black on both sides, and tack welded to the fuel cell frame. Also, the bolt and nut were loose enough that the ring terminal would easily move! As I replaced the tired, mismatched batteries, aftermarket battery clamps made the connection of 1/0 AWG wiring between them a snap. I also took this opportunity to tap an existing hole in the frame rail and ground the batteries to the frame directly.

With trunk-mounted batteries, the return path to the starter can get quite long. As shown, I tapped the frame rail (obviously, this car has been back halved) and used a 5/16–18 bolt to firmly secure the 1/0 AWG ground wire to the frame. In the front of the vehicle, a short run of 4 AWG connects the bellhousing bolt nearest the starter to the frame rail on the same side, completing the return path.

Shortly after this, I knew it was time to rip out all of the wiring in the car and start over from scratch. Unfortunately, at that time, I didn't know I'd be writing this book so I didn't take before pictures. Personally, I'm still surprised the starter even worked at all!

Battery is Drained Overnight

In Chapter 2 you learned how to use both a test light and a DMM to measure current draw. Now we put the DMM to use to solve a real world problem.

Example—2003 Ford Mustang GT
Symptom—Battery is dead after sitting for longer than 96 hours

I have a suspicion about what the problem is, but let's go through the motions. This vehicle has a bunch of aftermarket electronics, so it's a great candidate to separate the men from the boys. Currently, it has the following aftermarket electronics:

Audio Equipment
• AM/FM/CD Player
• (2) Audio Processors
• (2) Amplifiers, totaling 3,000 watts RMS in power
• (2) 18-inch Subwoofers
• (2) 6½-inch Component Speakers
• Neon Accent Lighting (above the woofers)
Security System
• CPU
• Shock Sensor
• Tilt/Motion Sensor
• Power Window Up/Down Convenience Module
• Auxiliary Power Source
• Siren
Radar Detector
• Front/Rear Hide-Away Detectors
• Instrument Panel located LEDs and Piezo Beepers
Go-Fast Goodies
• Water/Methanol Injection System
• Line Lock

• Boost Gauge
• Speedometer Calibration Box

OK, so that's a bunch of stuff in a Mustang huh? If you ever embark on such a project, it's helpful to make a legend to keep it all straight.

As I've done many installations like this over the years, I learned the value of adding centrally located fuse panels for the accessories. As the legend calls out, this vehicle has four of them and their locations are given. In addition, I provided the details of what's on each fuse and its value. (The specifics of the security system and its auxiliary source of power are kept a secret!)

In addition, the charging system of this vehicle has been extensively modified to keep up with the current demands of the audio system. It consists of:
• 200-amp Ohio Generator Alternator
• Optima Red Top Battery
• 100 Farad Rockford Fosgate Capacitor (used to soften the blow of the current requirements of the amplifiers, which is in excess of 300 amps at full power)
• 1/0 AWG Wiring Throughout
• Dash-Mounted Digital Volt Meter

Before taking measurements, it's important to separate the troubleshooting into two distinct sections—aftermarket electronics and OEM electronics, because it is possible that we could have a draw from one, the other, or both. In addition, as most late model vehicles are similarly equipped, this vehicle has been designed so that it automatically disables circuits that are unnecessary after the ignition switch has been

Cold Solder Joints

Solving the problem in the Lincoln power door lock circuit was easy once I identified the problem. But what if the relay contacts looked fine? The next step would have been to inspect the integrity of the soldering of components to the PC board itself in hopes of finding cold solder joints. A joint is the connection of an electrical component such as a resistor, capacitor, or semiconductor to the printed circuit board (or PCB) itself.

Not to be confused with cold solder connections, as described in Chapter 3, cold solder joints are a result of age. A number of issues cause this, but are not limited to: the type of solder used; electrolysis between the component, PC board, and solder; a high humidity or salt water climate; high current flowing through the joint; etc. Over time, a cold solder joint will result in high enough resistance

where the circuit no longer functions. Fortunately, they're easy to spot.

Pictured is the PCB from my garage door opener. It has suffered from poor range and I just haven't gotten around to fixing it. As the range has been reduced to pulling up to within two feet of the door, holding the remote out the window of the car, and pressing the button repeatedly, it's time to dig into it. Good solder joints appear shiny silver in color. Notice that many of the solder joints on the board have a dull gray color to them. Any one of these could be a cold solder joint. Numerous cold solder joints really affect how well a remote works.

Fortunately, this repair is simple. All I need to do is to get my soldering iron hot and remove the solder from any suspect cold solder joints with a vacuum type solder sucker (available at your local Radio Shack—yeah, I spend a bunch of time there). Then, re-flow fresh solder into the joint. When doing this, keep in mind that you only want to apply as much heat to the joint as necessary to get the solder to a liquid state. Heating the joint too much could result in component damage and/or cause a trace (the flat copper runners) to lift off of the board itself.

Now that I've repaired numerous cold solder joints and re-tuned the remote, I have all kinds of range! While this example was for a PC board in a garage door remote, it could have just as well applied to the black box I removed from the Lincoln. Now, I'm not encouraging you remove the ECM that controls your engine and attempt this, but this trick works great for simple modules or controllers in older vehicles, such as the Lincoln that you're faced with replacing anyway.

This printed circuit board from a Genie garage door opener will soon qualify as an antique. The two rows just to the left of the right-hand row of joints have solder joints that look suspect to me. Incidentally, these are the connections from the DIP switches to the only IC within this opener.

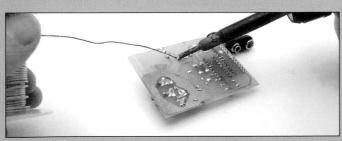

I reflowed solder into those two rows and found a few other suspect joints. A solder sucker can be handy here to remove old solder if there is a bunch of it in any joint.

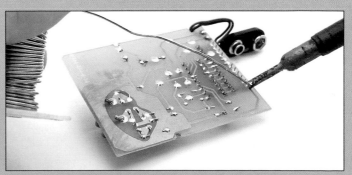

What the heck, I've got it apart, might as well flow solder into this row as well.

turned off, and the vehicles doors and trunk are closed for a period of time. This is commonly referred to as "sleep mode" or "hibernation" and minimizes the current the vehicle requires of the battery when it is left parked for an extended amount of time. Finally, it'd be kind of nice to know how much current Ford specifies the vehicle should draw when parked. I placed a quick phone call to a tech support specialist at my local Ford dealer and according to him, "Ford allows up to 50mA for a production vehicle." Good enough, let's dig into it.

Procedures

By following the procedures I outlined in Chapter 2, let's take an overall current draw reading with the ignition switch in turned off.

Meter Specifics

- Selector switch in the A position.
- Red probe in A and connected to positive battery post.
- Black probe in COM and connected to positive battery terminal.

When the battery in this vehicle is disconnected and then reconnected, this may cause the vehicle to exit its sleep mode, so we want to leave our meter connected for a few minutes. This allows the vehicle to go back into sleep mode so that we can get an accurate reading. In the case of this vehicle, the wait time was in excess of 10 minutes.

As I anticipated, the current draw has settled down. This is an accurate measurement of the current draw of everything in the vehicle with the vehicle parked. As you can see, our static current draw is 174 mA, and this is 124 mA higher than

2003 Ford Mustang GT – Key to Aftermarket Add-Ons

Underhood

Description	Location	Value
Main Audio System Fuse	Near Coolant Reservoir	200A

Auxiliary Fuse Box – In between drivers' shock tower and battery

Description	Location	Value
Interior Auxiliary ATC Fuse Panel Power	Position 1 (top left)	30A
Open	Position 2	
Open	Position 3	
Open	Position 4	
SS – SmartWindows	Position 5	30A
SS – Parking Lamps	Position 6	20A
SS – Main Power	Position 7	5A
Roll Control – Relay & Solenoid	Position 8	4A

Interior

Auxiliary ATC Fuse Panel – Behind carpeting on drivers' side of console

K-40 Radar Detector	Position 1 (top left)	1A
Blinder	Position 2	5A
Boost Cooler – Low Level Indicator	Position 3	1A
Boost Cooler – Controller & Pump	Position 4	20A
Roll Control – Interior On/Off Switch	Position 5	5A
Open	Position 6	
Open	Position 7	
Open	Position 8	

Multi Strand Cable – Behind shifter bezel on passenger side

Color	Function
Green	Trunk lid illumination relay
Yellow	Passenger door illumination relay
White	Drivers' door illumination relay
Blue	Woofer baffle Neon lighting relay
Red	+12V Constant from trunk aux fuse block
Black	Main system ground block in rear

Switches

Description	Location	Function
Black Rocker	Left of Defroster Switch	SS Valet / Programming
Black Rocker	Left of Traction Control Switch	Blinder On/Off
Black Rocker	Right of Traction Control Switch	Woofer baffle Neon lighting
Black Dual Knob	Left side of shifter bezel	K40 mode switch
Punch Bass	Center of shifter bezel	Bass control for T20001bd
Black Rocker	Right of cigarette lighter	Roll Control – Master On/Off
Red Rocker	Console	Roll Control On/Off

Description	Location	Indicates
Mini RED	Gauge Bezel, left	Low level in Boost Cooler reservoir
Mini BLUE	Gauge Bezel, left	Boost Cooler in use
BLUE	Console	SS Status

Trunk

Auxiliary ATC Fuse Panel – Passenger Side, rear wall – facing forward

Description	Location	Value
Source Unit	Position 1 (top)	10A
Processor power in spare tire well	Position 2	5A
Turn-On Relay	Position 3	5A
Neon Relay	Position 4	3A
Drivers' door illumination relay	Position 5	n/a
Passenger door illumination relay	Position 6	n/a
Trunk lid illumination relay	Position 7	n/a
Red wire in Multi Strand cable	Position 8	10A

Audio System Fusing – Drivers' side, above system capacitor

- ANL Fuse Holder, left

Description	Location	Value
T8004	Top	150A
T20001bd	Bottom	200A

- MAXI Fuse Holder, right

Open	Position 1 (top)	
Trunk Auxiliary ATC Fuse Panel Power	Position 2	40A
Open	Position 3	
Open	Position 4	

Note: The above-referenced relays are located behind the passenger side interior trim panel, behind the T8004 and crossover networks.

As Ford specifies 50mA, and I have almost four times that much, I've got some work to do here. It's easy to keep adding electronics to your vehicle and pay no attention to this. Then, one day you've got a dead battery and you're in troubleshooting mode!

Ford specifies. Although this doesn't sound like much, it is. This is the cause of the battery being drained when it sits for an extended period of time. Now, let's get to the root of the problem.

Step-by-Step

Believe it or not, even though this vehicle is stuffed full of electronics, this is actually a simple process. We just need to remove fuses individually until we find the circuit (or circuits) that is the source of the current draw. Then, we need to determine the accessory on this circuit that is responsible. When troubleshooting such a vehicle, start with the aftermarket electronics first, then to the OEM electronics.

1 Since there is an underhood aftermarket fuse panel right near the battery, let's begin by disconnecting each fuse one at a time. If there is no change in the overall current draw after removing a fuse, then re-insert it. (Note that according to the legend, fuse number 1 supplies power to the interior accessory fuse panel. Since I removed it and there were no

changes to the current draw, this rules out all accessories tied to this interior panel.)

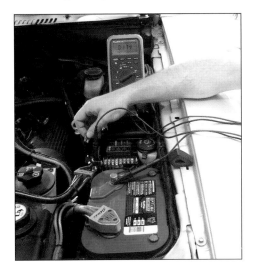

2 Since there was no change to the current draw, we can now proceed to the next step, which is removing the large ANL fuse from the fuse holder. This supplies power to the audio system as well as a second trunk-mounted fuse panel. Note that our current draw was reduced to 49 mA, a change of 125 mA.

3 Now that we've found a major source of current draw, we need to determine the accessory to blame. This necessitates that I reinstall this fuse to proceed.

4 Around the rear of the vehicle, access the accessory fuse panel on the passenger side of the vehicle and begin removing fuses one at a time as before. In this case, none of them resulted in any

change in the current draw, so we can rule out the accessories connected to them as culprits.

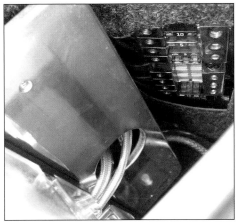

5 This leaves either the audio amplifiers or the capacitor as the culprit for this portion of our current draw problem. To determine this, remove the fuses for both amplifiers from the ANL fuse block to eliminate them. As the current draw didn't change, the storage capacitor is to blame as it is the only thing left on this circuit.

Unfortunately, this capacitor has a small parasitic drain as a byproduct of its design. I am left with two choices: remove it entirely, or just live with it. As my audio system consumes more current than the charging system can provide alone, and this capacitor really helps to overcome this problem, I elect to leave it in and drive the car more regularly. At the very least, I put a trickle charger on the battery if I do have to leave it for an extended period of time.

Because disconnecting the capacitor dropped the static current draw to 49 mA, below Ford's spec, I don't need to look any further. But what if I did, then what? Simple—I would need to continue the above procedures for the interior fuse panel, then the underhood fuse panel until the source of the problem is found. Start with the interior panel because the fuses in the underhood panel typically power multiple circuits. Remember, this vehicle can't enter the sleep mode with one of the doors open, which is a necessity when accessing the under dash fuse panel. No problem, I can close the switch in the door itself with a screwdriver. This allows the door to remain open,

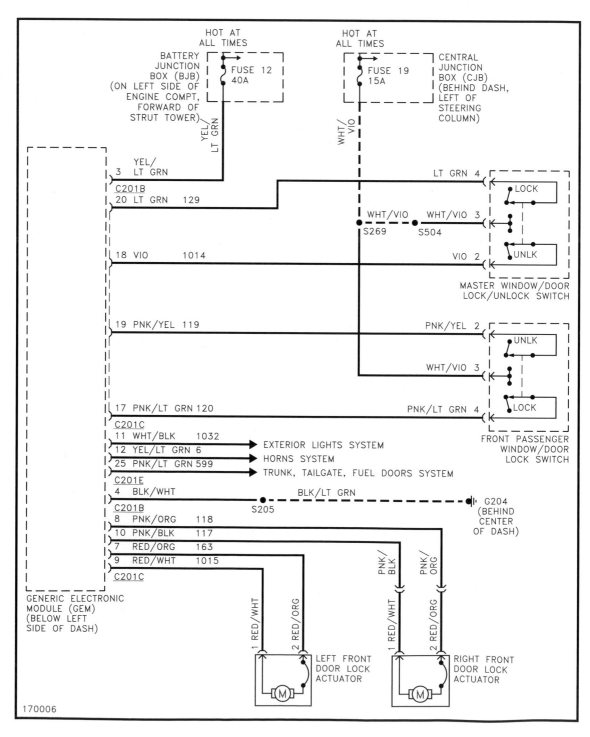

170006

which allows easy access the interior fuse panel.

This begins the countdown to sleep mode. Once the vehicle has entered it, I can resume my troubleshooting. (Just don't forget to pull up on the door handle before attempting to close the driver's door. This releases the switch, which in this case also happens to be the latch that secures the door around the striker to keep it shut.)

When you remove a fuse from either of the OEM fuse panels and you see a huge drop in current draw, refer to the owner's manual to determine which fuse supplies each accessory. If a fuse supplies power to multiple accessories, re-install the fuse and then disconnect each of the accessories one at a time so that you can determine which one is the problem. Typically, you can unplug them, thereby removing them from the circuit. Sometimes interfaces between a piece of aftermarket electronics and the stock electronics results in current draw issues. In these instances, isolate the aftermarket electronics to solve the problem. As long as you have the right tools and a little know-how, it doesn't take that long to figure out.

Intermittent Circuit Operation

These kinds of problems can be the most frustrating of all. Sometimes the accessory works, sometimes it doesn't, with no rhyme or reason. Worst of all, Murphy's Law ensures that it always works when you take it in for someone to look at it.

Example—Power door lock circuit in the 2003 Ford Mustang GT

Symptom—Switch in passenger door works intermittently

This kind of problem is easy to ignore—after all, the switch in the driver's door works just fine and that's where I sit, problem solved, right? Not so much. To help with the troubleshooting, I got my hands on a diagram of the circuit (Figure 7-4), courtesy of Mitchell.

At the end of the day, this circuit is fairly simple. Specifically, the circuit has the following components:
- Two lock/unlock switches.
- A GEM module.
- Two door lock actuators.

Although the diagram doesn't illustrate this, the following components also exist:
- Length of wire from each component to the GEM module.

- Plugs of some type in the kick panel area that facilitates removal of either one of the doors.

Furthermore, according to the diagram, the switches used are of the S.P.D.T. variety and rest open. At rest, they have no electrical connection. (These are simply "center off" switches.) In addition, the diagram shows that the switches switch +12 VDC only and since the actuators require both +12 VDC and ground to operate, we have to assume the GEM module contains some relays to make that happen.

Since we know the passenger switch is the only part of the circuit that is giving us trouble, let's concentrate our efforts there. I said above that it works intermittently. Specifically, neither the lock or unlock functions work all the time from this switch. (You already know too much; you're beginning to diagnose the problem already, aren't you?)

Procedures
Checking the switch itself.

Meter Settings
- Selector switch in the DCV Position
- Red probe in V/Ω
- Black probe in COM and connected to vehicle chassis ground

Step-by-Step

Note that, currently, the switch works fine.

1 Remove the passenger-side door lock switch so that its terminals can be accessed.

2 Connect the red probe of the DMM to the white/violet wire. This gives us a reading of +11.85 VDC.

3 Closely inspect this terminal and the connector itself for signs of a poor connection, corrosion, etc. We suspect that this wire is the culprit somewhere between the GEM module and the switch based on our symptoms, but it looks fine. Wiggle the switch/connector assembly while operating the switch in hopes that we can replicate the symptom—no go.

4 The next area to inspect is the plug above the passenger kick panel area that connects the door harness to the main wiring harness. (I just followed the harness as it comes through the jamb and then goes up into the darkness. Then, I removed the glove box to get better access to this remote area.) As pictured, there are two plugs high up in this area, but only one that contains the door lock wiring.

5 Unplug the plug and inspect both halves for poor connections or loosely fitting pins.

6 What do you know? The white/violet wire pulls right out of the plug on the wiring harness side—problem found!

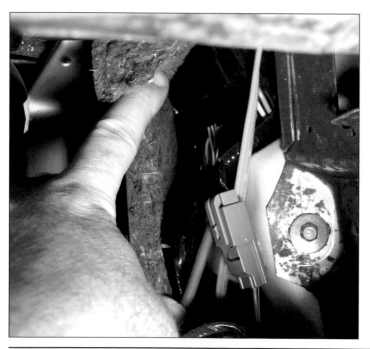

As this pin is actually in a plug with a lock retainer, this is quite unusual. As the pin was still in the plug, it did make connection some of the time to the mating pin in the other plug. And from time to time, it didn't. This explains why the circuit worked intermittently. To solve this problem, we just need to remove the lock from the front of the plug with a pick tool, snap the pin securely back into the plug, and reinstall the lock.

A problem such as this is likely a manufacturing-related issue and is relatively uncommon, but there you have it. Problem solved!

Now that you're versed in the basics of troubleshooting, there should be few problems you can't solve. Again, I hope you have an understanding of the thought process involved in each of the previous examples. Using simple, logical steps is always the best approach and almost always leads to the solution.

Knowing what you know now, can you imagine stabbing in the dark with a test light?

Now you know the difference between diagnosing the problem and making the appropriate repairs and replacing parts until you find the one that solves the problem. As I said earlier, there really is no substitute for experience when it comes to troubleshooting automotive electronics.

ADVANCED INSTALLATIONS AND INTERFACES

This chapter covers some of the more complex installations and interfaces. If you opened the book and flipped straight to here, you may choose to go back to the beginning, as this chapter makes the assumption that you know a great deal.

Specifically, this chapter covers:

- Interfacing with power door lock and power window circuits.
- Interfacing with power sunroof and convertible top circuits.
- Upgrading headlights to higher powered units.
- Adding an auxiliary battery.
- Adding an accessory fuse panel.

This is a lot of ground to cover. I think a great place to start is learning how to interface with the power door lock and power window circuits that I described in Chapter 5.

Interfacing with Power Door Lock and Power Window Circuits

Why on earth would you ever want to do this? Simple—maybe you'd like to add a keyless entry system or a security system that has keyless entry to your vehicle. Or, maybe you like the idea of being able to remotely open or close your windows. Personally, I love both of these features and have enjoyed these conveniences on numerous vehicles that my wife and I have owned since 1992 or so.

Power Door Lock Circuit Interfaces

When you make such an interface with power door lock circuits, really what you're doing is duplicating the efforts of the OEM switches and nothing more. Recall, the four most common circuits:

- Negative Pulse
- Positive Pulse
- Voltage Reversal
- Variable Voltage

For the sake of this explanation, I make the assumption that the keyless entry unit or security system, you are installing only has negative trigger outputs that have low current capability, say around 500 mA. Perfect to close the coil of a relay, but that's about it. If the unit you're installing has built in relays, it makes

the installation easier. Either way, everything shown here applies.

CAUTION: Before you start, it is imperative to verify the kind of power door lock circuit you're interfacing with. An improper interface could cause damage to the circuit, the unit you're installing, or both. In addition, you should always verify any wiring you plan to interface to with your DMM to be sure that you're connecting to what you think you're connecting to.

Negative Pulse: To interface a keyless entry feature with this switch, all you have to do is tie directly to the switch wires so that the CPU sends negative pulses to them when you press the buttons on the remote. This triggers the coils of the OEM relays, which operates the actuators, as it exactly duplicates what the OEM switches do (Figure 8-1).

See why this is my favorite type of door lock circuit now?

Positive Pulse: Interfacing is just like the negative pulse circuit, but you need to send +12 VDC and not ground to the switch wires to trigger the coils of the OEM relays. This

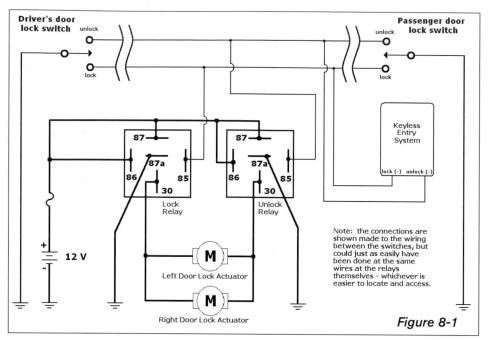

Figure 8-1

requires an additional pair of Bosch type relays (Figure 8-2).

Admittedly, many of the keyless entry systems and auto security systems available today have at the very least low-current outputs that are programmable as negative or positive pulsing. Check your installation manual to see whether the unit you're installing offers this feature. If

so, then the interface does not require the relays as it is very similar to the negative pulse interface once the outputs are programmed to be positive.

Pulsing Peculiarities: Many of the OEMs house the relays for the door lock actuators themselves within a module that is responsible for a host of vehicle functions, as is the case

with the GEM module in my Mustang (see Fig 7-4). As I discussed in the last chapter, some modules have been designed to enter a sleep mode (or hibernation, as some call it) after the vehicle sits for a period of time in an effort to reduce the overall current draw from the battery. As a result, some modules require more than a simple pulse to unlock the doors after the module has entered hibernation. (The GEM module in the Mustang does not.) At this point, the module may require an extended pulse or even multiple pulses to unlock the doors after the vehicle sits for an extended period of time. This is to first "wake up" the module, and then to unlock the doors.

As such, most keyless entry and security systems have this provision built in. This is typically an installer programmable feature and varies by manufacturer.

Voltage Reversal Rest at Ground: Interfacing with this kind of circuit is a little trickier. The interface is most commonly done between the master and slave switches, and the wiring can typically be accessed in the kick panel areas of most vehicles. A pair of Bosch type relays is all that's necessary to make the interface. I caution you to first determine which side the master switch is on before attempting this interface—the easiest way to do this is:

- Determine which of the wires is the LOCK wire with your DMM.
- Cut this wire in half and measure each side of the wire independently with your DMM.
- The half of the wire that has voltage on it when the LOCK switch is depressed connects to the master switch.

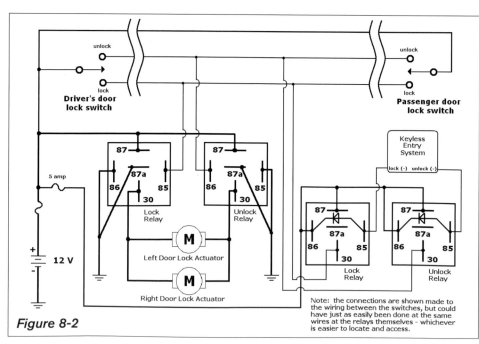

Figure 8-2

Look closely at Figure 8-3. This is another great example of the versatility of the S.P.D.T. relay. How would you do this otherwise? No amount of S.P.S.T. relays could pull this one off.

Variable Voltage: Recall, this kind of circuit (Figure 8-4) sends signals that vary in voltage level to a con-

Factory Wiring Diagrams

Where exactly do you find the wiring information for your vehicle? Your single best resource is a service manual that contained a wiring diagram of your vehicle, such as the diagram from Mitchell that I referred to

in Chapter 7. Remember, most auto parts stores carry a number of consumer manuals from Chiltons, Haynes, etc., and these may also be available to check out at your local library. Mitchell has such information available via its website at www.mitchell1.com. For a nominal fee, you can access every bit of information they have on a certain vehicle, including factory TSBs, for a period of time.

Finally, there are any number of sites on the Internet that may contain this information, as well. Like anything else on the 'net, some of it is good information and some of it is not. In the days before the Internet, I used my DMM to determine the function of any wire in a vehicle that I tied into and the same holds true today. You're simply asking for trouble if you neglect to do this. Here are some hints to make your job easier:

Hint 1: As you're simply duplicating the function of the OEM switches, you can pull them out and

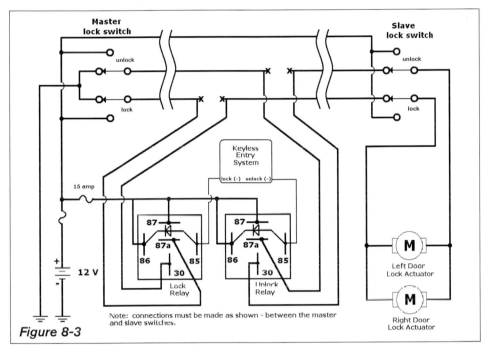

Figure 8-3

troller, which in turn operates the actuators. Interfacing with this circuit is also easy, you just need to know the value of the resistors used within the switch part of the circuit. In some cases you can use your DMM to measure the value of the resistors between the switch common (pole) and the input of the controller, while depressing the switch, of course; in other cases you cannot.

If you cannot make this determination with your DMM, you should contact the manufacturer's technical support department to get this information. If they are unable to provide this to you, then you might pay a visit to the dealer that you purchased the system from to begin with.

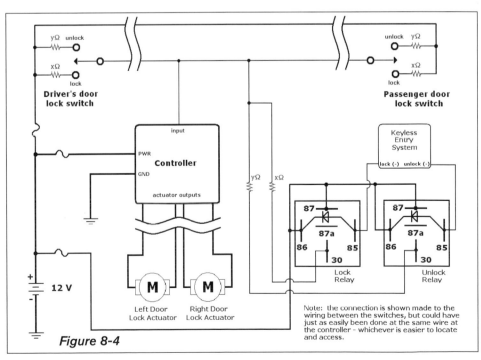

Figure 8-4

OEM Alarms

Many vehicles over the past 25 years have come straight from the factory with some kind of factory alarm. Most of them are simply noise makers, and I can't justify calling them security systems. If your vehicle is equipped with one, most likely you have to interface with its disarm wire when initiating an unlock command from any kind of remote device. Otherwise, you'll set off the OEM alarm when you open the door or attempting to start the vehicle after remotely unlocking it.

Although there is no way to cover all of the specific interfaces in this book, I'll show you one such interface. Logically, it would be similar to other interfaces, but the electrical specifics vary by vehicle.

Since most OEM alarms arm up within a certain time of you turning off the ignition switch, opening the driver's door, then closing all doors, they typically do not have an arming interface wire so there is typically no need to locate and interface with it. Again, there are exceptions to every rule so refer to the wiring diagram of your vehicle if in doubt.

Incidentally, when most OEM alarms are accidentally triggered, the operator is lost in regards to quieting them. We've all seen this a thousand times. In the event that the key fob is not able to silence the alarm, in most cases it can be silenced by:

1. Closing all doors of the vehicle.
2. Unlocking the driver's door manually with the key (sometimes turning two times).
3. If this doesn't silence the alarm, then enter the vehicle, put the key in the ignition and turn the switch forward to the IGN/RUN position.

This disarms most OEM alarms, thereby silencing them.

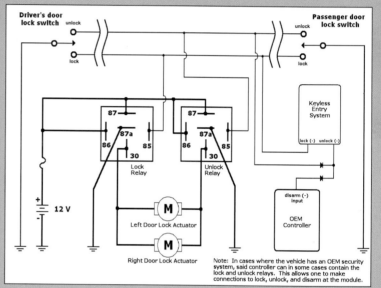

Note: In cases where the vehicle has an OEM security system, said controller can in some cases contain the lock and unlock relays. This allows one to make connections to lock, unlock, and disarm at the module.

see how they're wired. You can assume the following:

If both switches have three wires, they're more than likely wired in parallel.

- The gauge of wiring is 16-gauge or smaller; there is typically a pair of relays in the vehicle (or in a controller in the vehicle) that do the actual work—just like in my Mustang.
- The gauge of wiring is 14-gauge of larger, you may be dealing with an older GM dual coil system like I spoke of in Chapter 5.

- If one switch has four wires and the other has five wires, then you're more than likely looking at a voltage reversal rest at ground system.
- If the wiring to the switches is not obvious because the switches are part of an elaborate switch panel that encompasses numerous other switches, then you are more than likely to need the advice of a professional.

Hint 2: While you have the switches out, you can surely note the color of their wiring and verify

their operation with your DMM. Then, you can typically locate this wiring in the kick panel area for the interface—verifying this with your DMM, of course. In some vehicles, the harness comes through the jamb and into the kick panel area and then immediately goes up in to the darkness of the dashboard, as in my Mustang. In these cases, it may be easiest to do the interface within the boot between the door and body (unsnap the boot at the body and door and slide it partially into the door to make accessing the wiring easy), or at the switch itself by running your wiring through the boot in the jamb and into the door. I've seen a few cases where this was extremely difficult. If you're attempting to connect to a negative or positive pulse circuit, you can always stick your head under the dash and listen for the click of the relays themselves to determine their location. The relays could be external or built into a controller. Either way, it may be easiest to make the interface there. This is exactly what I did in the Mustang, as the GEM module was easily found just above the driver-side kick panel.

Hint 3: For both negative- and positive-pulse (low-current) door lock systems, you can use an ATC fuse holder with a 1-amp ATC fuse in it to test the interface before you actually make it. After you've verified the wiring with your DMM, of course. This is how to do it:

- Clip the fuse holder assembly to either the plus or minus clip of a cigarette lighter adapter such as the one shown—negative for negative pulse and positive for positive pulse (obviously, right?).

- Touch the bare end of the other side of the fuse holder to the switch wire you're going to interface with.
- The actuators should lock or unlock depending on which wire you've connected the fuse holder to.

You're not likely to damage a door lock circuit with a 1-amp fuse because it blows immediately if you accidentally connect it to the wrong wire. If the locks work with the 1-amp fuse trick, they'll surely work with your keyless entry system.

Hint 4: Assume that wiring information from the Internet or a buddy is a guess at best. Do not connect to any wiring without verifying it with your DMM first! Blue wire in the driver-side kick panel? There might be twelve of them that fit that description.

Power Window Circuit Interfaces

The main difference between interfacing with power door locks and power windows is that power windows operate individually of one another. The circuits can be very similar, but you will have two or four unique power-window circuits in most vehicles. Although the driver's door can sometimes have the switches for all of the power windows, I've never made my interfaces there. For vehicles with express or venting features, this is certainly not the place to make the interface because these circuits are in between the switches and motors.

I know this is going to sound like a hassle, but the tried-and-true way to interface with power windows is to do so at the window motors themselves. Yes, this means that you have to remove the door panels to access the wiring to each individual motor, and that you have to run wiring into

the doors, but this is the way the pros do it.

Following are the interfaces for the circuits I outlined in Chapter 5. For these examples, I assume:

- You're interfacing with a pair of windows.
- You have a pair of low-current auxiliary outputs from your CPU to work with.
- You'd like for one channel to roll both windows up and the other channel to roll both windows down.
- These low-current outputs remain (or can be programmed to remain) constant as long as you hold the button down on the key fob. (Many keyless entry systems and security systems allow the installer to program the auxiliary outputs to be pulsed, timed, or latched. When using them in this application, you need to program them to be pulsed. A one-second pulse is not sufficient because this would require several button presses to fully raise or lower a window. Rather, you want the output to be active as long as you hold down the button on the key fob.)

Voltage Reversal Rest at Ground: No different than the power door lock circuit of the same variety, a pair of Bosch-type relays is all that's necessary to make the interface. Note that this means one pair per window.

Even though Figure 8-5 shows only two switches, the interface is identical for multi-switch systems as the interface is made at the window motors directly. As you can see, you need eight relays to make this kind of

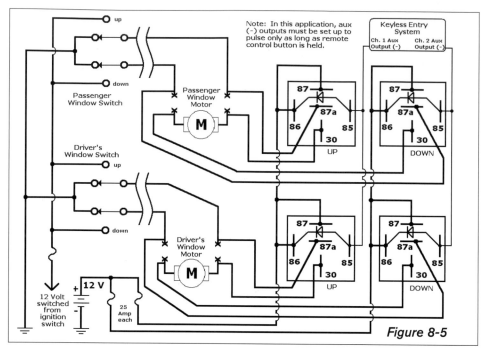

Figure 8-5

the doors to access the motor wires as there are no modules between them and the motors and no master/slave switch arrangement for the passenger window.

Most auto security manufacturers sell window roll-up modules that do the up part automatically when you arm the system. The interface with them is much the same, except for a trigger wire between the security system and window roll-up module instead of the auxiliary output channel. Because they have on-board relays, external relays are not required. Some of these even include one-touch features for any window you connect to them. Over the years, I've installed a bunch of these from many different manufacturers. One of the best things about them is that they don't require an auxiliary channel to do the up feature, just the down.

interface in a four-window vehicle.

Voltage Reversal Rest Open—Power Windows Only: Even though this circuit's net result is the same as the Voltage Reversal Rest at Ground circuit, the interface required is radically different. Interfacing with this kind of circuit is a little trickier, and it requires two pair of Bosch-type relays per window, which is twice as many as a voltage reversal rest at ground window circuit (Figure 8-6).

As I mentioned in the Chapter 5, this is the way GM did the windows in the Gen III Camaro (1982–1992). At least in those vehicles, you can make the interface at the switches themselves versus having to go into

Interfacing with Power Sunroof and Convertible Top Circuits

Power Sunroof Circuit Interfaces

As I discussed in Chapter 5, power sunroof circuits can be more similar to power door lock circuits than to power window circuits. At this point, you know enough to interface with them with one exception—using a window roll-up module to do the job automatically.

As I said before, these mechanisms can be very fragile. Continuing to power the motor after the sunroof has reached the end of its travel can take its toll on the mechanism rather quickly. If you're making an interface to the auxiliary outputs of a unit and intend to operate the sunroof manually (but remotely), you're typically fine making this interface at the

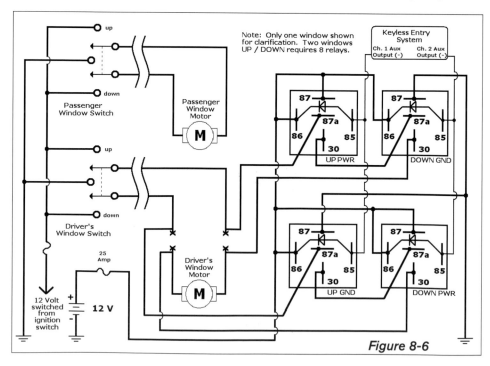

Figure 8-6

switch itself and duplicating its efforts. On the other hand, if you intend to use a window roll-up module to close the roof automatically, you're well advised to make the interface at the sunroof motor itself and interface the module with the sunroof's limit switch. This ensures that the module doesn't power the motor, even for a brief time, if the sunroof is closed. Be advised that these interfaces can involve removing the headliner entirely to access the wiring. If you decide to undertake such an interface, shop around for a window roll-up module that has an input designed to interface with this limit switch.

Convertible Top Circuit Interfaces

Think of a convertible top as a very high-current power window. As the switch itself cannot support the current required of the convertible top motor, a pair of high-current relays is typically located near the convertible top. If you desire to operate the top remotely, you're advised to use auxiliary channels of your unit and duplicate the efforts of the switch. Again, choosing a system with auxiliary outputs that can be programmed to be active as long as you hold down the button on the key fob is the way to go. I do not recommend window roll-up modules of any type for this application, even ones of the high-current variety.

Be advised, though, that the following are challenges that you need to be aware of:

- The latching mechanism: If the top has manual latches, and many do, then they have to be manually unlatched before it can be operated remotely.
- If the top comes down hard when closing it, and you have

to help it down slowly with your hand to avoid it crashing down on the windshield frame, there will be no way to prevent this when closing the top remotely—you may choose to do open only.

Either way, this is a hit at the local burger stand!

Upgrading Headlights to Higher Powered Units

For many years now, this has been a popular upgrade for older vehicles. High-powered halogen or xenon headlights consume far more current than the stock head lightswitch, hi/low beam switch, and wiring were designed to accommodate. To avoid damaging the wiring or switches as discussed in Chapter 4, add a few relays as shown in Figure 8-7.

Notice that now the entire OEM circuit only powers the coils of the relays. This greatly lessens the load on this circuit, generally speaking. In addition, since this new circuit uses larger gauge wiring and connects directly to the battery, these lights have plenty of current going to

them. Feel free to mount the relays under the hood, just be sure to insulate them properly and mount them (with screws!) so that their terminals point down to keep water out of them.

HID (high intensity discharge) kits are also quite popular, and many of the kits on the market have been designed to plug into the stock headlight harnesses. Ballasts install between the stock headlight plugs and the new HID lamps because the lights require a higher operating voltage and have unique "start-up" requirements. In some cases they can actually draw less current than the stock incandescent lamps they're replacing.

Adding an Auxiliary Battery

Let's say that you needed to add a single auxiliary battery to your vehicle for whatever reason. We've discussed how to determine when auxiliary battery(s) are necessary, now let's discuss what's required to install one. The two challenges are the physical installation and connecting the battery electrically.

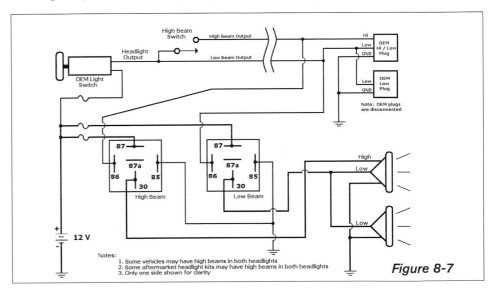

Figure 8-7

Where there is a will, there is a way. The owner of this vehicle figured out how to tuck four PowerMaster XSPower D1000 batteries inside the passenger frame rail of his 1999 Chevy Silverado 2500 truck. These batteries are used to supplement the audio system in the truck. (Courtesy Matt Logan)

Physical Installation

Obviously, this chews up some real estate in any vehicle. In that regard, there are a few considerations:

- Mount batteries externally under the hood, in the bed of a truck, in the undercarriage, or inside the frame rails, which is safest. (When possible, they should be protected from the elements.)
- When mounting a second battery under the hood, said battery should be mounted in a suitable tray and properly tied down.
- When mounting a second battery in some other place, it needs to be solidly mounted in a suitable rack, tray, or enclosure. Any of these need to be solidly mounted to the vehicle.
- Batteries installed in an enclosure of any type need to be vented to the outside of the vehicle for safety.
- Batteries installed in the passenger compartment should only be installed in a suitable enclosure and need to be vented to the outside of the vehicle for safety—I prefer sealed batteries in these applications.

I'm not really a big fan of batteries installed in the passenger compartment of a vehicle, but in some cases this is the only place it can go. If you choose to do this, it's probably a good idea to make the cabin of your vehicle non-smoking, so there's absolutely no chance of igniting battery fumes.

Connecting the Battery Electrically

Now that you've mounted the battery itself, you have to connect it to the vehicle's charging system. You have three choices when doing so:

- Wire the battery in parallel with the OEM battery.
- Wire the battery in parallel with the OEM battery via an isolating solenoid.
- Wire the battery via a battery isolator.

No matter the application you choose, the battery negatives must be connected to a point of very low resistance. Now, let's look at each scenario so that you can pick the one that's right for your application.

Wiring a Battery in Parallel with the OEM Battery: The main reason to do this is to have additional current available to the vehicle's starter. If this is the case, there is no reason to isolate the two batteries and the installation is simple. This is the one type of installation where it's mandatory to use the same kind and type of battery as the stock one, otherwise they can feed off of each other when the vehicle is parked, causing them to go dead. In addition, if the stock battery has in excess of 10,000 miles on it, you should consider installing a pair of fresh batteries, as you want them to be close in age.

This is a common upgrade for big trucks or work trucks, and in most cases the second battery can be installed under the hood. As the Big Three all make diesel trucks, they typically leave room under the hood for a second battery tray, which is sometimes available for purchase at the parts counter, making this job easy. Incidentally, if I have to put the battery somewhere else besides

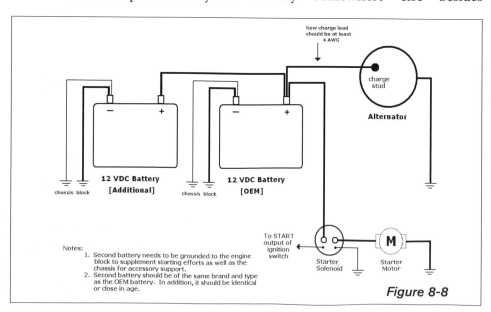

Figure 8-8

under the hood, I choose to isolate it via one of the other methods.

Figure 8-8 is the diagram to do this.

Use the same gauge of cable the OEM uses for the stock battery cables for this connection, unless it's considerably longer. In that case, increase the gauge of the cable based on its length—remember, this battery will be used to supplement starting the vehicle. Note that there are no fuses between the batteries as they are unnecessary in an underhood installation. I used to use them, but after years of noticing the OEM wiring from one to the other with no fuses, I don't. The main reason they do not use them is because the fuse(s) limit current, which is contradictory to why you're adding the battery to begin with.

Since you're adding this battery to supplement starting of the vehicle, its negative cable needs to be connected to the engine block in the same manner as the OEM battery. (If the batteries were mounted right next to one another, it is acceptable to tie their negatives together directly.) In addition, you should connect a smaller gauge strap from the negative terminal to the chassis in the same manner as the OEM battery.

It goes without saying that you need to properly anchor the positive cable connecting the two batteries together and keep it out of the way of moving parts as well as the hood latch mechanism or hinges for obvious reasons. A short in the middle of this cable could ruin your day.

The next two cases are where you've added a high-current accessory to the vehicle and upgraded the charging system accordingly (refer to Chapter 6). Now you'd like to be able to also use this accessory for an

extended period of time with the engine off and the ignition key in the ACCY position without danger of depleting the starting battery. You know, play the stereo with the windows down at the park for a few hours and then get in and start the engine with a fresh battery—how convenient!

Wire the Battery in Parallel with the OEM battery via an Isolating Solenoid: With the key in the IGN/RUN position, both batteries are tied together in parallel, which will allow the alternator to charge them both while the engine is running. With the key off or in the ACCY position, the auxiliary battery is totally disconnected from the charging system as is the high-current accessory. In this case, the battery does not have to be the same type and kind as the starting battery. In many cases, a deep cycle battery may be a better choice for the auxiliary battery due to the nature of its use.

Regardless of where you install the auxiliary battery, this is also a simple installation Figure 8-9.

Solenoids for this use are commonly available in 80 and 200 amp sizes and your local car stereo or electrical supply store typically stocks a few sizes of them. The current capability of the solenoid required is determined based on the amount of current the auxiliary accessory and battery requires. For a long time, hot rodders have used Ford starting solenoids for this purpose as well. I should note that OEM starting solenoids are not really intended to pass continuous current through their contacts, so I don't recommend their use.

Notice that this installation requires protection to be safe. Two ANL fuses are each mounted within 18 inches of the auxiliary battery, as shown. A third is required near the solenoid to protect the run of wiring between the solenoid and the auxiliary battery should the battery be

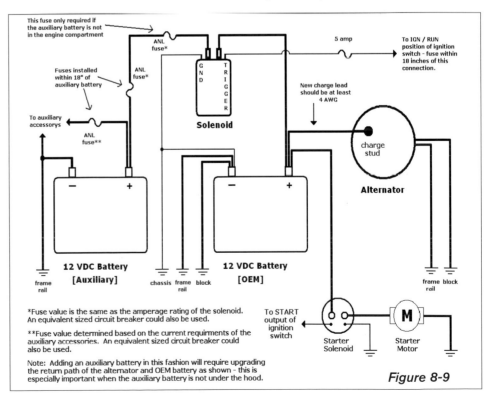

This fuse only required if the auxiliary battery is not in the engine compartment

Fuses installed within 18" of auxiliary battery

ANL fuse*

ANL fuse*

To auxiliary accessorys

ANL fuse**

GND TRIGGER

Solenoid

5 amp

To IGN / RUN position of ignition switch - fuse within 18 inches of this connection.

New charge lead should be at least 4 AWG

charge stud

Alternator

− +

12 VDC Battery [Auxiliary]

frame rail

− +

chassis frame rail block

12 VDC Battery [OEM]

frame block rail

*Fuse value is the same as the amperage rating of the solenoid. An equivalent sized circuit breaker could also be used.

**Fuse value determined based on the current requirments of the auxiliary accessories. An equivalent sized circuit breaker could also be used.

Note: Adding an auxiliary battery in this fashion will require upgrading the return path of the alternator and OEM battery as shown - this is especially important when the auxiliary battery is not under the hood.

To START output of ignition switch

Starter Solenoid

M

Starter Motor

Figure 8-9

located somewhere other than the engine compartment. You could also use heavy-duty, manually resettable circuit breakers for this job. Either way you go, be sure and select the fuse/breaker size based on the length and gauge of wire between the batteries that you're using, which is determined by the current requirements of the accessory.

Wire the Battery via a Battery Isolator: For many years, this was the most recognized way to add an auxiliary battery. In fact, this was the only way the military did it. As I said a few chapters ago, a battery isolator is really nothing more than a pair of very high-current diodes mounted in an aluminum heat sink. There are three studs on an isolator, and they are typically labeled A, B1, and B2.

For whatever reason, a lot of folks just don't understand this interface. I think the confusion sets in because the natural process is to connect the stock battery to the B1 terminal, when in reality the stock charge lead from the alternator, as well as any-

thing else that was tied to the alternator output stud, connects to this terminal as shown in Figure 8-10.

Recall, the big cable on the stock battery is for the starter motor and nothing else. As you can see, this is quite different from the other two methods and at no point are the batteries connected together—vehicle running or not. Remember, diodes require seven tenths of a volt to be "turned on," so you have at least seven tenths of a volt delta between the A stud and either of the B studs. This is why many folks choose to use an isolating solenoid instead.

When choosing an isolator, keep in mind that all of the current the alternator is capable of making will pass through the isolator. Given this, choose an isolator that is able to pass 20 percent more current than the alternator can produce. If you have a 150-amp alternator, you need a 180-amp isolator. So the $29 unit at the local auto parts store won't cut it! High-current isolators are quite large, and can be a challenge to physically

mount under the hood of a vehicle.

Be aware that on some vehicles, especially those fitted with a one-wire alternator, the alternator does not work properly unless you use an isolator with an "exciter stud," which is labeled with an E. This stud is typically tied to the IGN/RUN output of the ignition switch via a small circuit breaker. In addition, the alternator may require a slightly different harness with a sensing lead that can be tied to the B1 terminal on the isolator so that the alternator will work properly. Since this varies by vehicle, refer to the manufacturer of the isolator.

Either way, when you start the vehicle, you should use your DMM to verify 13.8 to 14.4 VDC present at the A stud and roughly seven tenths of a volt less present at each B stud.

To make the best use of an isolated auxiliary battery, there are a few things to consider. Let's say that you did add a high-powered audio system and wanted to be able to play it with the key in the ACCY position for an extended period of time with minimal current draw. In addition, you've chosen to go the route of using an isolating solenoid for your auxiliary battery. Here's how to do it:

- Connect the audio amplifier(s) directly to the auxiliary battery.
- Connect ancillary low-current accessories, the radio for example, to the auxiliary battery via a relay that is triggered when the ignition switch is in the ACCY position.

Turning the ignition switch to the ACCY position would allow the audio system to operate independently of the starting battery (Figure 8-11). In addition, the ancillary devices would not draw current from the starting battery, only the

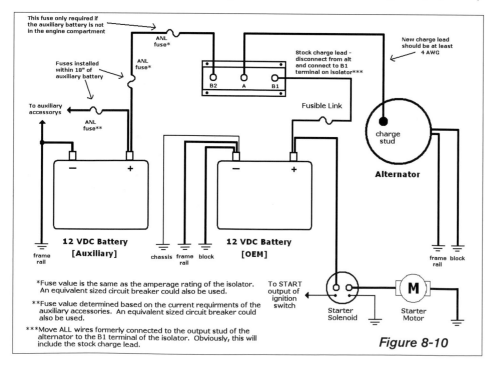

Figure 8-10

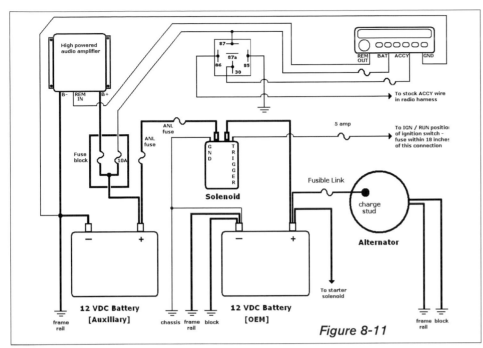

Figure 8-11

Check out the custom-made buss bars in this high-powered audio installation. The batteries are installed in such a way that their posts do not line up. The combination of bus bars and short 1/0 AWG jumpers allow for an easy connection, as well as excellent serviceability. (Courtesy stevemeadedesigns.com)

Determine the correct gauge of wiring based on the accessory's current requirements and use it for these connections. Another alternative is to use brass bars for these connections, but that is a whole lot more work. No fuses should be used between these batteries, and only one connection to the vehicle's chassis (preferably the frame) is required.

coil powering the relay, and that is minimal.

Incidentally, these same considerations hold true when using either an isolating solenoid or a battery isolator. Remember to turn off other accessories, including the dome light(s), to minimize draw on the starting battery. This ensures minimum current draw from the starting battery.

If your accessory requires two or more auxiliary batteries, then connecting the additional batteries to the first is really quite simple. Mount the batteries as close together as possible and connect them in parallel as shown below.

Wiring a pair of batteries in parallel is a snap. Just connect the pluses (positive terminals) together and the minuses (negative terminals) together. As shown in the Olds, those connections are done via 1/0 AWG wiring and aftermarket battery clamps.

Adding an Accessory Fuse Panel

Let's say that you plan to add a number of aftermarket electronic accessories and you need a nice, simple, and safe way to interface them to your vehicle's charging system. In addition, you'd like the ability to add more accessories down the road as your budget permits. No problem, it's time to add an accessory fuse panel.

A second fuse panel you say? How hard is that going to be? Believe it or not, this is one of the simplest and safest upgrades that you can make. A good example of when to do this is in my Olds. A single aftermarket ATC fuse panel provides a way to safely and easily power a number of high-current accessories that could not be tied to the aftermarket Painless Performance fuse panel that I chose to build the wiring harness around.

These are readily available from all the major parts houses and in some cases, your local auto parts store. This fuse holder has only one input, so you have to use relays with it for accessories that are powered off of the ACCY or IGN/RUN circuits. Here are the accessories that I have connected to this fuse panel, from top to bottom:

- Fan 1 circuit
- Fan 2 circuit
- Starter solenoid trigger relay
- Headlight relay
- MSD 6-BTM Ignition
- Cigarette Lighter
- Trans-brake
- Spare
- Start buttons on firewall for

adjusting the valves (I typically only put the fuse in when I need these, otherwise I leave it out.)

As many of these circuits are only required when the vehicle is running, a number of relays are required in conjunction with this fuse panel to accommodate this. When installing such a panel, take into consideration the combined current requirements of each of the accessories it powers. Just because they fit, it doesn't mean you can fill the slots with 40-amp fuses; this panel cannot pass that much current through it. In addition, this panel accommodates up to a single 6 AWG or a pair of 8 AWG wires for its input, I elected to use a pair of 8 AWG.

Other types of aftermarket fuse panels are also readily available, like the one that I used under the hood of my Mustang.

I got this one at my local auto parts store. As it easily comes apart, one could cut the common strip at any point so as to make some fuses

hot all the time, and other fuses powered by the ACCY or IGN/RUN circuits. This is just fine for a number of low- to medium-current accessories.

That about covers it for installing aftermarket electronics of all kinds, or does it? Turn the page and find out!

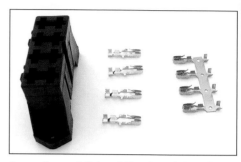

I purchased this at the local Pep Boys for less than $10. Assembling one of these is not very difficult, and your pin-crimping tool can crimp all the loose pins (assuming your tool will accommodate this size of pin). If you choose to leave the other four pins connected, you connect the appropriate number of cables to it based on the overall current requirements of all of the accessories connected to it.

This nine-position ATC fuse panel is quite nice. The panel has an AWG input, and the outputs are located on the barrier strip on the left. Just crimp on a fork connector and go. I got this one at a local car audio retailer.

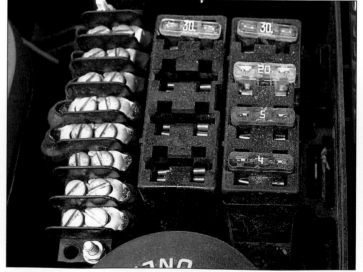

The fully assembled fuse block looks like this. I added the barrier strip (on the left) to make it simple to connect to the aftermarket panel in the previous photo. I chose this panel because of space constraints and input flexibility.

BUILDING A WIRING HARNESS

This chapter covers the last major topic—harness basics. In addition, I'm going to present a number of examples that tie together what you've learned in the first eight chapters of the book. I chose examples that I feel most readers of this book will be likely to attempt.

Harness Basics

This is one of my absolute favorite parts of wiring—assembling harnesses. Over the years, I've made thousands of harnesses for projects.

You get the benefit of that experience here, as I assure you that I've made all the mistakes! There are only two considerations: the accessory came with a harness and you need to "prep" it for installing it in the vehicle, or the accessory did not come with a harness and you need to build one from scratch and then install it in the vehicle.

Prepping a Harness

Again, this is a case where your new accessory came with a wiring harness of some kind. Take a

moment to inspect it to be sure that it is truly ready to install, rather than get in the vehicle and start wiring it up only to find out that:

- Some or all of the wires are not long enough.
- It isn't complete—more wiring is needed to complete the install than was provided.

Having installed thousands of aftermarket accessories over the years, let me assure you that maybe 1 percent of the included harnesses are truly plug-and-play. And even those will benefit from a little prepping on the bench prior to their installation. This example starts with a new piece of gear for the Mustang—a Pioneer Premier AM/FM/CD player.

Car stereos have come a long way. This unit has a number of features that only a few years ago would have been impossible to imagine in a single DIN head unit, the following being the main ones: iPod interface via USB, Bluetooth capability, Audio from Bluetooth-equipped storage devices, cell phone syncing for your Bluetooth cell phone.

This deck has a really slick interface for iPods and accessories.

This is the complete kit from Pioneer. As you can see, I've already taken care of the physical mounting of the radio as it is mounted in the custom 3/8-inch billet aluminum panel that is shaped identical to the stock radio. Below the radio is a Dakota Digital Volt Meter that allows me to keep tabs on the voltage at my amplifiers directly.

As such, this radio has a number of *guzintas* and *goes-outtas* as well as a USB cable and microphone that need to be installed to use the iPod and hands free features so it makes for a really good example.

Looking at the included harness, I notice right away that the ACCY lead and the remote lead are much shorter than the ones on the radio I'm replacing with this one. This needs to be addressed to ensure that my installation goes smoothly—better to do it at the bench.

Step-by-Step

1 Secure the harness so that the wiring is facing you.

2 Group and tape the power, ACCY, and ground wiring together. (Note: I extended the accessory wire slightly by soldering and heat shrinking another 8 inches of 18-gauge Red wire to the one Pioneer included)

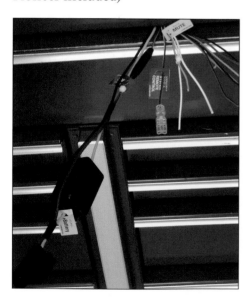

3 Group and tape the speaker leads together.

4 Group and tape the remote out and mute input leads together.

5 As my Mustang has two amplifiers, I do not require the speaker outputs of the radio so I insulate them with tape to prevent them from accidentally shorting to the chassis; same goes for the mute input lead.

Now that the harness is prepped, I can install it in the vehicle in a much neater fashion than would have been possible if I had done this in the car. A couple of cable ties, and this radio is ready to install.

6 Once in the vehicle, I connected the power, ACCY, and ground wiring. As the audio system is fairly elaborate, I decided to make these connections to the main power and ground distribution in the rear of the vehicle. (If your audio system is not so elaborate, you should install a female plug, so you can easily connect to the factory radio harness without cutting any wiring. This plug is readily available at your local car stereo retailer.)

7 I connected the remote output terminal to the trigger lead for the processor and amplifiers.

8 Route the USB cable under the center console and into the storage compartment at the rear of the console—this is where I locate my iPod.

9 Route the microphone cable up the driver-side A-pillar, securing it in place with duct tape (the good stuff please!) and mount it to the headliner with the included mounting bracket.

Now that all the cables are coming out of the radio opening, note that I've left plenty of length so that the radio can easily be installed and removed and they are neatly grouped together.

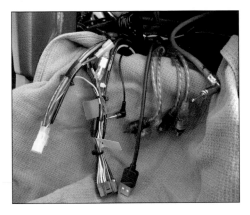

Finally, note the number of connections to the radio itself:
- Main harness.
- USB cable—to the iPod.
- 1/8-inch audio jack—to the microphone.
- Antenna.
- RCA cables for the amplifiers.

Admittedly, this was a simple harness prep. Something like a keyless entry or auto security system is a more involved prep. When do you know it's time to make your own harness? When the harness you have won't support the equipment you're adding.

Building a Harness from Scratch

This requires a bit more planning and "stuff" on your end than simply using, or even modifying slightly, a harness that came in the box with your new accessory. Let's first discuss the planning.

Planning the Harness

Before you can actually make the harness, you need to determine a few things:

- Define the objective.
- Outline the considerations.
- List the parts required.
- Draw a diagram.

Define the Objective: Skip this part, and you could spend days or even weeks trying to sort it all out after the fact. This isn't terribly difficult to do, but you need to have a firm understanding of what the harness needs to accommodate. For example, let's revisit the example I gave you in troubleshooting the electric fan circuit in Chapter 7.

I built this circuit and harness from scratch. These were the objectives of this circuit.

- Turn on a pair of cooling fans automatically when:
  a. The engine was running
  b. The engine temperature had reached 180 degrees
- Turn on the cooling fans manually via a dash mounted switch that could override the automatic feature when:
  a. The key was in the IGN / RUN position
  b. The ACCY switch on my panel was ON

Outline the Considerations: We can only determine what these considerations are after we've defined the circuit's objective. As we have, let's first consider the basic parts the harness will connect together and its routing:

- Pair of 16-inch Spal puller fans mounted to the radiator; each

require 22 amps of current according to the manufacturer.
- Thermostatically controlled switch tapped in the intake manifold near the water neck.

- Dash-mounted override switch—already in the Painless Panel as it were.

- Passage through the firewall safely.
- Source of power—in this case, we can use the accessory fuse panel mounted to the firewall on the passenger side.
- Proper safety via the correct fusing.

List the Parts Required: We know that we will need a pair of 30-amp relays to operate the fans, as the switch can only handle 10 amps or so. Before we go any further, we need to decide where these relays can be located so that we can determine the gauge of wiring to

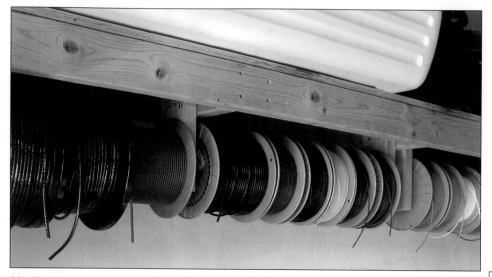

Having some primary wire on hand certainly makes your wiring tasks easier. Yeah, you've probably got a box under a workbench somewhere full of odds and ends, but you're going to need a good selection of wire when you start building harnesses.

use. I chose a spot on the firewall above the transmission hump to mount the relays. As this is less than 15 feet away from the fans, we know that 10-gauge is the way to go. Let's list the parts needed to complete the build:

- Three 30-amp S.P.S.T. relays (sure, you can use S.P.D.T. relays like I did as either will accomplish the same job here).
- 50 feet or so of 10 AWG wiring.
- 180 degree thermostatically controlled S.P.S.T. switch.
- Insulated female push-on terminals (blue and yellow in this case) for connection to the relays.
- Quick disconnects between the thermostatically controlled switch will provide an easy way to disconnect the harness from the manifold if it has to come off for any reason.
- Other miscellaneous crimp connectors to connect the harness to the plugs on the end of the fans, power to the

relays to the accessory fuse box, ground connections, etc.
- Split loom tubing to cover the wiring under the hood.
- Cable ties to anchor the wiring.

As the vehicle already had a snap busing in the firewall large enough to accommodate the wiring, we will utilize it. Of course this job also calls for all the regular wiring tools.

Draw a Diagram: Pull out a sheet of paper and sketch it out. This saves you the trouble of forgetting something simple.

Now, it's time to consider the things that are handy to have on hand when embarking on such projects. What will you need?

Required Stuff

When it comes to assembling your own harnesses, you really only need a few things:

- Wiring of the correct gauge and color.
- Plenty of it to choose from.
- Proper connectors.
- 3M Super 33+ tape—Use it to

group a harness (rather than ties that can get hung up in jute or around other body work).

Let's say that you only had red and black wire on hand in 10-, 12-, 16-, and 18-gauge. That's eight rolls of wire, a bunch, but only two colors. Although you could make a harness from this, it'd be next to impossible to tell what was what in a harness of any size. For that reason, I recommend that you have at least the following wire at your disposal:

10 AWG	12 AWG	16 AWG	18 AWG
Red	Red	Red	Red
Black	Black	Black	Black
		Yellow	Yellow
		Blue	Blue
		Brown	Brown
		Green	Green
		Orange	Orange
		Purple	Purple
		White	White
		Gray	Gray

As you can see, I believe in having plenty of connectors on hand to choose from. Pictured is about half of what I keep on hand.

You can use half as many colors of 16 and 18 AWG, but there really is no way that you can have too many. As your project increases in complexity, the amount of wiring choices you need increases exponentially. You can find suppliers that sell such wiring in bulk. You always pay less per foot for a big roll than for a small roll, and this pays off in the long run. As I do a lot of wiring projects, I also keep on hand 8 AWG, 4 AWG, and 1/0 AWG in at least Red and Black.

In addition, you need crimp connectors of all types and sizes. This can also be a major investment, but again shop for them in bulk. Although it sounds like a lot, a pack of 100 connectors won't last as long as you think it will—especially now that you're comfortable with wiring in general.

Building Your First Harness

Before I show you how to build a harness from scratch, let's talk about some fundamental harness-building basics. Here they are:

- Plan your work as you just learned.
- Build your harness on the bench, not in the vehicle.
- Group wiring together that will run in a common direction.
- Use 3M Super 33+ tape to keep your work together.

Harness Construction Project

Example: Installing aftermarket door lock actuators
Vehicle: 1972 Olds Cutlass

I covered this circuit in Chapter 6 in my discussion of relays.

Before we do the actual building,

let's follow the guidelines I provided previously, starting with planning.

Define the Operational Objective: Add the convenience of power door locks to a vehicle without them. Specifically, we want to be able to:

- Operate them with a single console mounted switch
- Allow for a future addition of a keyless entry system

Outline the Considerations: Right away, our objectives tell us about the harness we're going to have to build as we know:

- Harness must route into both doors.
- Relays need to be located under the dash, centrally is preferable.
- Switch needs to be located centrally in the dash so that both driver and passenger can reach it.
- Power will be sourced from the accessory fuse box mounted to the firewall on the passenger side.

Since I'm building this from scratch, I'll elect to trigger the relays via negative pulse from the switch. In addition, I'll install quenching diodes across the coils of the relays. These steps make it a snap to add a keyless entry at some point down the road.

List the Parts Required:

- Two aftermarket door lock actuator kits
- An S.P.D.T. Center OFF momentary switch (SPAL Part # 3700050)
- Two S.P.D.T. relays
- Two diodes
- Associated crimp connectors
- Super 33+ tape
- Wiring
- 12 AWG—For the main power and ground

- 16 AWG—Between the relays and the actuators as they require less than 5 amps of current each and the wiring run to them is about 10 feet each (20 foot total run as we have to go to and back)
- 18 AWG—For the low-current connections to the switch
- 15 amp ATC fuse

The parts required for this project. Anytime I embark on a project like this, I lay all the parts out to be sure nothing is missing.

Lay Out the Harness: This is actually a pretty simple harness to build, as we can assemble nearly all of it on the bench. This installation will actually have three separate harnesses going in three different directions:

- From the relays to the driver-side of the vehicle, through the jamb, and into the drivers-door to connect to the actuator
- From the relays to the passenger side with two sub harnesses:
a. To the source of power at the accessory fuse panel
b. Through the jamb and into the passenger door to connect to the actuator
- From the relays to the dash mounted switch

Step-by-Step

1 Secure the relays upside down in a bench vise so you can easily wire them.

2 Wire the relays as shown in diagram 7-2 on page 106. Note the quenching diodes across the coils, as well as a second pair of trigger leads, in anticipation of adding a keyless entry system to this at a later time.

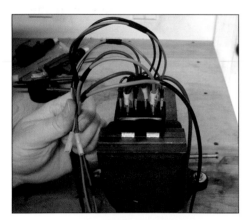

Note the four sub-harnesses in addition to the power and ground: left actuator harness, right actuator harness, switch harness, and keyless entry harness (with the red push-on connectors).

3 Note that I've left my self plenty of length for the harnesses that go into the doors—16-gauge wire is relatively inexpensive and we don't want to have to extend this because it wasn't long enough.

Look closely at the quenching diodes. One is installed across the coil of each relay.

(I've always used blue and green wires for aftermarket door lock actuators. This appears to be a standard.)

Note how nicely things are grouped together based on which way they are routed in the vehicle. I always secure my harnesses high in the dash and never under the carpet for a job like this.

4 Mount the relays.

5 Ground the wiring connected to terminals 87a to a suitable location.

6 Choose a location for the switch and drill a hole if

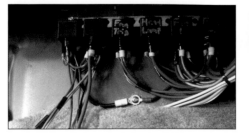

necessary (as an entire interior re-work is in my Olds future, this switch will find its way into a custom center console).

7 Route the switch harness from the relays to the switch location, properly anchoring this along the way.

8 Route the wiring toward the kick panel areas of the vehicle, being sure to anchor it up high as you go.

Note the new Green and Blue wiring routed neatly along an existing harness going up and over the steering column on its way to the driver-side kick panel.

Note the Green and Blue wiring tied neatly to an existing harness as it makes its way to the passenger-side kick panel.

9 Since this vehicle does not have a boot between the body and the doors, we must drill holes and install snap bushings—remember to drill the holes in the body higher than the ones in the door to keep water from getting into the body by traveling down the harness.

Installing a snap busing in the door itself can be a tricky matter. In this case, I was able to sneak my entire drill into the interior of the door and drill it from the inside out. Of course, a right-angle drill would certainly make this job easier.

10 Run the harnesses into the doors and cover with split loom tubing.

Notice that I secured the split loom tubing to the wiring in the jamb via the electrical tape method I shared with you in Chapter 6. Not only does this look neat, it keeps wiring itself hidden as the door is opened and closed over the years.

11 Secure the wiring away from moving parts, such as the window regulator and door lock mechanism.

This is an interior shot of the passenger door. Note that the wiring comes through the snap bushing, and it is anchored to the door itself.

12 Connect the wiring to the actuators themselves.

I elected to cut off the wimpy bullet connectors that were on this actuator in favor of some fully insulated push-on connectors. As they're in the interior of the door itself, I filled them with white lithium grease. Look closely at the two silver screws to the left—these secure the actuator itself to the back of the metal.

13 Connect and install the switch.

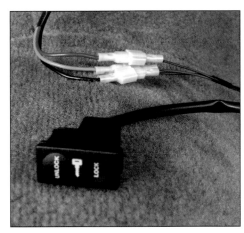

As my center console in the Olds isn't finished yet, I just laid the switch on the transmission hump so that I can verify operation. The system works great!

14 Connect the power lead to the fuse box and insert the 20-amp fuse.

15 Try the system.

Everything should work correctly. In the event that the motors operate backward from what you intended, then you can either reverse the wiring at the motors directly or at the relays—whichever is easier. This is not a big deal so don't fret. As I used Green for lock and Blue for unlock throughout, this was not an issue this go.

Although I didn't cover the mechanical part of the actuator install, it's really quite simple. After you've connected them to the door unlock/lock rods within the door, you need to verify that you can still easily manually unlock and lock the doors with both the key and interior plunger. If not, you may have to play with the alignment to get all to work smoothly. Better to determine this while the door panel is off!

The hardest part of the job was drilling the holes in the door and body to get the wiring from the body and into the doors. The second most difficult part of this install was lying on my back and routing cable overhead with my feet around the headrests of the seats.

Installing a Multi-Function Harness

This is no more difficult than installing a single-function harness. Let's say that you wanted to add power windows and power door locks. Most aftermarket power window kit manufacturers sell pre-assembled wiring harnesses that vary slightly based on location of the power window switches. The switches can be located in the doors or centrally, such as in a center console. If I was installing both power windows and power door locks, I would install the wiring harnesses to them simultaneously—this greatly cuts down on the amount of work required as both require sub harnesses run into each door and common switch locations.

Let's say that you had such a vehicle with a center console and wanted the power door lock and power window switches located next to each other in the console. Then, you need the pre-made power window harness that was designed for console-mounted switches. At this point, you need to either build your own harness for the power windows or buy a pre-made harness.

When it comes to installing these two separate accessories, proceed as above to Step 7. Then, begin the installation of the power window wiring harness by laying it loosely in the vehicle based on the direction the sub-harnesses need to go. From this point on, treat the installation of these harnesses as if it were a single installation and follow the remaining steps with both harnesses.

As you're routing, it's easier to treat multiple harnesses and sub harnesses as one when anchoring them—up high and out of the way, of course. Compare this to what you typically see drooping out from under the dash of even the nicest of custom-built cars at the shows. It's the behind-the-scenes stuff that counts in such wiring jobs.

When you're building and installing harnesses, the time you spend on the details makes the difference. Here are a couple of common pitfalls to avoid.

Pitfall #1—Short Wiring: Short wiring is the act of using just enough wire to get to a specific component or controller. Keeping serviceability in mind, there may be times when something needs to be removed, such as the center console in the example I just gave. In this case, you would need to use enough wiring to allow the switches to be easily unplugged from their respective harnesses in the event the center console needed to be removed for whatever reason. As the door lock relays, door lock actuators, and window motors are permanently mounted, this is not nearly as important for them. Yet, consider if a relay were to fail and needed to be replaced. Your wiring must allow for this.

Pitfall #2—Ease of Removal: Consider the use of Molex plugs to be able to quickly remove something that the harness passes through. You learned how to assemble these in Chapter 3. Consider again all the plugs in the kick panel of my Mustang, pictured in Chapter 7. This allows the entire door to be easily removed by a body shop in the event that it needed to be replaced.

There's no telling what kind of vehicle you might be working on or what kind of a project you build. Keep these kinds of plugs in mind to make disconnecting harnesses quickly a

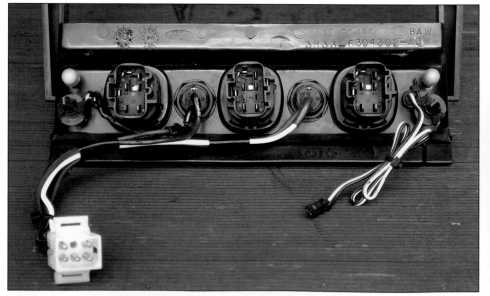

The connector for the valet switch for my security system is on the right and it is pre-terminated with a small plug—how handy that it came terminated this way. Notice how the Radio Shack six-pin connector makes the pair of switches and LED a snap to disconnect should this panel need be removed for any reason.

snap. When disassembling consoles and dashboards in vehicles, take notice how often the OEMs use these types of plugs for this very reason.

Thinking about serviceability as you're doing an installation saves yourself time in the long run. The most common thing that I run across are switches, lights, and indicators installed in removable dash panels with no thought given to easily disconnecting them. A great example of this is the dash panel surrounding the radio in my Mustang. Note the switches and LED that I added. I installed a Molex type plug to allow for easy removal. Yup, I got it at Radio Shack.

If you're installing a switch, light, LED, or any other controller or indicator in a removable panel, it will be difficult to remove the panel with all the different wires going to the back of it, especially if they're

Mounted in the trim panel around the instrument cluster in my Mustang are a pair of LEDs for monitoring operation and low fluid level of the aftermarket water/methanol-injection system. A couple quick disconnect push-on connectors allow this panel to be easily and quickly removed.

short wired. Now imagine a mechanic at the dealership faced with removing the same panel. They will probably just start cutting wires. If nothing else, use quick disconnects for ease of disconnecting.

Pitfall #3—Mummifying: While it is true that the OEMs typically enshroud their harnesses entirely with tape, this isn't really necessary or desirable to do when you're adding a harness. The OEMs typically use a special harness tape for this, which can be several inches wide and with a radically different adhesive than electrical tape. Using electrical tape to mummify a harness becomes expensive in a hurry.

As a result, many choose to use the "cheap" tape for this duty. Don't fall into that trap because it creates a gooey mess over time. Trust me when I tell you that there are few things messier than troubleshooting a problem in such a harness in the heat of the summer where you have to cut the cheap tape off to get to the wiring inside.

Over the years, I've typically mummified only security system harnesses in order to make them to be indistinguishable from the factory harnesses. This is one of the ways professional auto security installers ensure that your security system isn't vulnerable to the thief in a hurry. If you do elect to mummify a harness

for any reason, use the good tape—yup, 3M Super 33+!

Documentation: it is always a good idea to Document your work. Whether you're building a simple harness or multi-function harness, taking a few minutes to write down the color of wires you used for what will save you a bunch of time should you have to troubleshoot this some time down the road. In addition, should the circuit consist of multiple components, you may also write down their location.

This won't take you much time if you take a minute and document the info down as you go. Should you decide to sell the vehicle down the road, this will make the future owner's day.

Well, this kind of brings me back full circle. I began the book telling you what inspired me to write it to begin with—the wiring malady in my Olds. Funny how that worked out, but it was certainly fitting. I hope that you've enjoyed what's between the covers. With any luck, this book will find its way into your garage and soon be covered in greasy hand prints—nothing would make me happier than to know that I helped you get your wiring job done easily!

Next time a buddy tells you how much they dread wiring, just smile...as it's now second nature to you!

Passenger-Side Harness Through Firewall

Red 12 ga.	MSD box power
Blue 10 ga.	Starter solenoid trigger
Blue 16 ga.	Electric fan relay trigger
Dual 12 ga. reds	Power to fan relays
Yellow 18 ga.	Trans temp gauge
Black 12 ga.	Trans brake (+)
Dual 8 ga. blues	Main Power to auxiliary fuse box

RESOURCES

Autotronic Controls Corporation
1350 Pullman Drive, Dock # 14
El Paso, TX 79936
(915) 857-5200
www.msdigntion.com

Fluke Corporation
6920 Seaway Boulevard
Everett, WA 98203
(425) 347-6100
www.fluke.com

Mitchell1
14145 Danielson Street
Poway, CA 92064
(888) 724-6742
www.mitchell1.com

Ohio Generator
134 N. Chapel Street
Louisville, OH 44641
(330) 875-6677
www.ohiogen.com

Painless Performance
2501 Ludelle Street
Fort Worth, TX 76105
(817) 244-6212
www.painlessperformance.com

Powermaster Motorsports
7501 Strawberry Plains Pike
Knoxville, TN 37924
(865) 688-5953
www.powermastermotorsports.com

The Ramsey Consulting Group, Inc.
16023 S. 35th Way
Phoenix, AZ 85048
(480) 706-9828
www.ramseyconsultinggroup.com

Rockford Corporation
600 South Rockford Drive
Tempe, AZ 85281
(480) 967-3565
www.rockfordcorp.com

Steve Meade Designs
www.stevemeadedesigns.com

*How To Build High-Performance
Ignition Systems*
by Todd Ryden
CarTech Inc.
3996 Grand Avenue
North Branch, MN 55056
(651) 277-1200
www.cartechbooks.com

Basic Installer Study Guide
by Consumer Electronics Association
2500 Wilson Boulevard
Arlington, VA 22201-3834
(703) 907-7689
www.mecp.com

Advanced Installer Study Guide
by Consumer Electronics Association
2500 Wilson Boulevard
Arlington, VA 22201-3834
(703) 907-7689
www.mecp.com

Notes

Notes